9780130564160

BASKETBALL'S
PERCENTAGE OFFENSE

BASKETBALL'S PERCENTAGE OFFENSE

Robert Cimbollek

Parker Publishing Company, Inc.
West Nyack, New York

© 1972 BY

PARKER PUBLISHING COMPANY, INC.
WEST NYACK, NEW YORK

ALL RIGHTS RESERVED. NO PART OF THIS
BOOK MAY BE REPRODUCED IN ANY FORM OR
BY ANY MEANS WITHOUT PERMISSION IN
WRITING FROM THE PUBLISHER.

Library of Congress Cataloging in Publication Data

Cimbollek, Robert (date)
   Basketball's percentage offense.

   1. Basketball--Offense.   I. Title.
GV889.C5   796.32'32   72-3973
ISBN 0-13-056416-8

PRINTED IN THE UNITED STATES OF AMERICA

DEDICATION

I would like to dedicate this book to my loving wife, Judy, and to my children, Kimberly and Robby, for the daily inspiration they give me.

What Percentage Basketball Will Show You

BASKETBALL'S PERCENTAGE OFFENSE is a truly all-purpose attack designed to allow a team to master just two offensive systems which are flexible enough to permit the team to be in complete charge of its own destiny. This is accomplished by employing techniques which govern the speed at which the game is played and by using methods which put the controlling percentage components at the command of the disciplined ball-control team.

The methods and techniques that will put a team in command are found in the percentage-controlled, penetrating, patterned, continuity offense, which patiently and systematically strives for the close-to-the-basket, high-powered percentage shot that will function against any type of defense.

This book presents methods and techniques which enable a team to have at its disposal an offense that will work successfully against any and all defenses, regardless of type. This system of play enables the high school coach to solve one of the most difficult problems he must face . . . that of trying to develop and install an offense which will work against all of the different defenses a high school team will be forced to meet during the course of a season, and yet one which will be simple enough for high school players to comprehend and execute successfully. Probably secondary to this problem is that of not having enough time to prepare a team to meet these varied defenses.

Because BASKETBALL'S PERCENTAGE OFFENSE is a ball-control type of game, any team that employs this type of system must expect to face many different types of defenses, because other teams will want to try to force it away from the use of control tactics. This was the major reason for the development of an offense that could work against anything that was thrown at it. In developing the All-Purpose Attack of BASKETBALL'S PERCENTAGE OFFENSE, all of the aforementioned difficult factors were taken into careful consideration, and this book presents a proven style of play that works successfully against any of the following defenses and situations:

Man-to-Man Defenses	*Zone Defenses*
Normal	1-2-2
Sagging	1-3-1
Switching	2-1-2
Tight Overplay	2-3
Half-Court Pressure	2-2-1
Full-Court Pressure	Half-Court and Full-Court Presses
Combination Defenses	*Fluctuating Defenses*
Half-Court Man-to-Man and Zones	Changing from Man-to-Man into a Zone and back again

At the same time, it is a well-disciplined percentage-controlled offense that can obtain the high-percentage shot by perpetually penetrating the defense until the defense commits a mistake that results in an easy basket.

It is inconceivable to have a special offensive pattern for each of the previously listed defenses, because there would be just too many offensive patterns to be used, so that high school players would never be able to learn to operate them effectively with a high degree of confidence. Yet, it is still extremely difficult to have just five or six patterns to cover the many situations that a team will face and really be ready to handle them confidently with a high degree of success.

The theory behind the All-Purpose Percentage Offense is that it is *better to know one play thoroughly than to be confused about half a dozen* . . . It is much like Aesop's Fable about the *fox that went to the dogs* . . . The fox knew a thousand ways to fool the dogs, but he couldn't decide which one to use. Thus, as he was taking time to decide . . . he went to the dogs. Whereas, the cat had but one avenue of escape and it always worked . . . He would quickly scurry up a tree to safety. *Better to know one play thoroughly than to be confused about half a dozen.*

This is the philosophy of the All-Purpose Percentage Game in relation to both the offensive and defensive approaches used in modern-day basketball. This approach can be readily applied to the problems previously mentioned . . . too many things to cover and too little time to do it in . . . that coaches face every day of the season.

The all-purpose attack has just two basic formations and two basic options, that can be run separately or by rotating, reversing or combining them, to give a team enough flexibility to meet any man-to-

What Percentage Basketball Will Show You 9

man or zone defense. Four special adjustment techniques give the offense the added surprise element needed to keep the defense honest at all times.

The success of the minimum offensive patterns to be learned lies in the ability of the coach and his players to execute slight, but extremely effective adjustment techniques when the defense starts to change, "play" the play, perform sagging or switching tactics or apply pressure.

This book shows a step-by-step procedure for employing the adjustment techniques that the All-Purpose Percentage Offense has to use to counteract all of the defensive changes and techniques opponents might employ in trying to stop the attack. These simple, but very effective adjustment techniques are designed to set up the defense and allow the offense to still get the high-percentage shot it is seeking.

The easy-to-learn two basic options and their special adjustment techniques are devised so that after the two basic options are mastered, time may be spent on teaching and learning the proper execution of these options and their needed adjustments against all defenses and situations. Proper execution is the key to the All-Purpose Percentage Offense.

Material is presented that illustrates how a coach can take average or below-average players and blend them into a strong working unit with the capability of overcoming a superior opponent. By relying on BASKETBALL'S PERCENTAGE OFFENSES, a team may have a better chance to overcome any type of defense, survive a poor shooting night or lighten the loss of a regular starter, because it gives the team something solid to fall back on and to go to in a real tight situation, instead of having to rely on the skills of an individual player or on lady luck. The Percentage Game takes the pressure off the individual player and puts it where it really belongs . . . on the coach and on team play . . . because the Percentage Offense dictates who will do what, and when and where he will do it.

By employing and utilizing the All-Purpose Percentage Offense, a team will find itself well-prepared to meet the hardships of the most difficult part of its schedule—the tournament playoffs. Most states in the country determine their high school state champions by regional, district and state tournament playoffs. Players and coaches face tight, pressure-packed games where a loss eliminates them from further competition. It is in this type of game situation that the All-Purpose Percentage Offense really comes to the fore.

The confidence, poise, discipline, teamwork and mental and physical condition that is developed by this style of play will carry a team through the many problems it must face in tournament play

... that of playing two or three consecutive days with little or no time to prepare for the next opponent; meeting the unexpected, such as injuries, illness or an opponent's sudden change in strategy; playing before large crowds in large auditoriums or fieldhouses and the problem of fatigue—thus making the percentage shot of even more importance.

I strongly believe that a team which has an All-Purpose Percentage Offense to fall back on has a decided psychological and physical advantage in tournament competition, because if the system was effective enough to get a team to the playoffs, then the team must have mastered the system to a high degree of skill and is well-prepared to meet any situation with confidence.

This book will give a step-by-step account of the methods and techniques used for developing the All-Purpose Percentage Offense. By following the procedures outlined here, a team should improve as the season progresses, so that by tournament playoff time, it should be just reaching its peak, prepared to face any situation by using the same basic formations and options and by making the necessary simple adjustments in the offense to solve the situation at hand.

BOB CIMBOLLEK

ACKNOWLEDGMENTS

High School Coach: Fred "Red" Barry
College Coach: Del Merrill
Personal Friend: Bob Kelley
Brother-in-Law and Assistant Coach: Gerald "Red" Briggs

Contents

What Percentage Basketball Will Show You 7

1. *The Foundation of the All-Purpose Percentage Offense* . . 17

    The Merits of the All-Purpose Percentage Offense . . . The Percentage Shot . . . The Percentage Shot Areas . . . Getting the Percentage Shot Against Any Defense . . . Using the Ball-Control Theory to Obtain the Percentage Shot . . . Essential Attributes of the Coach, Players and Offense in the Percentage-Controlled Game . . . Advantages and Disadvantages of the Percentage-Controlled Offense . . . The 10-Point Game Strategy . . . Players' Reactions to Playing on a Percentage-Controlled Team.

2. *Building the All-Purpose Percentage Offense* 35

    Player Positioning . . . Importance of Disciplined Options . . . Continual Player Movement . . . Continual Ball Movement . . . Simplified Signals for Play Options . . . Penetrating Patterns Designed to Get the Percentage Shot . . . Positioning Offensive Rebounders for the Second and Third Shots . . . Maintaining Disciplined Defensive Floor Balance . . . Employing the Special Offensive Adjustment Techniques . . . Maneuverability from Man-to-Man Offense to Zone Offense . . . Utilizing the Time Clock . . . Other Necessary Elements to Play Successful Percentage Basketball . . . The Two All-Purpose Percentage Formations.

3. *Setting Up the Percentage Man-to-Man Attack* 48

    The Five Cutter Formation . . . The Development of the Five Cutter Offense . . . Getting into the Five Cutter Offense . . . The Outside Options . . . The

13

Identical Inside Option . . . Rotating to the Outside Options . . . Rotating to the Identical Inside Option . . . Interchanging the Outside Options and the Identical Inside Option . . . Using the Special Adjustment Techniques Against the Sagging, Switching and Anticipating Defenses . . . Handling the Tight Man-to-Man Front-Court Pressure . . . Verbal Release Call . . . Dribble Release Move . . . The Stack to the Identical Inside Option . . . The Strong-Side Safety Valve . . . The Auxiliary Offense to the Five Cutter Attack.

4. *Breaking Man-to-Man Pressure Defenses with the All-Purpose Offense* 127

Meeting Pressure Defenses . . . Aims of Pressure Defenses . . . Active Presses . . . Passive Presses . . . Dribbling into the Outside Options . . . Dribbling into the Identical Inside Option . . . The Auxiliary Offense to the Five Cutter Attack . . . Using the Identical Inside Option Full-Court . . . Operating the Stack Full-Court . . . Box Special Setups . . . Facing Half-Court Man-to-Man Pressure.

5. *Using Percentage-Controlled Movement Against Zone Defenses* 153

Employing the All-Purpose Formations . . . Player Movement Offenses . . . Ball Movement Offenses . . . The Five Cutter Offense with Player Movement . . . The Five Cutter Offense with Ball Movement . . . The Auxiliary Five Cutter Offense with Player Movement . . . The Auxiliary Formation with Ball Movement . . . Attacking Combination Defenses with the Identical Inside Option . . . Solving the Fluctuating Defenses with the All-Purpose Percentage Attack.

6. *Centering Zone Presses with the All-Purpose Percentage Offense* 191

Objectives of Zone Press Defenses . . . The Real Secret of Breaking Any Zone Press Defense . . . The Two Rule Play . . . Centering the Even-Front Full-Court and Half-Court Zone Presses with the Five Cutter Formation . . . Centering the Odd-Front Full-Court and Half-Court Zone Presses with the Auxiliary Formation . . . Special Techniques for Coaching Zone Press Offenses.

Index **235**

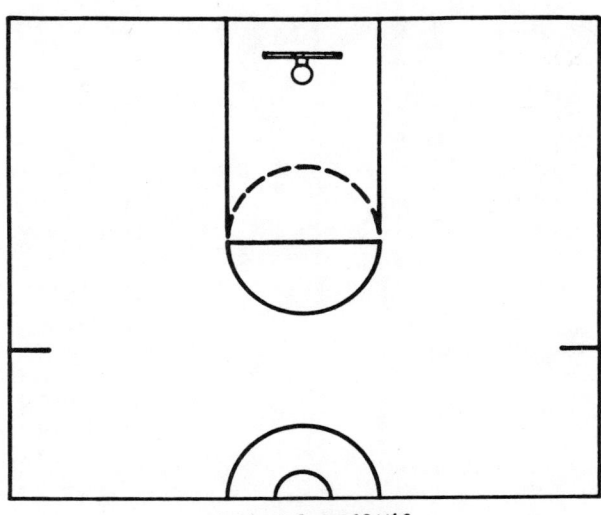

KEY FOR DIAGRAMS

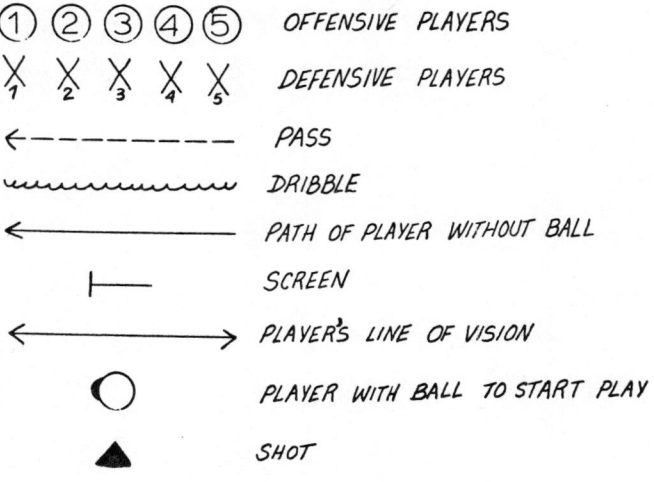

CHAPTER 1

The Foundation of the All-Purpose Percentage Offense

During my high school coaching career, the teams I have coached have always been considered very conservative ball-control teams that based their game on the percentage factors. Whereas many people feel that we are basically a ball-control team, I like to think that we are instead a percentage-controlled team that uses the percentage factors to put the law of averages in its favor.

The percentage factors we are constantly striving for are: (1) the high-percentage shot close to the basket, which has a better then 50-50 chance of being successful; (2) a percentage-controlled offense which allows our teams to control the tempo of the game and the amount of time that we have the ball and our opponents do not; (3) a tough man-to-man defense designed to frustrate our opponents because they do not have the ball more than one-third of the time, for we control it so long on offense that they become very anxious to shoot the ball as soon as they get it. We have found that our players are very willing to work extra hard on defense because they only have to spend one-third of the game playing it.

This percentage-controlled style of play has been very good to us over the years, and we have tried to make the necessary yearly adjustments in our system so that our opponents could not read our offensive strategy like an open book. The biggest problem we encountered was that of having to employ too many offensive patterns to cover all the different defenses that our opponents threw at us, and not having enough time to prepare properly for these defenses. We have constantly been searching for an offense that was still mainly a percentage-controlled system that could do the job against any type of defense, and yet would still remain simple and effective enough for high school players to comprehend and execute.

We have always used a percentage-controlled continuity type of offense, and over the years we have used different kinds of shuffle offenses, various backtraps and combinations of shuffles and backtraps because we liked the percentage situations that occurred from such offenses. We have also incorporated several types of continuity attacks with the shuffles and backtraps to give us a well-balanced offense. We adopted features of each of the aforementioned offenses that we felt were best suited for us, along with some of our own ideas, and blended them all into the All-Purpose Percentage Offense. We have used this all-purpose attack now for several seasons and have had great success with it, in spite of varying calibres of team talent.

Some of the teams had excellent individual talent, some had average ability and one team had below-average ability, yet all of them were able to do the job against most of the different defenses they were forced to encounter by using the All-Purpose Percentage Offense.

The Merits of the All-Purpose Percentage Offense

The chief merits of the All-Purpose Percentage Offense are that it can be used against any type of defense, has only two offensive formations and each formation has only two basic options. The options are quite simple and easy to learn, and within several practice sessions, a team can have its entire offense mastered and take the rest of the practice time to develop the All-Purpose Percentage Offense to its fullest potential. It can do this by concentrating on the four special offensive adjustment techniques and maneuvers which make it a real All-Purpose Offense, capable of working against any defense successfully. This offense will also allow a team to spend at least half of its practice time on defense, because you have eliminated one of the biggest time consumers in coaching basketball—that of having too many patterns to be learned in too short a time.

The Foundation of the All-Purpose Percentage Offense

The all-purpose attack eliminates the problem of having to use the standard offensive setup of two guards, one center and two forwards because the offense moves five men on each option to five different floor positions, so that once you have started the offense it makes no difference what type of players are in the lineup at any given time, as long as you are running the All-Purpose Percentage Offense.

This also makes it very easy to substitute for a player and not for a position because every player must know the assignments for each play for each floor position. The all-purpose attack also makes it possible to operate successfully without exceptional individual talent because the offense is based on playing the percentages, with emphasis on disciplined team play.

One of the biggest reasons we were able to develop the all-purpose attack into a functional cure-all is because we believe in the theory that if our patterns will work well in front court, then they should be able to work full-court and we should be able to get the same desired results—PERCENTAGE BASKETBALL. Thus, we run our man-to-man offensive patterns exactly the same full-court as half-court, and we do the same thing with our zone offenses. By making the simple special offensive adjustment techniques which will be discussed later in Chapter 3, we can use the two basic options of the offense in spite of whatever defense is set up against it and regardless of the fact that it is full-court, half-court or three-quarters court.

The Percentage Shot

The foundation of the All-Purpose Percentage Offense is the percentage shot. Many offenses are designed to get the percentage shot, but they never really define what type of shot a percentage shot is. The All-Purpose Percentage Offense has a specific definition of what constitutes a percentage shot. There are three types of percentage shots we look for when employing our offense.

The Moving Layup Shot

This is a layup shot on the move, where the player usually takes the ball while moving and lays it off the backboard. Most often the player does this off his own dribble or when he receives a pass while on the move from a teammate. This type of shot usually occurs at the end of a fast break or on a give-and-go option in the front-court offense.

The Stationary Power Shot

The stationary power shot is the shot that is the most commonly used in the All-Purpose Percentage Offense. It is taken from the power lane, which is shown in Diagram 1-1. It is an area 1 to 6 feet in

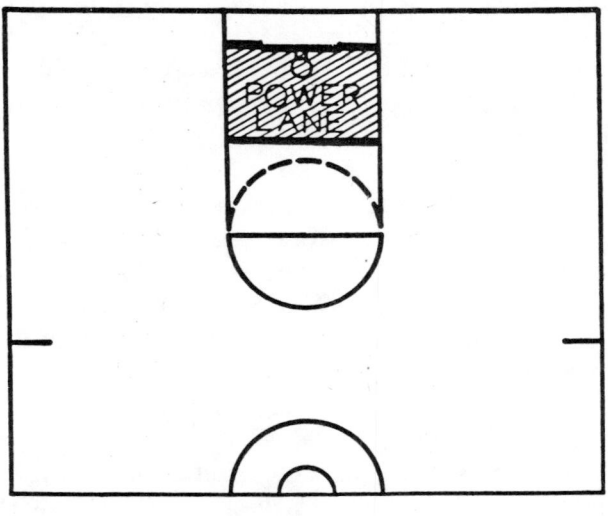

Diagram 1-1

length which encompasses the front of the basket, running perpendicular to the key lines of the bucket on each side of the hoop. The player, upon receiving the pass, stops, pivots to square himself to the basket (by pointing both his feet on a straight angle with the center of the rim) and after squaring himself, jumps straight up in the air, playing the ball off the backboard at the top of his jump. The player should release the ball at the point in his jump that he feels himself suspended in the air, before he starts to descend to the floor. The player must bend his legs enough so that he can get a great deal of explosive leg power and jump up through the defensive man guarding him. The stationary power shot is the shot that the All-Purpose Percentage Offense is always looking for, and we feel that it is the real heart of the offense. This shot is not an easy one to execute because of the heavy traffic that develops in the power lane, and a team must spend a great deal of time working on the fundamentals of this shot. It is designed to get many 3-point plays and draw fouls. *Coaching Hint:*

The Foundation of the All-Purpose Percentage Offense

The stationary power shot is never shot on the move. The player must stop before he shoots the ball.

The 6 to 15 Footers

If we do not get the moving layup or the stationary power shot, then we look for any other shot that is no further than 15 feet from the basket, provided it is not a forced shot. When defining a forced shot, the players should be told that if they have to dribble the ball in order to get free to get the shot off (unless it is on a clear drive to the basket), then it is definitely a forced shot, because the system did not develop the shot—the player developed it on his own. Players may execute either the jump shot or the one-hand set shot, depending upon the individual player and what type of defense is being used against the All-Purpose Percentage Offense. A further description of a forced shot will be discussed later in the ten factors for determining the criteria for a percentage shot, which follow.

The Criteria for Selecting the Percentage Shot

We must now immediately establish the criteria of what is to be considered before a shot can be taken in the All-Purpose Percentage Offense.

What constitutes a good high-percentage shot for one player may not be considered such for another player. This must be taken into serious consideration. The coach and the player must establish what type of shots each player will be allowed to take and from what area on the floor. If the player is open but his shot does not emerge, then he must pass up the shot. The following ten factors must be taken into careful consideration before a player takes a shot in the percentage system, especially if it is not a moving layup or the stationary power shot:

(1) The period of the game.
(2) The time remaining in that period.
(3) The score of the game.
(4) The margin of the score and who is ahead.
(5) The coach's instructions during the last time-out, or a signal from the bench as to what type of shot should be taken.
(6) Each individual player's shooting ability from the area at which the player has the ball. This should be established by the coach and the player, based on past shooting performances.

(7) Teammates' positions on the floor for offensive rebounds and defensive responsibility.

(8) The player must be squared to the basket. Both feet must be facing the basket. Diagram 1-2 illustrates this point.

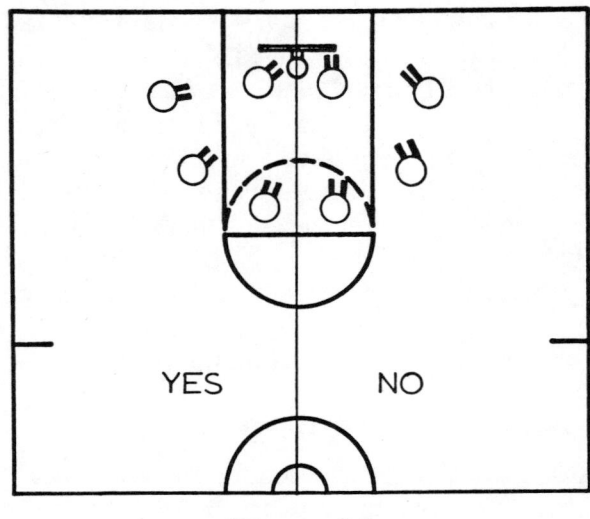

Diagram 1-2

(9) The player must feel very confident that he can make the shot.

(10) The player must actually be surprised if he should miss the shot.

The ten factors listed above must all be known and on the positive side, and if they are not, then the player should not take the shot. If a player is not sure if he should take the shot and there is some doubt in his mind that he can make it, then again the shot should not be attempted.

Players should know at all times what the score is, how much time is remaining in the period and what period of the game it is. The players should look at the scoreboard each and every time the official's whistle blows to make sure they gain the desired information about the period, time and score. There is adequate time available to look at the scoreboard every time the whistle blows on each violation called, because the official has to get the ball and give it to the team that has just gained possession of it, before the ball can be put back into play.

Instant reaction based on the ten factors that must be used before a shot is taken may seem to be a lot to ask of a player in the heat of battle, but he should have acquired the needed information regarding

The Foundation of the All-Purpose Percentage Offense

score, time and period before the ball is put back into play. However, with allotted practice time devoted to the different score, time and period situations, players can be schooled and disciplined concerning when to shoot on these three counts. It is important to mention that during practice time when a player takes a shot he shouldn't have, he should be corrected immediately, on the spot, regardless of whether the basket was made or missed. He must be corrected so that he does not take that same kind of shot again in an identical game situation.

The player's individual shooting ability, established by the coach and the player working together; the coach's instructions on what type of shot may be taken, based on each player's shooting range; the position of offensive rebounders and defensive responsibility on the part of at least one player, are all techniques that can be mastered by the players, provided the coach has complete control over the team at all times. The coach must discipline his team so that it is second nature for the players to know a good percentage shot from a poor percentage shot, depending on the situation at hand.

It is important to note that when we refer to disciplined players in this book, it does not mean discipline in the form of punishment, but instead discipline over each player's self-control. There is a big difference between these two kinds of discipline in basketball.

Drills that teach the player to square his feet to the basket before shooting and develop his confidence in his ability to make the shot must be provided, so that he can have an opportunity to practice these important techniques.

Many times during the course of a game individual players should be told what type of shots they may take as individuals or as a team, depending on the time, score and period formula. Some players may be allowed to take the unmolested moving layup only or both the unmolested layup and stationary power shot, but not the 6- to 15-foot shots. Some players, especially the smaller ones, may not be allowed to take any of the layups or stationary power shots if they are guarded at all. Some players should be allowed to take any of the percentage shots. The coach should take full responsibility in determining the shooting policies. However, one thing should be stressed at all times. When a player attempts a shot he should not have taken in practice or in a game, then he must be corrected the moment it occurs, regardless of the outcome of the shot, and if the player takes the poor shot again during that same practice session, then he should be made to run some penalty laps around the gym to think about his mistake. If he takes the poor shot later on in a game situation, then he should be taken out of the game, regardless of the score. *Players must know when to shoot and when not to shoot.*

The Percentage Shot Areas

The front court is divided into four shooting percentage areas, as shown in Diagram 1-3. Zone one encompasses the 6-foot area in front of the basket, running perpendicular to the key lines of the bucket

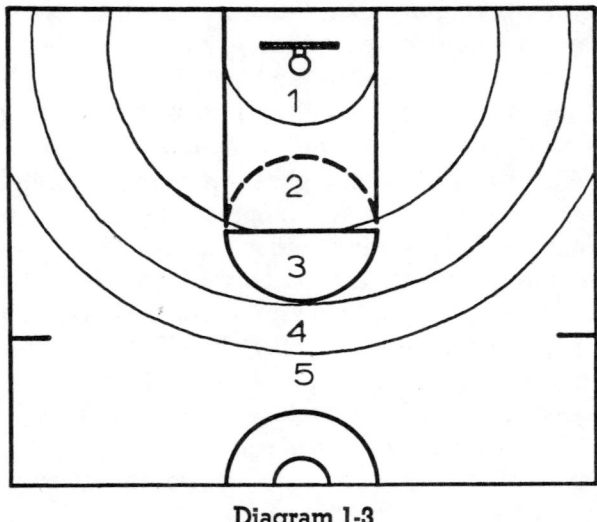

Diagram 1-3

area on each side of the basket. It is in this area that the unmolested layup, the stationary power shot and the offensive rebound power shots or tap-ins are taken.

Area two is the 6- to 15-foot zone, which goes from the basket to the foul line and moves around both sides to the end line. It is in this area that we get our secondary choice of shots if we cannot penetrate area one. It is in both of these areas, one and two, that we like to take our shots when teams are playing us straight man-to-man on defense.

Area three is the 16-foot to 21-foot distance from the basket, which goes to the top of the foul circle and around both sides to the end line. The only time we take shots in this zone is when we are facing zone defenses and cannot get any of the in-close percentage shots in areas one and two. We do not shoot from area three unless it is absolutely necessary or if we should happen to have an outstanding one-hand set shooter.

The Foundation of the All-Purpose Percentage Offense

Area four is the 21- to 25-foot distance from the basket where we hope our opponents will be forced to take their shots. Our team should *never* take a shot from this area unless it is a last-second shot at the end of a period. (Area five is 25 feet from the basket. According to American Basketball Association rules, any shot made from this distance or farther counts 3 points. This area has no place in high school basketball.)

As is quite self-explanatory, the farther away from the basket a shot is taken, the lower the odds are that the shot will be successful. It is in areas one and two that we should take all of our shots from the All-Purpose Percentage Offense, and it is in areas three and four that our defense should force our opponents to take most of their shots. An excellent example of where the shots were taken from on the floor, using the All-Purpose Percentage Offense during an actual game, and where our opponents' shots were taken from against the Percentage Defense, is shown in actual game charts illustrated in Diagrams 1-4 and 1-5.

Getting the Percentage Shot Against Any Defense

One of the safest and surest ways of getting the percentage shot against any type of defense is with a patient, patterned, disciplined percentage-controlled offense that has good penetrating player move-

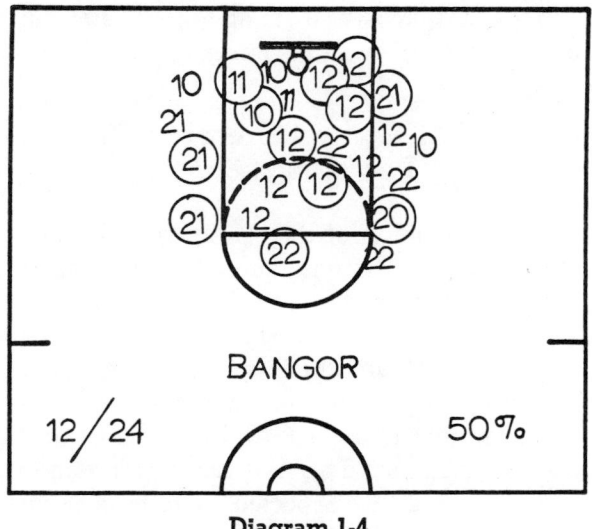

Diagram 1-4

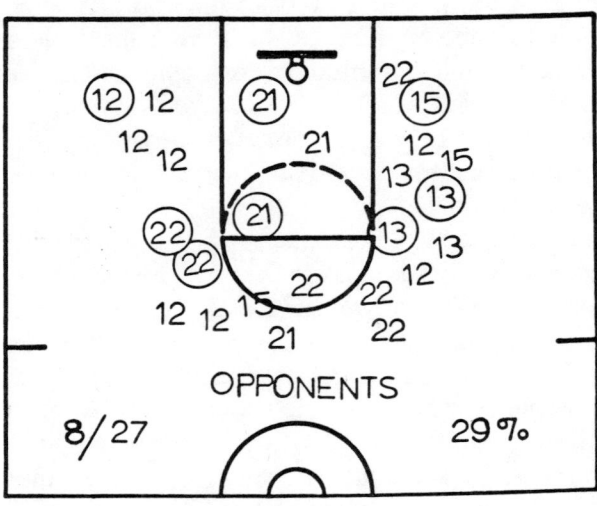

Diagram 1-5

ment without the ball, and an attack that has excellent continuity, so that the defense can never relax without paying for it.

This does not mean that a pattern of this nature is only for man-to-man defenses; it should also be able to do the same thing against zone defenses. The longer a team can move players and the ball in a continuous pattern that puts strong pressure on the defense in the high-percentage scoring areas, as shown in Diagram 1-3, the more difficult it makes the job for the defensive team and the greater the chances are that the percentage shot will eventually develop.

Using the Ball-Control Theory to Obtain the Percentage Shot

Whereas, the foundation of the All-Purpose Percentage Offense is the percentage shot, the foundation of the percentage shot is the percentage-controlled tactics that are derived from the ball-control theory of offense. The majority of basketball teams today use the fast-break, up-and-down, back-and-forth or run-and-shoot offense. Most teams expect to bring the ball up the floor quickly, make one or two passes, shoot the ball and race back down the court to play defense, and then have their opponents do just about the same thing. When their opponents do not do as expected in today's modern run-and-shoot game, then the teams that base their entire game on running and shooting have a great tendency to become extremely upset and frus-

The Foundation of the All-Purpose Percentage Offense

trated. They want to run and shoot and spend as little time as possible playing the tough game of defense. The opponent's players (especially their star) may become very upset over the fact that they may not be able to get their points, thus they may hurry and force their shots whenever they get the ball. (The type of player who hogs the ball is usually more interested in how many points he makes rather than in overall victory. This tends to upset his teammates.) The ball-control team presents a very serious psychological problem for the run-and-gunners (if nothing else) in using control tactics. Also when the ball-control team gets ahead, they can become even more deliberate and fussy concerning the type of shots they take, and this forces the run-and-gunners into dangerous and careless action.

Also by playing a ball-control game, the opponents have to spend much more time on defense than normal. A good, disciplined ball-control team should have the ball up to 65% of the game, which means the opponents, who are used to playing no more than 50% of the time in the trade-and-shoot game, must spend 15% more time chasing players on defense as they run through their deliberate and tough-to-defense offensive patterns. Defense is more tiring physically and psychologically than offense. Also, usually a ball-control team's offensive patterns are designed so that defensive players must spend a great deal of time moving backwards at fast speeds in order to defense the patterns successfully. This is definitely very tiring to the defensive player.

Our theory of ball control is: Keep the ball in your possession until the kind of shot that is desired develops; make your opponents spend a great deal of time on defense, thus making the defense become frustrated and upset. This puts the percentage factors in the hands of the ball-control team.

Essential Attributes of the Coach, Players and Offense in the Percentage-Controlled Game

To play successful percentage-controlled basketball, a team must have a coach, players and an offensive system that will work together toward a common goal, that of winning—the coach and every member of the team all believe in each other, in themselves and in the system they will use. The first essential that will be discussed is the attributes a coach must have to be successful in the percentage-controlled game. Before a coach can expect his players to run a winning percentage-controlled attack, he, himself, must be willing and able to do the following things:

(1) Develop a thorough knowledge of his individual players, their strong points and their weak points.
(2) Have a thorough knowledge of what he wants to accomplish, how he wants to accomplish it and when he wants to accomplish it.
(3) Have a thorough knowledge of the offense he wants to use.
(4) Be able to follow plays or movements and correct mistakes and make adjustments that will make the offense go.
(5) Be able to remain calm at all times and think under fire and pressure.
(6) Be able to introduce special adjustment techniques quickly and confidently.
(7) Have strong player and team discipline, so that players do not question his decisions but instead believe in them.
(8) Insist and see to it that patterns are being run properly; even if a player does something he should not do and it works, he should be corrected on the spot, whether it is a shot or an incorrect technique or pattern.
(9) Have confidence in his system, his players and himself, so that he will stay with all three when the going gets rough.
(10) Be willing to take full responsibility for losses, provided his players did what they were told to do.

The second essential a percentage-controlled team must have is players with the following attributes:

(1) Players willing to accept discipline for self-control.
(2) Players who believe in percentage-controlled tactics due to the coach's continual citing of past success records of teams using this style of offense.
(3) Players who want to play team basketball.
(4) Players willing to work for the good shot.
(5) Players willing to sacrifice individual glory for the good of the team.
(6) Players with at least average ball-handling skills (passing skills, not dribbling skills).
(7) Players capable of shooting 65% from the foul line.
(8) Players who are coachable and can take positive criticism.
(9) Players who love to play basketball.
(10) Players who want to win first and score their points second.

The Foundation of the All-Purpose Percentage Offense

The third essential a percentage-controlled basketball team must have is a set patterned attack designed to move the opponent continuously and relentlessly, until the defense makes a fatal mistake that allows the percentage shot to develop. A good percentage-controlled attack should have the following attributes:

(1) Must provide for good floor balance.
(2) Must move players to different positions on the floor each time an option is run.
(3) Must have a discipline continuity pattern designed to move five players in such a way that each player knows what to do at each position on the floor and when and how to do it.
(4) Must have patterns that move the ball by passing instead of by dribbling.
(5) Must have easy, identifiable signals for each option.
(6) Must provide good offensive rebounding for at least three players.
(7) Must have at least one back assigned to defensive responsibility at all times.
(8) Must be able to work against all types of defenses.
(9) Must be fun and enjoyable to perform.
(10) Must be challenging to the players.

Advantages and Disadvantages of the Percentage-Controlled Offense

Like any offensive system that is used in modern-day basketball, the percentage-controlled attack has both advantages and disadvantages that set it apart from the most commonly used offenses. However, the advantages far outweigh the disadvantages when the offense is directed at controlling the ball and the tempo of the speed at which the game is to be played. The following 20 advantages should be fully understood by both coaches and players before attempting to play the percentage-controlled game:

(1) It develops individual and team discipline.
(2) It develops no fear of playing in close games, as the percentage-controlled team is involved in many more close games than any other type of team.
(3) It eliminates careless play, for the ball means something to the

percentage game, because when the offense has the ball, opponents cannot score.

(4) It involves all the players as an integral part of the offense; many run-and-shoot, free-lance teams involve only one or two men at a time in their offensive plays, with the remaining three players becoming standing spectators.

(5) It develops player confidence, poise, pride and team cohesiveness, an "all for one" and "one for all" esprit de corps.

(6) It determines the tempo at which the game is to be played.

(7) It limits the opponent's fast-break opportunities.

(8) It helps improve the defense because you do not have to spend as much time on defense; therefore, it is easier to work that much harder on defense, psychologically speaking, because the players know that soon they will have the ball again.

(9) It is an excellent way to stall to protect a lead and still get the high-percentage shot when the defense commits an error.

(10) It makes the defense work harder and longer; therefore, it tires sooner.

(11) It makes the defense commit more fouls.

(12) It makes it easier to survive a poor shooting night.

(13) It upsets the run-and-shoot, free-lance players mentally, by frustrating them and not allowing them to do what they like to do—shoot.

(14) It provides for a balanced scoring attack; the offense dictates who is going to shoot, not the players, and it determines when and where the shot will be taken.

(15) It is an excellent way to get the second and third shot on the offensive board, because the movement of five players makes it more difficult for the defense to box out moving players than standing players.

(16) It is easier to substitute players, as all players must know all the assignments for each position in the offense; therefore, it is easier to adjust to foul difficulties, player injuries, sickness and the like.

(17) It is easier for the players to get used to the type of shots they will be taking.

(18) It allows you to have possession of the ball at least two-thirds of the game.

(19) It takes the pressure off individual players and puts it squarely where it belongs, on the coach and on team play.

(20) It makes it extremely difficult for opponents to prepare for a percentage-controlled team because they usually have to use

their second group of players to perform the percentage-controlled team's patterns, and if the opponents are a run-and-shoot team, then they will have a great deal of difficulty in giving their first team an authentic facsimile of the real thing. This is also true of the opponents' preparation for the man-to-man defense, especially if the opponents are a zone team like at least 75% of the run-and-shoot teams. It is very hard for the opponents' second string to give their starters the true picture of a strong and penetrating percentage-controlled offense and a tough man-to-man defense. Usually this forces the opponents into a hope-and-pray situation where they hope the percentage-controlled team does not get an early lead. The opponents know what the percentage-controlled team is going to do, but there is little they can do to prepare for it, or they may become overconfident because they had little trouble handling their second team's man-to-man imitation and they were able to stop the continuity patterns cold. This may give the opponents a false sense of security which they will probably pay for come game time.

Because any offensive system a team uses has distinct advantages, it must also have some disadvantages. The percentage-controlled offense has some disadvantages, but they are far less in number than those of the run-and-shoot, free-lancing teams. The following five disadvantages must be fully understood by the coach and his players in order to make the percentage-controlled game successful (by learning how to overcome the disadvantages and turn them around to help the offense):

(1) Probably one of the most difficult things a percentage-controlled offense must do is continue to play deliberately, even if they get 10 to 15 points behind in the game. They must stick to their attack and have faith in it.

(2) Usually they must stay fairly close to the opponents to be truly effective.

(3) They must be a ball-control and percentage-controlled team all season long; you cannot play the control game one week and run-and-gun the next. A team must start its season as a control team and end the season as a control team in order to be effective.

(4) It is difficult to educate your fans to appreciate this style of play as they usually do not find it too exciting.

(5) This style of play will not bomb weak opponents like the run-and-gun teams do.

These are the five disadvantages of the percentage-controlled offense. However, probably the most difficult thing about the percentage offense is that it is not easy to teach and coach true percentage-controlled basketball, unless you really work at it and believe in it. This, however, is not a disadvantage, but a state of mind, and it can be overcome by experience and success, which can be derived from the percentage-controlled game.

The 10-Point Game Strategy

We feel that whenever we get a 10-point lead against a man-to-man team, we should become very picky and fussy about the type of shot we want our players to take, regardless of the time left in the period or the game. Usually we should take nothing but the moving layup shot or the power shot, provided the players are 100% sure they can make the shot.

Many times against a good zone defense, if we can get a 10-point lead, we will just hold the ball and make the defense come out after us from their regular zone formation, because the responsibility for action lies with the defensive team in this situation. We have gone for as long as 4 or 5 minutes in one stretch just moving the ball from player to player in order to force the zone team to come with their zone or go man-to-man against us. As the zone comes out after us in a half-court type of zone press, we look for the base-line power shot, and when we get it, we will shoot it. However, the player must be 100% sure he can make the shot.

Many times zone teams will stay in their zone even when they are 20 points behind, hoping that their opponents will keep shooting the low-percentage outside shot and eventually cool off. In fact, the zone will encourage the outside shot in hopes of making this strategy work to their advantage. Remember, when a percentage-controlled team gets ahead by 10 points in a game, it is equivalent to a run-and-shoot team having a 20- to 25-point lead. The percentage-controlled team should not be concerned with how much they can beat their opponent, but just be satisfied with their hard-earned victory.

Players' Reactions to Playing on a Percentage-Controlled Team

Probably one of the most overlooked factors of playing a percentage type game is the players' reactions and attitudes concerning their feelings about playing this type of game. I have talked to our

The Foundation of the All-Purpose Percentage Offense

players many times about this factor. Usually, they favor such a system once they have played the game in this manner and have been successful with it. Players like to know what is expected of them in any given situation, and the percentage-controlled game gives them this information. Average or a little above-average players like the idea of playing together as a team, because they know that they all are an important part of the whole and must do their individual job if the team is to experience success.

Players do not like to stand around and watch other players go 1-on-1 or 2-on-2 while they do nothing to help (they are not supposed to move because they may interfere with the players who are in possession of the ball or who are involved in a two-man play). Players want to move, not stand around like dummies. In the percentage-controlled offense, every player moves every time an option starts. Each player has his assignment to carry out, and each player's job is as important as his teammate's.

Players like the idea of the coach being responsible for making most of the decisions, and they also like the idea of the offense dictating who is going to take the shot, when he is going to take the shot and from what area. This prevents one of the most distasteful things about basketball, that of having a player going on his own, lone wolfing so to speak. Many times such hogging of the ball leads to team-morale and discipline problems because some players are very greedy and selfish when it comes to giving up the ball. The percentage-controlled offense will definitely uncover the type of player who is more interested in his point average than in team victory. There is no question that the free-lance, run-and-gun teams have many more morale and discipline problems, because there is only one ball and there are five players who want it.

The last and most important feature of the players' reactions to playing the ball-control game, based on the percentage factors, is that it takes the pressure off the individual players and puts it where it should be—on the coach and on team play. How many times have you heard coaches, players and fans alike blame an individual player because he had a poor night offensively, and complain that if the player had been on his shooting game his team would have won instead of being beaten? I feel that it puts too much pressure on a boy to shoulder him with such heavy responsibility. There are only a very few high school basketball players who want to carry this degree of responsibility on behalf of their coach, their teammates, their fans and themselves. Players appreciate a coach's willingness to accept full responsibility for defeat, if the players carried out their orders to the best of their ability. When a percentage-controlled team loses a game, you can never put the blame on individual performances; instead it falls exactly where it should, on the coach and on the performance of the team, not on individual players.

I feel that this in itself is reason enough to play percentage-controlled basketball. Players are human beings, and they should be treated as such. No player does anything wrong intentionally. When a coach can take away many of the pressures and fears that players have as individual personalities, then the instrument that he uses to accomplish this objective must have many outstanding features.

CHAPTER 2

Building the All-Purpose Percentage Offense

In Chapter 1, in covering the section on the essential attributes of a percentage-controlled offense, 10 factors relating to these essential attributes were listed. These 10 attributes were not discussed at any great length. Chapter 2 is devoted to covering these 10 major attributes in complete detail, plus how to use the special offensive adjustment techniques, how to fully utilize the time clock and an introduction to the two all-purpose offensive formations that are used in the All-Purpose Percentage Offense.

Player Positioning

The positioning of the players in any percentage-controlled offense is extremely important, as well as the patterns that the players are going to execute. Players should be positioned so that in the original formation the best ball handler controls the ball at all times until the team goes into the disciplined, controlled attack. The big men should be at the low-post areas and the shooters on the wings (Diagram 2-1), because as you run a continuity attack after the first time through the pattern, the big men usually are going to the basket and your shooters

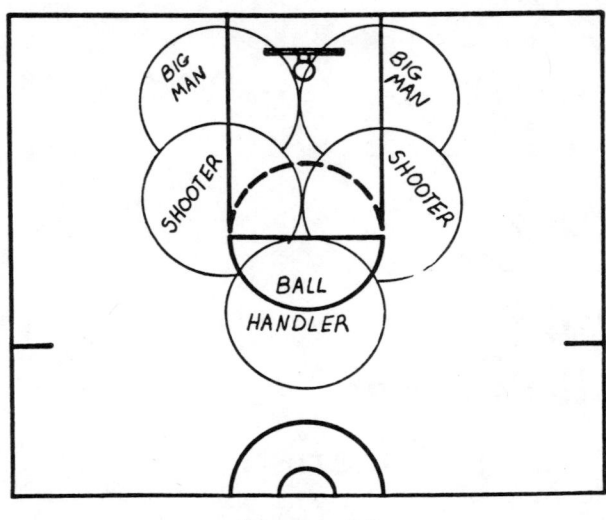

Diagram 2-1

should be coming to the ball in some type of shuffle offense (at least every other time the option is run).

Importance of Disciplined Options

The importance of disciplined options cannot be overstressed. Players must know precisely what they are trying to accomplish, how it is going to be done and when it is to take place. The offense must be so disciplined that the players react to the situation at hand without having to think about it. What to do in a given situation must come automatically to them, sort of an instantaneous involuntary reflex reaction. There is no room for the free-lance move in the percentage-controlled offense, unless it is used as a special offensive adjustment technique, which will be discussed and explained later on in this chapter. In an offense that moves four or five men on each option, it is imperative that each man does his job correctly, because if one man makes a mistake, the timing of the option probably will be interrupted and the option's progress will be unsuccessful. This results in disciplined assignments breaking down and the team finding itself without the proper number of offensive rebounders, a fast break stopper (a man who is supposed to have defensive responsibility out of position when the shot is taken), etc.

If players are forced to execute the correct techniques and assignments for each play option, then they should have little, if any,

Building the All-Purpose Percentage Offense

problems with missed assignments. The coach must take the time to correct any error in running the assigned option, regardless of the outcome of the option. The error must be corrected on the spot just like in a situation where a player takes a poor shot, or a shot at the wrong time, which is successful . . . the player must understand what the error was and what he must do to correct his mistake, so that he will not do the same thing again. This is the real key to the importance of disciplined options. Recognizing the mistakes and correcting them, regardless of the success of the outcome of the option, must be done if the option is to be run to perfection. By correcting player mistakes in this way, there is no doubt in the player's mind as to what he is supposed to do and when he is supposed to do it in any given situation—*leave nothing to chance.*

Continual Player Movement

The player's movement must be controlled at a specific rate of speed. Basketball is not a game where a player can be racing at 100 miles per hour or at a 100% output. Unless a player is cutting off a backtrap screen, he should usually be going about 75% of his maximum speed output in order to operate effectively. By running under a controlled speed, the player can use the special offensive adjustment techniques when the defense forces him to do so. If a player is running at an "abandon" rate of speed, he will not see the maneuvers that the defense may make to stop the play.

The player's movement in a percentage-controlled offense must be continual, with no wasted motion. The patterns must be so organized that the offensive player is continually keeping his defensive man on the move, never allowing him a second to relax or anticipate what is going to happen. The All-Purpose Percentage Offense is a five-man pattern which has every man moving each time an option is run through. The distance that each player has to cover in the option depends on what position he is at when the option is started. Usually the shortest distance a man has to cover in this attack is when he is the first man to get the ball after the option has been initiated.

The biggest advantage of continual player movement is that with five players, each moving in a predesignated pattern, and different distances from each position on each option, the defense is forced to move backwards a great deal of the time. This is the most difficult of all defensive techniques for a player to master . . . that of defending an offensive player who has several choices of maneuvers to free himself to go to the ball from different areas on the floor, while moving backwards or sideways without the ball. Eventually a defensive mistake should occur, and then the offense has its percentage shot. It may not happen the first time through the option or it may not occur the fourth time through—perhaps it will be on the tenth try—but some time a defensive player will make a mistake and the offensive pattern will have successfully achieved its objective.

Continual Ball Movement

Second only to continual player movement is continual movement of the ball with as little dribbling as possible. By combining continual player movement and continual ball movement, you are forcing the defense into an endless parade of follow-the-leader movement. The disciplined options should be so designed that after just one pass the ball is in a position to be moved by just one more pass to a player cutting into a high-percentage scoring area. This is extremely important because the more passes and dribbles it takes to create action, the easier it is for the defense to relax and not have to work so hard. Remember, it is easier to follow ball movement if the defensive player's man does not have the ball than it is for the defensive player to watch his man when he does not have the ball and many players are moving at the same time. Therefore, there should be much more player movement than ball movement once the option has been started.

Simplified Signals for Play Options

The signals that are used for a percentage-controlled offense should be visual ones based on what a designated man with the ball does on a designated spot on the floor. The signal should not be so obvious that the defense can read it well in advance of the start of the play. Verbal and hand signals are poor cues for a percentage-controlled team. The players must know what the signals are for each option they are going to run from the different offensive formations they have, and they must be based on what the man in the signal position does with the ball and what he does after he passes the ball. These are player action signals and are much more difficult for the defense to pick up. Because of the noise and pressure of a game, many times verbal or visual hand signals cannot be picked up every time by each player. But, by setting up designated positions for the forma-

Building the All-Purpose Percentage Offense

tion, preplanning the signal position and deciding previously what the man in the signal position does after he gets rid of the ball, it is much easier for each player to pick up the signal. This cuts down on the number of broken plays due to players not catching the signal of which option is going to be run.

Penetrating Patterns Designed to Get the Percentage Shot

The type of patterns that a percentage-controlled team runs must be designed to put a great deal of pressure on the defensive players, so that when a mistake has been made the offense can capitalize on it immediately. The patterns must be executed perfectly. They should take one man to the basket to receive the ball and then take him to a corner on the same side of the ball if he receives the ball in the power lane. Each pattern should also take another player to the ball preferably to the foul line (Diagram 2-2). It must have these two penetrating cuts on each and every option in order to be effective enough to

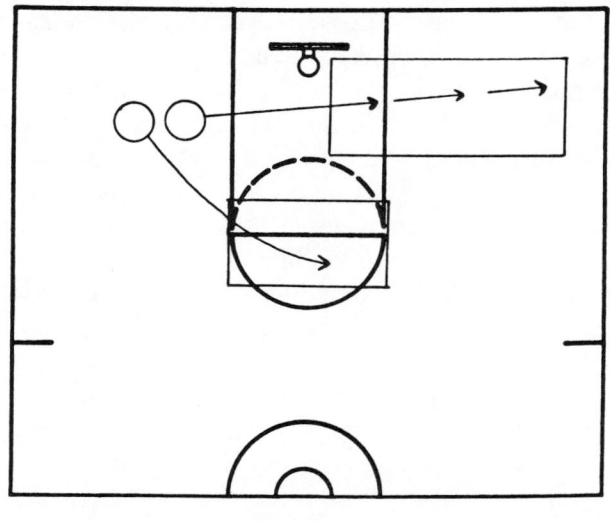

Diagram 2-2

keep the individual defensive players occupied. The pattern that puts a lot of pressure on the defense is one that moves all five players each time an option is run. Patterns that move only four players make it much easier for the defense to sag, switch or "play" the play, because the defensive man guarding the man who is not moving out of one particular area can help out a great deal. Therefore, the penetrating patterns must be a five-player offense each time an option is run. Each player must have a solid understanding of each option and how to execute each pattern from the five different positions, and he must be able to perform the special offensive adjustment techniques from each option that are designed to overcome the sag, switch or anticipating the play on the part of the defense. The patterns must be functional to allow the player to be able to adjust without hesitation. They must be simple but effective.

Positioning Offensive Rebounders for the Second and Third Shots

In order for a percentage-controlled offense to be successful, it must get the second and third shot on the offensive board. This must be done by sending at least three and one-half players to the offensive board every time a shot is taken. The positions of these players on the floor must be so arranged that they are able to get the proper angle and the spot at which the ball will come off the rim or backboard on the missed shot. The percentage-controlled offense has a big advantage when it comes to offensive rebounding, for the players usually know when the shot is going to be taken and where it is going to be taken from on the floor. Because they are familiar with these two factors the players usually can sense where they should go, for they know that they have a pretty good idea where the ball is going to rebound if the shot is missed. The players develop a sort of sixth sense when it comes to offensive rebounding, as they are used to the shots that are taken and where they are going to go on the rebound.

Players can be drilled on how to prejudge the flight of the ball after it hits the rim. Great natural offensive rebounders are born with this instinct, but any player can be taught how to anticipate where the ball is going. Percentage-controlled teams are usually excellent offensive rebounding teams because they see the same shots taken over and over again in practice and games. Since the shorter the distance from the basket the shot is taken the less distance the ball will rebound from the basket if it hits the rim, the percentage-controlled team knows that the ball will probably come down within an 8-foot area from the basket. This is where the patterns should station the three rebounders on each and every shot, in a circular formation, to cover this 8-foot circular area.

Building the All-Purpose Percentage Offense

Another big advantage to offensive rebounding in a percentage-controlled attack is that usually each offensive player is moving when the shot is taken, and it is much harder for a defensive player to block out a moving man than a stationary one. Before a player can become a good offensive rebounder he must be a good defensive rebounder (in order that he may know what to look for when he is on offense and his defensive man is trying to block him off the offensive board). Any percentage-controlled offense or ball-control offense must have options that always put at least three men to the offensive board on every shot that is taken, in order to be an effective offensive attack designed to cash in on the percentage factors of the percentage shot.

Maintaining Disciplined Defensive Floor Balance

In order for a percentage-controlled team to be capable of stopping its opponents' attempts to speed up the tempo of the game, the offensive pattern must offer a definite way in which to stop the opponents' fast break. Every time a shot is taken the offense must have one man heading toward the mid-court area while the ball is in flight, and he should be facing his own basket before the ball hits the rim or goes in, as shown in Diagram 2-3. It is this player's responsibility not to allow an opponent to get behind him. The player who has

Diagram 2-3

this responsibility will depend upon the player who is moving away from the basket at the time the shot is taken (it is never the same man). The offensive pattern should determine who is going to have the deep defensive responsibility. The other man on defense is the one who is assigned to go to the foul line on the shot. This player is a half-and-half man. He is half a rebounder because he may pick off any deep rebound from the basket, and he is half a defender because he can interfere with the opponent's outlet pass on an attempted fast break. A good percentage-controlled attack with a pattern that allows for three and one-half men to go to the offensive board and one and a half men to stay back on defense will seldom be beaten to their opponent's basket by the fast break, and a team that can cut down their opponent's fast break has an excellent chance of winning because many teams count on their running game for at least half of the points they score. By cutting off the running game you force the fast-breaking team to slow their tempo down, and this is what will upset them the most.

In order to have men at these two important positions on each shot, players again must be disciplined to know automatically which people have these responsibilities, depending upon what position they find themselves in when the shot is taken. Players must be given rules to follow governing these two important assignments. The All-Purpose Percentage Offense has two such rules that are simple but effective in governing which players will have defensive responsibility on the shot. These two simple rules will be discussed in Chapter 3 concerning man-to-man offenses and in Chapter 5 dealing with zone offenses.

Employing the Special Offensive Adjustment Techniques

Much has been said in Chapters 1 and 2 about the special offensive adjustment techniques. Any percentage-controlled offense must have special maneuvers which can be employed against defenses that do the following things:

(1) Sagging tactics off the ball.
(2) Switching techniques on any screen away from the ball.
(3) Anticipating the play by being in front or ahead of the offensive cutter at all times—"playing" the play.
(4) Tight-denial man-to-man pressure tactics.

Building the All-Purpose Percentage Offense 43

Each and every player must be taught how to identify such defensive changes and what he should do at each position to counteract any of the defensive maneuvers. The players should also know how to set the defense up to take advantage of how the defense is playing. This is one of the biggest factors in the success of the All-Purpose Percentage Offense. These special offensive adjustment techniques will be discussed in complete detail in Chapter 3.

Maneuverability from Man-to-Man Offense to Zone Offense

For an offense to be a truly effective all-purpose attack, it must be flexible enough to change from a man-to-man attack to a zone offense and vice versa, without changing the fluency of the offense. Because the All-Purpose Percentage Offense operates from out of just two formations, one being an odd-front attack and the other being an even-front attack, it is very easy for a team to change their offense from zone to man-to-man or man-to-man to zone without changing the basic offensive formation, as both formations can work against either zone or man-to-man defenses. Since the offense is primarily a five-player moving attack, it is very easy to determine when a defensive team has changed its defenses, as the players are moving continuously—when no one is cutting with them then it has got to be a zone, and if defensive men move with the cutters then it has got to be a man-to-man defense. At this point, the question of matchup defenses might be brought up. This is no problem for the All-Purpose Percentage Offense because the cuts that are run from either formation can automatically be adjusted to send the cutters into the corners, which is usually one of the most widely used and highly successful maneuvers in handling the matchup defense. Also, by going from an even-front setup to an odd-front setup in the All-Purpose Percentage Offense, or from an odd front to an even front, this technique presents a difficult problem for the matchup defense. It makes the job of actually matching up players very frustrating. Due to all the movement of the all-purpose percentage attacks, after the first series of cuts the matchup has been virtually eliminated. The techniques and patterns used for meeting the fluctuating or changing matchup defenses will be explained thoroughly in Chapter 5.

We have found that usually the players, themselves, can pick up the type of defense being used against them as they run the regular basic All-Purpose Percentage Offense, thus eliminating the need to call a time-out that could be put to more of an advantage at a later point in the game.

Utilizing the Time Clock

The time clock is a very important instrument in the percentage-controlled offense. To be a truly ball- and percentage-controlled team, it is a necessity to have possession of the ball at least two-thirds of the game or approximately 22 minutes of the game's 32 minutes. From the opening tap, a manager trained in running a stopwatch, that will start-stop-restart without erasing the existing time, should be used to keep track of the time the offensive team has the ball in its possession for each quarter of the game. He should be instructed to start the watch each time the offensive team gains possession of the ball (regardless of how it gains advantage of it) and stop the watch each time the defensive team or the opponents gain possession of the ball. The manager must be trained to recognize when the official time clock is stopped and started, so that he can keep an accurate record of the time with regard to the actual amount of time the ball is in play. An example of this would be: When the opponents are called for a violation and the official clock is stopped, the manager waits until the ball is put in play and starts his watch at the same time the game clock is started.

At the end of each quarter, the manager records the total time that exists on the stopwatch—this is the time that our team had the ball in its possession during the quarter. By taking this total and subtracting it from 8 minutes, he gets the amount of time the opponents had the ball during the period. This should be done for each quarter and totalled, for each half and for the entire game. The reason for this is that the percentage-controlled team must set its goal of 22 minutes or more of ball control for each game, and this is the only sure way a team can be positive that it is attaining its goal.

Why the importance of 22 minutes of ball possession to the percentage-controlled team? The main objective of this is based on the theory that if a team has the ball in its possession, it is automatically worth 4 points—the 2 points the offense can score and the 2 points the opponents cannot score . . . a team cannot score unless it has the ball. Many times a percentage-controlled team's best defense is its offense. Also this means that the possession team has to play only about 10 minutes per game on defense while its opponents, who are usually used to going 50-50, must spend 22 minutes or so on defense.

This presents many psychological advantages for the percentage-controlled team. Knowing normal man-to-man defensive play requires so much physical exertion over a 50-50 time period, our players are willing to work extra hard on defense. They realize that they are only going to have to play about 10 minutes of it. Usually they have been on offense for a fairly long period of time when they have to go back and play defense, and the tendency of our opponents to put the ball up in the air as soon as possible means that we will probably not be on defense for any great length of time. Also, having the ball about 22 minutes of the game puts a great deal of pressure on our opponents' offense and defense, because the run-and-shoot teams are used to being on the go back and forth, and they have to establish a rhythm of running and shooting to be really effective. They become easily upset and frustrated when they cannot go, because as soon as they shoot the ball and we can gain possession of it, they know that they are going to have to spend a lot of time on defense. Defense is something that many run-and-shoot teams do not want to play because it is much more tiring physically, as the defensive player must travel sideways and backwards and must go when his man goes—this is definitely tiring psychologically as well as physiologically. Of course when we talk about following the men around wherever they go, we are referring to man-to-man defense. Zone defenses also have a problem, as they have to shift very quickly in order to cover the assigned areas that individual players in the zone must cover. This too can become very tiring, perhaps more so psychologically than physically, whereas man-to-man defense tiredness is based on the opposite theory.

Other Necessary Elements to Play Successful Percentage Basketball

Probably the two other necessary elements needed for playing successful PERCENTAGE BASKETBALL is that the percentage-controlled offensive patterns the players must run have to be fun and enjoyable to execute. That is, the patterns and cuts must be designed so that the players really like to run them. Also the patterns must be extremely challenging for the players, so that they do not become bored by the repetition that must take place in order to learn and perform the movements and assignments correctly. Players take great pride in being able to show that they know their assignments backwards and forwards. This is where the special offensive adjustment techniques come in handy, because they are definitely challenging and sometimes difficult to learn and execute in the correct way in the right situation. Players enjoy being challenged and being able to meet the challenge successfully. There is a great sense of individual and team pride and accomplishment when five players play together to make a set patterned play work to perfection and score 2 points.

The patterns of a percentage-controlled offense must be imaginative but effective, simple but challenging and conservative yet enjoyable. The All-Purpose Percentage Offense offers all of these essential elements.

The Two All-Purpose Percentage Formations

Now is the time to reveal the basic two all-purpose percentage offensive formations. They are not unique, but instead are two generally and widely used formations; however, it is not the formation itself but what is done from these setups that is extremely effective. The basic formation that is used about 80% of the time is the 1-2-2 formation, as shown in Diagram 2-4. It has one point man, two wing men and two low-post men in the original formation. Just by moving

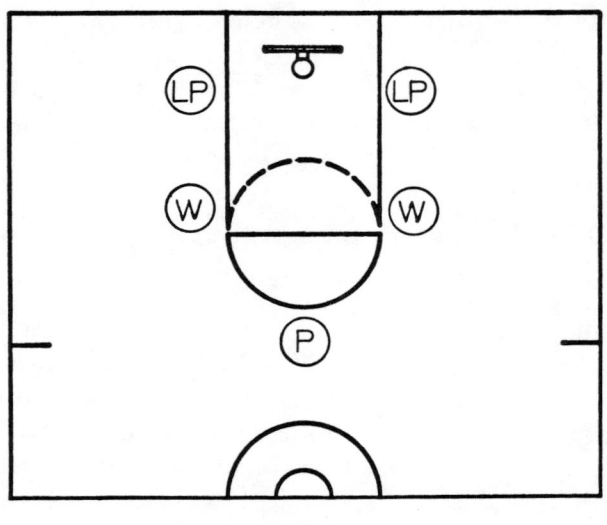

Diagram 2-4

one player from either side of the wing positions, the offense can be set up into a potentially strong weak-side, strong-side attack that will throw a combination shuffle and backtrap at the defense in such a

Building the All-Purpose Percentage Offense 47

manner that the defense will not be able to stop the ball from getting to the most dangerous position on the floor to set up the percentage shot.

The second formation is a supplement to the 1-2-2 formation, and it is used approximately 20% of the time. It is a basic 2-3 low setup, as shown in Diagram 2-5. It has two guards and two forwards, who position themselves low near the basket on the foul line extended, and a low-post center man who stays on the same side as the ball is on at all times. This 2-3 offensive setup is used mostly as a decoy to get into the 1-2-2 formation, except when it is used against zone defenses.

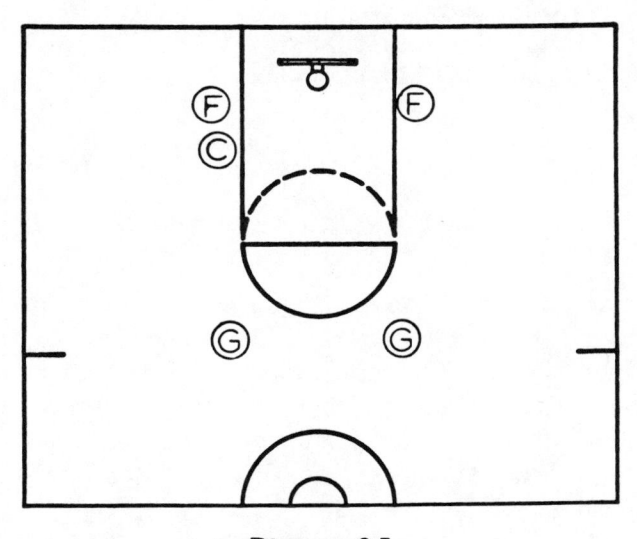

Diagram 2-5

CHAPTER 3

Setting Up the Percentage Man-to-Man Attack

The Five Cutter Formation

The Five Cutter Formation is the offensive alignment that will be used in the All-Purpose Percentage Offense approximately 80% of the time. The Five Cutter Formation is a compact 1-2-2 offensive setup, with several slight adjustments of the techniques used in the percentage-controlled offense. Diagram 3–1 shows and describes the positions the players assume in the original formation. The formation has a point man who is shown as the number 1 man, two wingmen numbered 2 and 3 and two low-post men numbered 4 and 5.

The point man is the best ball handler on the team, and he tries to take the ball to the top of the foul circle even with the basket before starting the offense. The wing men are stationed even with the foul line and tight to the key line as it extends to meet the foul line. The left-wing man is the 3 man and the right-wing man is the 2 man. Both wing men must be tight to the foul line. The low-post men are stationed directly in line with the wing men on their side of the key line. They are tight to the key line and on the 8- by 12-inch divider that separates the first two players on each key line on foul shots. The left-post man is the 5 man and the right-post man is the

Setting Up the Percentage Man-to-Man Attack

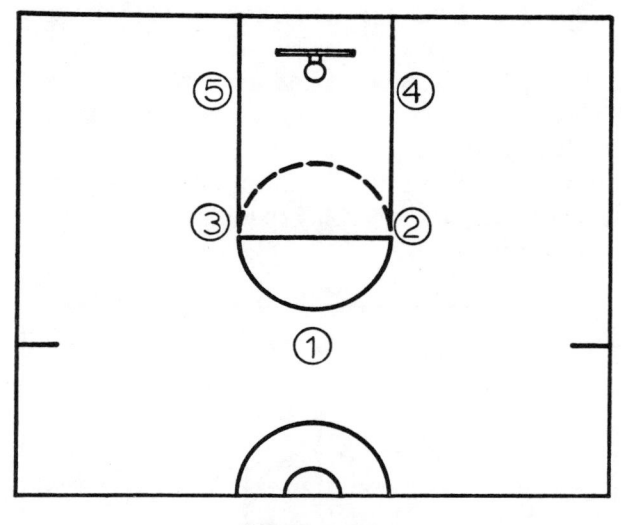

Diagram 3-1

4 man. By numbering the players and the positions on the floor in this manner, the left positions are the odd numbers and the right positions are the even numbers.

After each individual option or play is executed, the offense will still be in the original Five Cutter Formation, if the option does not result in a try for a goal. Each time the offense is run from one side of the court and a shot is not taken, the ball is now on the other side of the court; this is called "turning the offense over." It just means that the offense has started on one side of the court and did not get a shot, so it has been turned over to the other side of the court, and it is ready to start over again, immediately, in the original 1-2-2 Five Cutter Formation.

The Development of the Five Cutter Offense

We have always run some form of backtrap or shuffle continuity in our offensive patterns. However, there were always three things that seemed to be drawbacks to these fine offenses. We found it very difficult to get the ball to the weak side of a basic shuffle setup because the defense would play real tight on the weak-side man. They knew that in order for a shuffle offense to be really effective, the ball had to go to the weak-side man in order to start the attack. Thus, the defense would force us to go to the strong side of the formation, which did not offer options that were as effective as those of the weak-side cuts. The

Setting Up the Percentage Man-to-Man Attack

defense also could read our formation immediately because the basic shuffle formation is a strong-side–weak-side formation. As our guards brought the ball up, all the defense had to do was see which side of the court the high-post man was set up on, and they automatically knew where the ball was going to go before we could get our offense set up. Diagram 3-2 shows the problem of the weak-side–strong-side formation and the denial pressure overplay that can be put on the weak-side man in a shuffle formation.

STRONG SIDE   WEAK SIDE

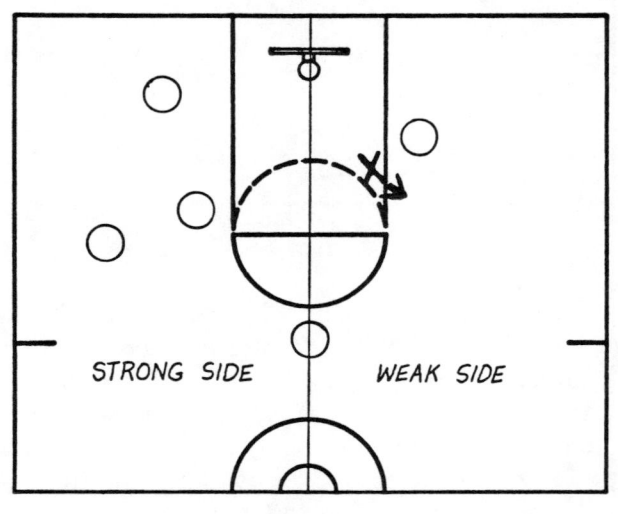

Diagram 3-2

Another serious problem we encountered was that when the high-post man would set himself up as a stationary screen for the strong-side wing man to run his man into after the ball had gone to the weak side, the defensive man watching the strong-side wing man would sag off the wing man, even to the point of being behind the high-post man setting the stationary screen (Diagram 3-3). Because this defensive maneuver cut down on the effectiveness of this basic shuffle concept, we either had to make an offensive adjustment or not use this option of the shuffle.

Every year we used the shuffle and backtrap continuity attack, we found it increasingly harder to be as effective as we had been the season before. We finally came to a point where we either had to find the solution to these two pressing problems or drop these offenses and go to a different type of offense. Because the shuffle and backtrap continuity offenses had been so successful for us over the years, the thought of dropping these excellent team offenses was very depressing. So we went to work on how to solve these difficult problems.

Setting Up the Percentage Man-to-Man Attack 51

Finally, after much searching and experimenting, we came across a formation that would not let the defense know which side the weak side or strong side was going to be on until after two passes were made. Also, because we liked the backtrap theory, we had the man who was setting the backtrap screen on the strong side of the floor change assignments with the low-post man on the same side of the floor. We also had the man setting the screen change his technique for applying the screen. Instead of having the man set a stationary screen and then have the strong-side wing man run his man into the screen, we had the man setting the screen go headhunting and actually set his backtrap screen on the defensive man who was guarding the strong-side wing man, as shown in Diagram 3-4. This meant that the man setting the screen had to go to the point on the floor where the defensive man was to set the screen, directly on the strong-side wing man's defender. This technique of setting the backtrap screen on the defensive man, instead of setting a stationary screen to have the cutter run his man into, had been extremely effective.

By finding a formation that takes care of the defensive tendency to overplay the original weak side and by adjusting the backtrap

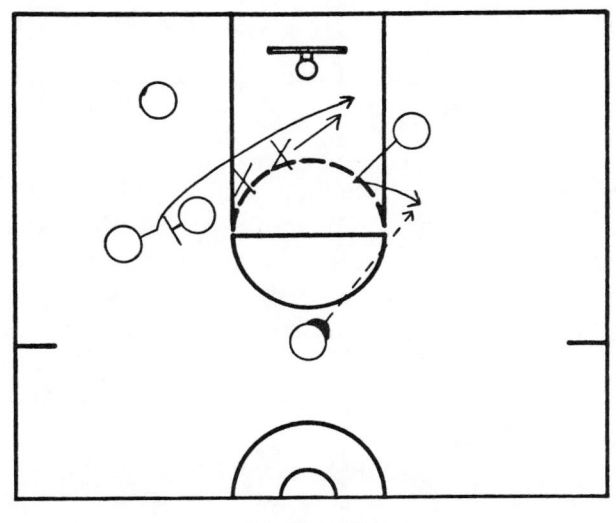

Diagram 3-3

screen technique, we have been able to continue using the shuffle and backtrap continuity offenses and principles with a great deal of success. We have also been able to develop a real, effective All-Purpose Percentage Offense, and these two adjustments have played a big part in the success of this attack.

Diagram 3-5 shows how we start to get into the weak-side–strong-side formation from the original 1-2-2 setup, thus reducing the defense's ability to deny the pass to the weak side. This is accomplished by not giving the defense enough time to see which side is going to become the weak side until it is too late to do anything about allowing the ball to get to one of the wing spots. The time the defense has to react to the 1-2-2 setup to the weak-side–strong-side formation has been cut to almost half of what it was in the original shuffle concept.

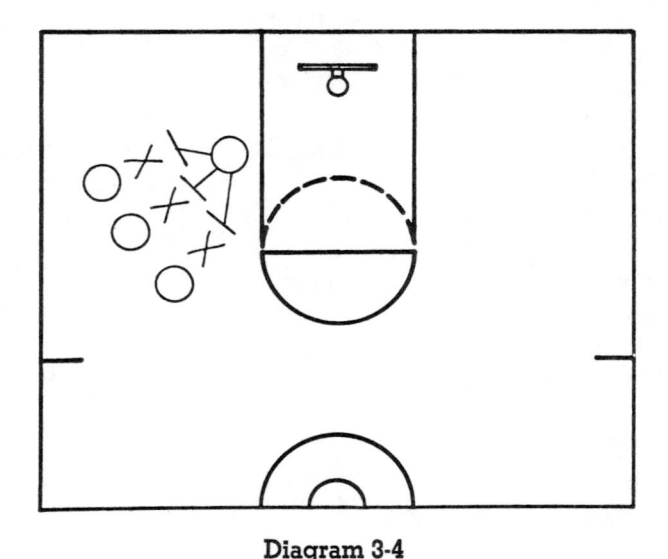

Diagram 3-4

The point man brings the ball up and stops his dribble at the top of the foul circle. He immediately has an option of passing to either wing man. As soon as the point man stops dribbling, both wing men make a sharp V (in-and-back move) to free themselves. They should try to get the ball even with the foul line and about 5 feet from the key line extended. Of course, the defense does not know which wing man is going to receive the ball. This keeps the defense relatively honest. If the point man cannot get the ball to either wing man because of the pressure that the defense is putting on the wings, then one of the low-post men just flashes into the middle to get the ball. He either gets the shot, as shown in Diagram 3-6, or the wing man on the same side of the court as was the low-post man (who now has the ball) just back-doors his man and cuts to the basket on a straight line to receive the pass from the low-post man for the easy layup (Diagram 3-7).

After the defense has been burned a couple of times by this maneuver, the offense should have very little trouble in getting the ball to the wings in order to start the offense.

Diagram 3-5

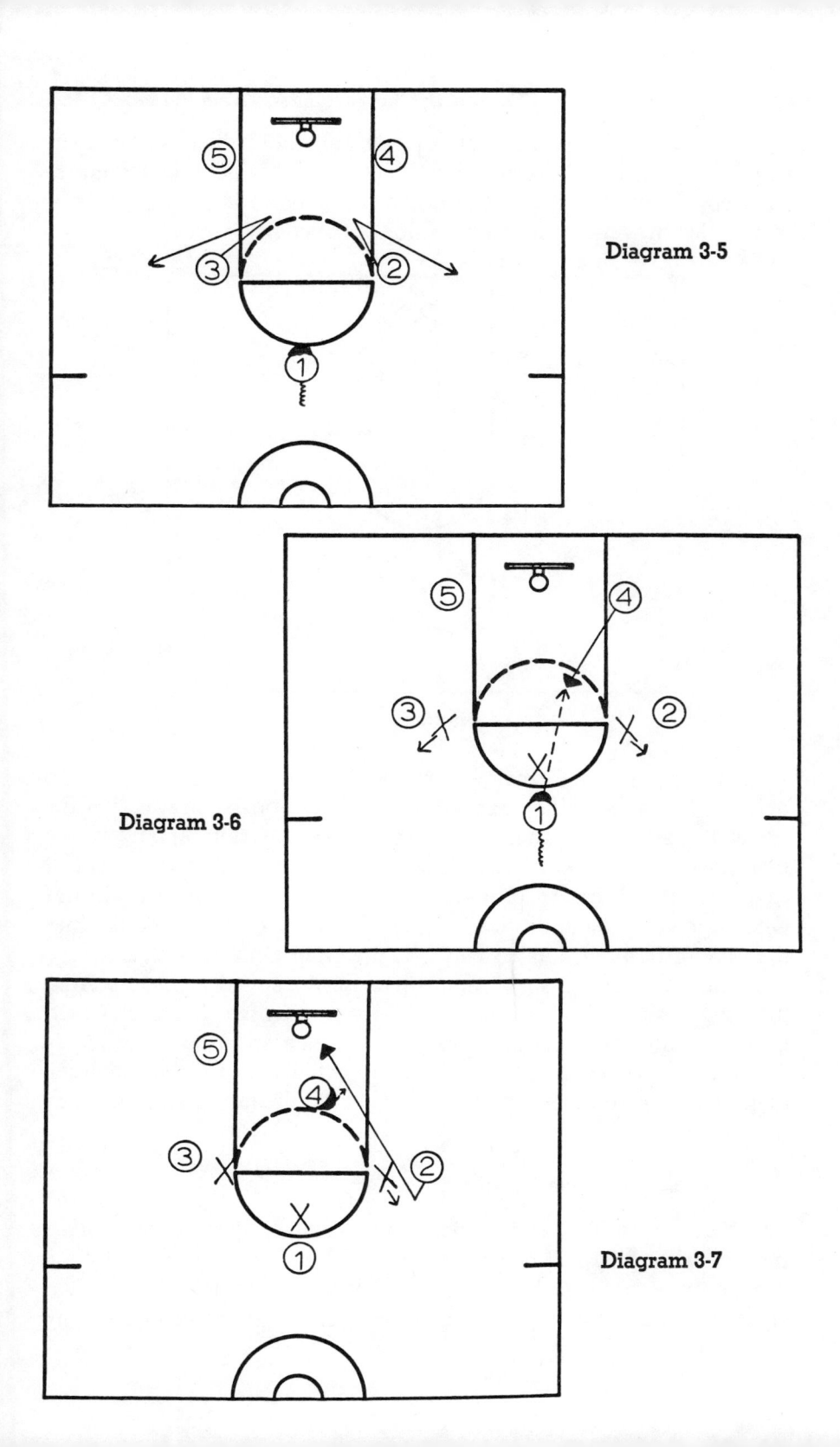

Diagram 3-6

Diagram 3-7

Diagram 3-8 has the 1 man passing to the 2 man. The 2 man now has two options concerning where to pass the ball. He can either pass the ball back to the 1 man at the point, or he may pass to the 4 man at the low-post position on his side of the court.

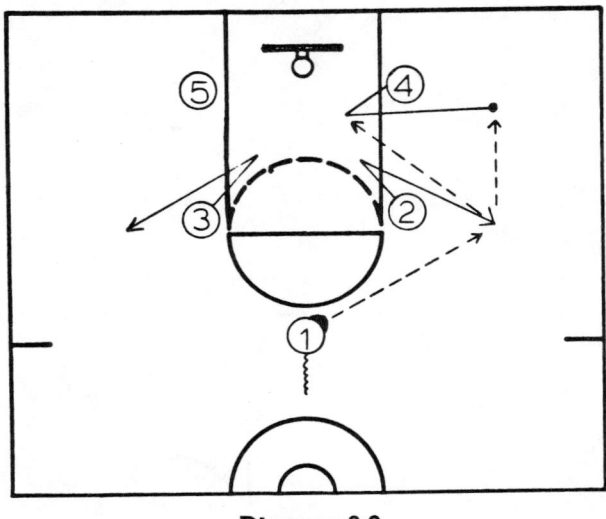

Diagram 3-8

Another problem that was created by the defense in trying to defense the basic shuffle weak-side–strong-side formation was that the signal for the play option to be run was usually determined by the man at the top of the foul circle who had the ball, and this made it easy for the defense to pick up the offensive cue. The Five Cutter Offense is very unique in that it is not the point man who determines the play to be used, but instead it is the wing man who receives the pass and becomes the signal man. Because the signal is coming from the wing position (usually in any odd-front offensive formation), and the signal most often comes from the point man, it makes it extremely difficult for the defense to pick up the signal because the defensive players are usually looking for the play to originate from out front in the middle of the court.

The Signals for the Five Cutter Offense

The signals that will be used to determine what option will be run and what play will be run from the option are determined by the wing man with the ball. Of course the point man has the original choice, because he may pass to either wing man. After one of the wing

Setting Up the Percentage Man-to-Man Attack 55

men receives the ball from the point man, he becomes the man to watch for the signal. After the wing man has made his pass to either the point or the base-line low-post man on his side of the court, the signal for the option that he wants run is given. The wing man first determines what option is going to be used, and this is signaled by his passing to either the point or the low post. He then determines the play that is going to be executed by his maneuver after his pass. This is done by his either cutting through to the key area or by staying put after his pass, regardless of where he passed the ball. Diagram 3-8 shows the two choices the wing man has after he receives the ball from the point; Diagram 3-9 shows the alternates the wing man has after he passes the ball to the low-post man and Diagram 3-10 shows his choices if he passes the ball back to the point man. Remember, regardless of who the wing man passes to, he must either cut through the bucket area toward the basket or remain in his position. He either stays or goes.

When teaching these signals and the techniques used in administrating them in the All-Purpose Percentage-Controlled Offense, it should be stated here and now that in the beginning it will be quite difficult for the other four players, other than the wing man with the ball, to pick up the wing man's original option signal and then his play signal, because they are not used to watching a wing man for the signal to determine what the offense should do. It usually takes quite a bit of hard, concentrated work in this area till the other players disci-

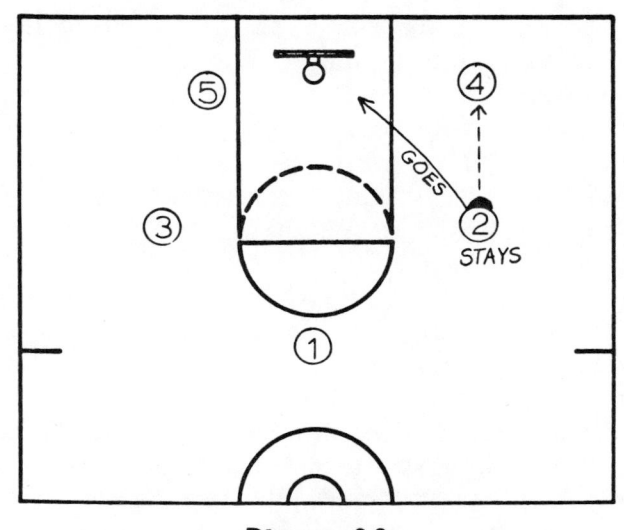

Diagram 3-9

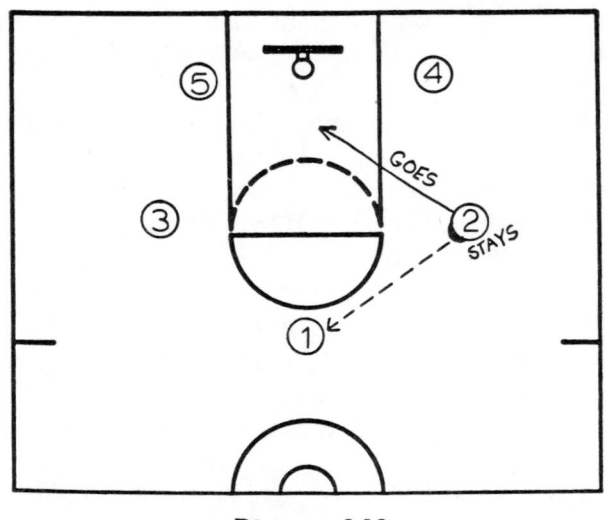

Diagram 3-10

pline themselves to watch the wing man instead of the point man. However, do not become too discouraged if they seem slow to pick this technique up. As you will see when you first start these signal techniques, because it is hard for the offense to discipline themselves, you can imagine how hard it is for the defensive players to pick up the signals, for they too are not used to having the signals come from the wing man. Not only will the defense not be able to pick up the signal man right away, but usually they will experience a great amount of difficulty in picking up the play signal because it comes after the second pass, and it is determined by a player in the wing position, not the point position.

After the wing man passes the ball to the low-post man on his side of the court, who has broken out to the corner, even with the wing man with the ball, the 2 man who passed the ball to the 4 man cuts through, looking for the return pass of a simple give-and-go option. If he does not get the ball, he cuts directly to the opposite-side high-post position at a point where the foul line and key line meet, and now we are in a weak-side–strong-side formation (Diagram 3-11). If the wing man passes the ball back to the point man, he cuts through the bucket area and goes over to the same position he was in when he passed to the base-line man and then cut through but did not receive the return pass. This is shown in Diagram 3-12 where again the offense is in a weak-side–strong-side setup, and we got into this formation without too much difficulty. You will see later on in the chapter,

Setting Up the Percentage Man-to-Man Attack

Diagram 3-11

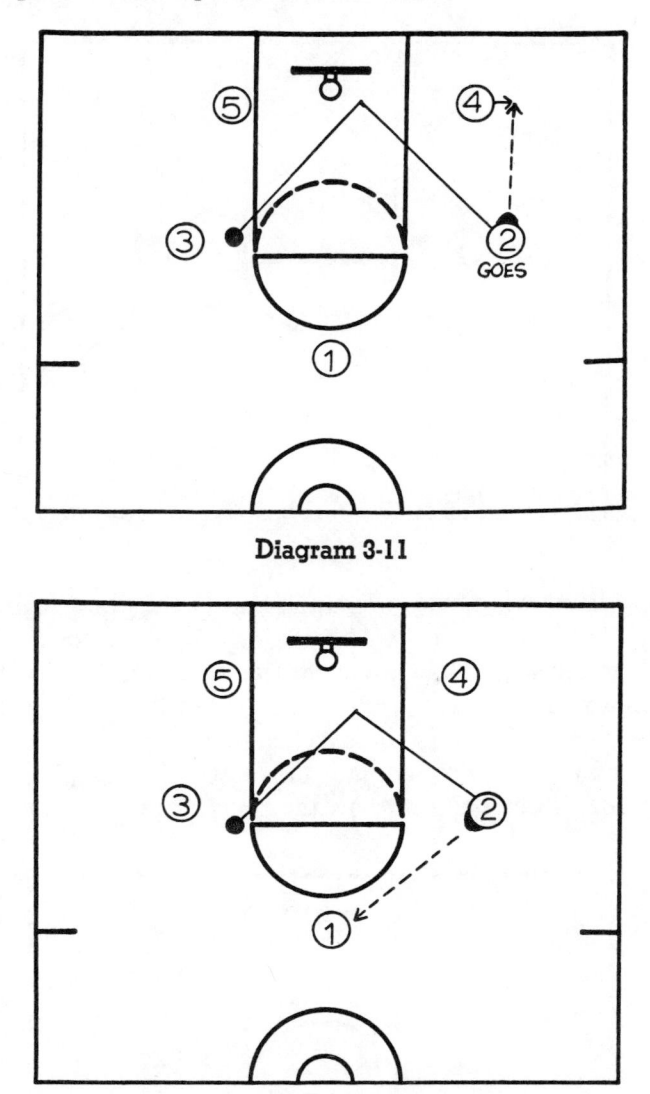

Diagram 3-12

when we discuss the Identical Inside Option, how really effective this technique of getting into the weak-side–strong-side formation is.

Many times the man cutting through, after he has passed to the wing man, stops in the bucket area and posts himself. If his defensive man is not alert, then he can get the quick, short jump shot, and if he is not open, then he quickly clears the bucket area and goes to the high-post spot, as shown in Diagram 3-13.

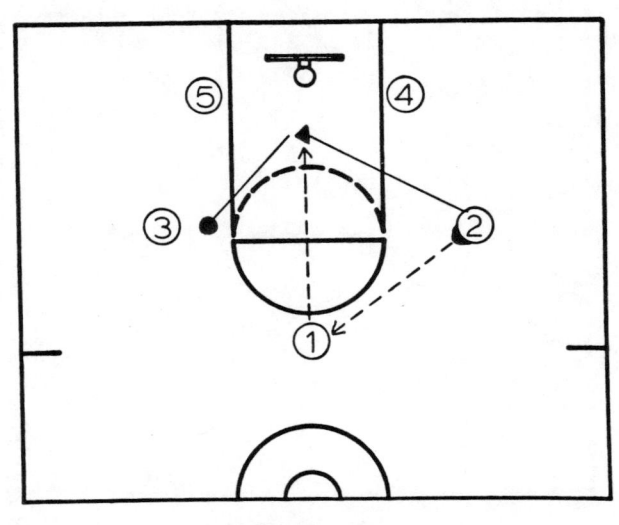

Diagram 3-13

Also, if the wing man passes the ball to the point man and does not cut or go through, then this is the key for the opposite-side wing man to cut through. Now we have the same weak-side–strong-side formation, except that it is on the other side of the court, as illustrated in Diagram 3-14. This is an excellent technique to use when the defensive players seem to feel that they have picked up the signal for the wing man's cut on a pass to the point. Executed correctly, this

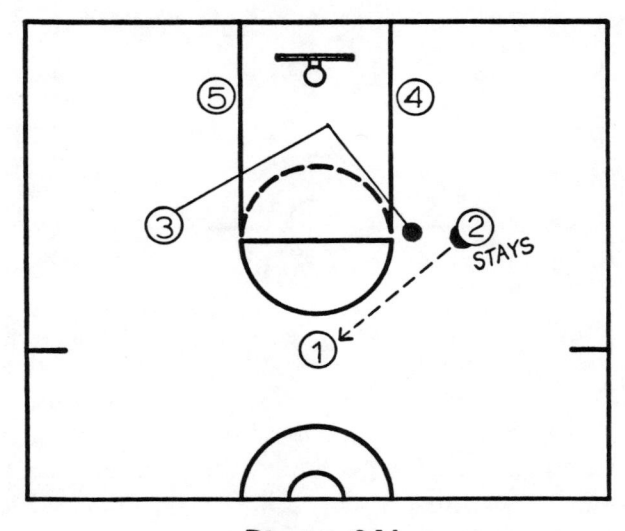

Diagram 3-14

Setting Up the Percentage Man-to-Man Attack 59

technique presents an excellent adjustment maneuver to get the offense into the weak-side–strong-side formation, without the defense being able to pick up the offensive cue to have the opposite wing man cut through instead of the wing man with the ball.

If the wing man with the ball has difficulty in getting it back to the point or to the corner because the defensive players put on tight pressure by overplaying their men, then we use the same offensive technique that we used when the point man had difficulty in getting the ball to the wing men, as was shown in Diagram 3-6. Diagram 3-15 shows what happens when pressure is applied to the point and corner.

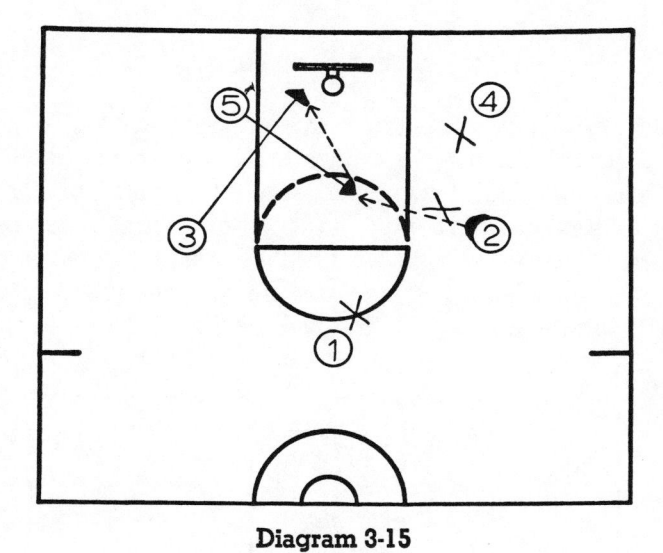

Diagram 3-15

The opposite-side low-post man, the 5 man in this instance, just flashes to the middle to get the ball from 2. He can shoot or he can feed the wing man who was on his side of the court, the 3 man, on a back-door maneuver that results in the easy shot. This again will keep the defense honest. This is also an excellent way of getting the ball to a big man and not allowing the defense to sag on him, because they are too busy covering the passing lanes that are used to start the Five Cutter Offense.

The development of the Five Cutter Offense was brought about by the three situations that cause us a great deal of trouble in using the shuffle and backtrap concept. These three problems were:

(1) Difficulty in getting the ball to the weak-side position to start the offense.

(2) Difficulty in having the high-post man stand stationary and having the strong-side wing man run his man into the screen, thus allowing the defensive man an opportunity to sag around the high-post man and "play" the play.

(3) Difficulty in concealing the signals for the plays to be run because they were always given by the man who was at the point.

We feel that the Five Cutter Offense, developed from the shuffle and backtrap theory, combined with the adjustments we made in correcting the three major difficulties encountered in using these excellent offensive attacks, has given us a far more potent offense.

Getting into the Five Cutter Offense

As has already been shown, the offense is started by getting the ball to either of the wing positions. The wing men should be positioned tight to the foul line extended, and they should break out to get the ball as soon as the point man stops dribbling. After one of the wing men receives the ball, he must be ready to start the offense. Diagram 3-16 shows the 1 man passing to the 2 man. At this point the 2 man should look quickly to the 4 man, who should move into the

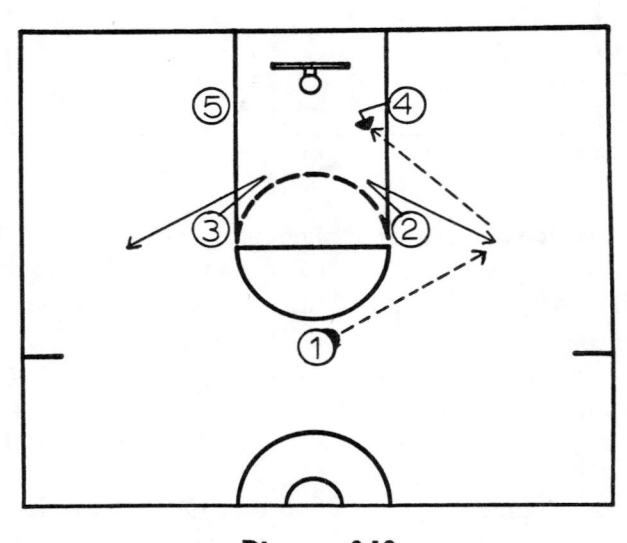

Diagram 3-16

bucket area to get in a better position to receive the ball from 2. If the 4 man is open, then he should be fed by the 2 man. If the 4 man is not open, then he should do one of the three following things:

Setting Up the Percentage Man-to-Man Attack 61

(1) Move quickly to the corner on the side of the ball and line himself up even with the wing man (Diagram 3-17).

(2) Move quickly to the high-post area on the opposite side of the court (Diagram 3-18).

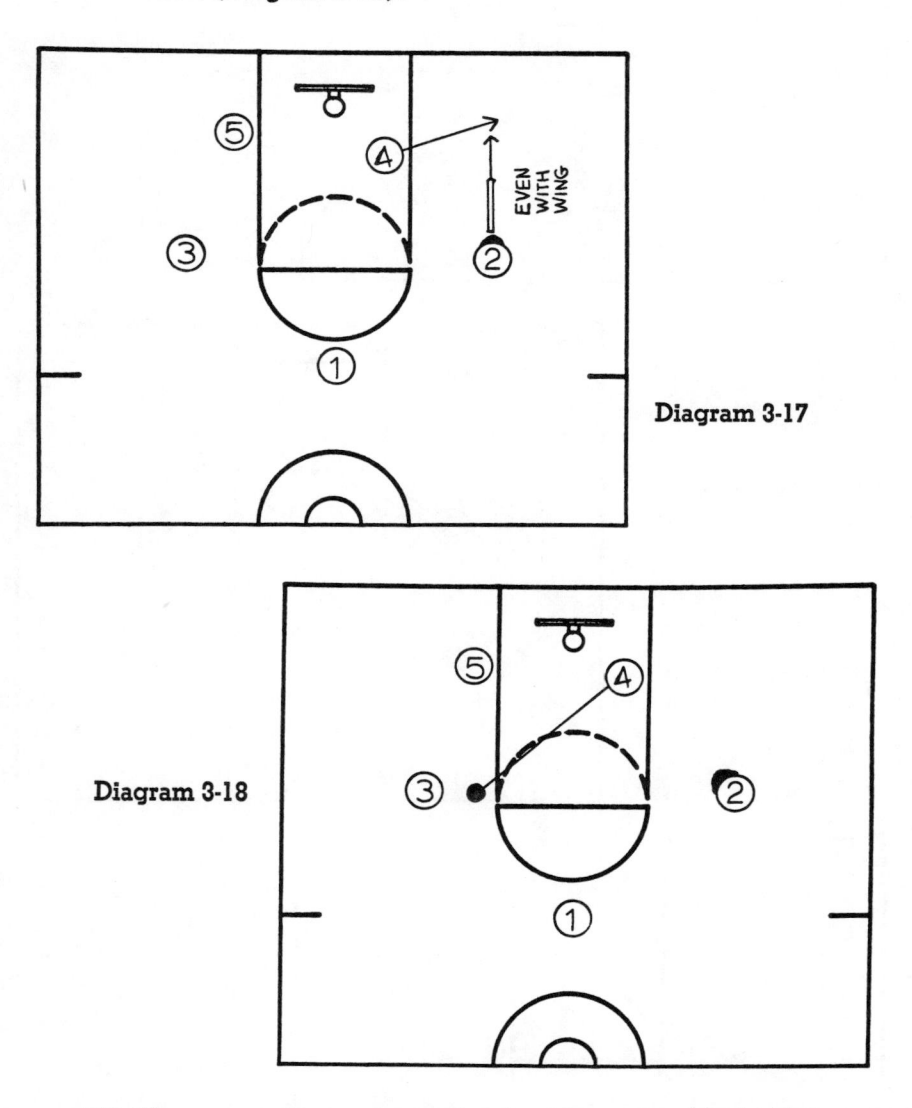

Diagram 3-17

Diagram 3-18

(3) Move up and set a screen for the wing man with the ball, and then he should screen roll as the wing man comes off his screen. The wing man should look for the shot off the post man's screen (Diagram 3-19), or he should feed the post man rolling to the basket, as shown in Diagram 3-20. If neither of these two options

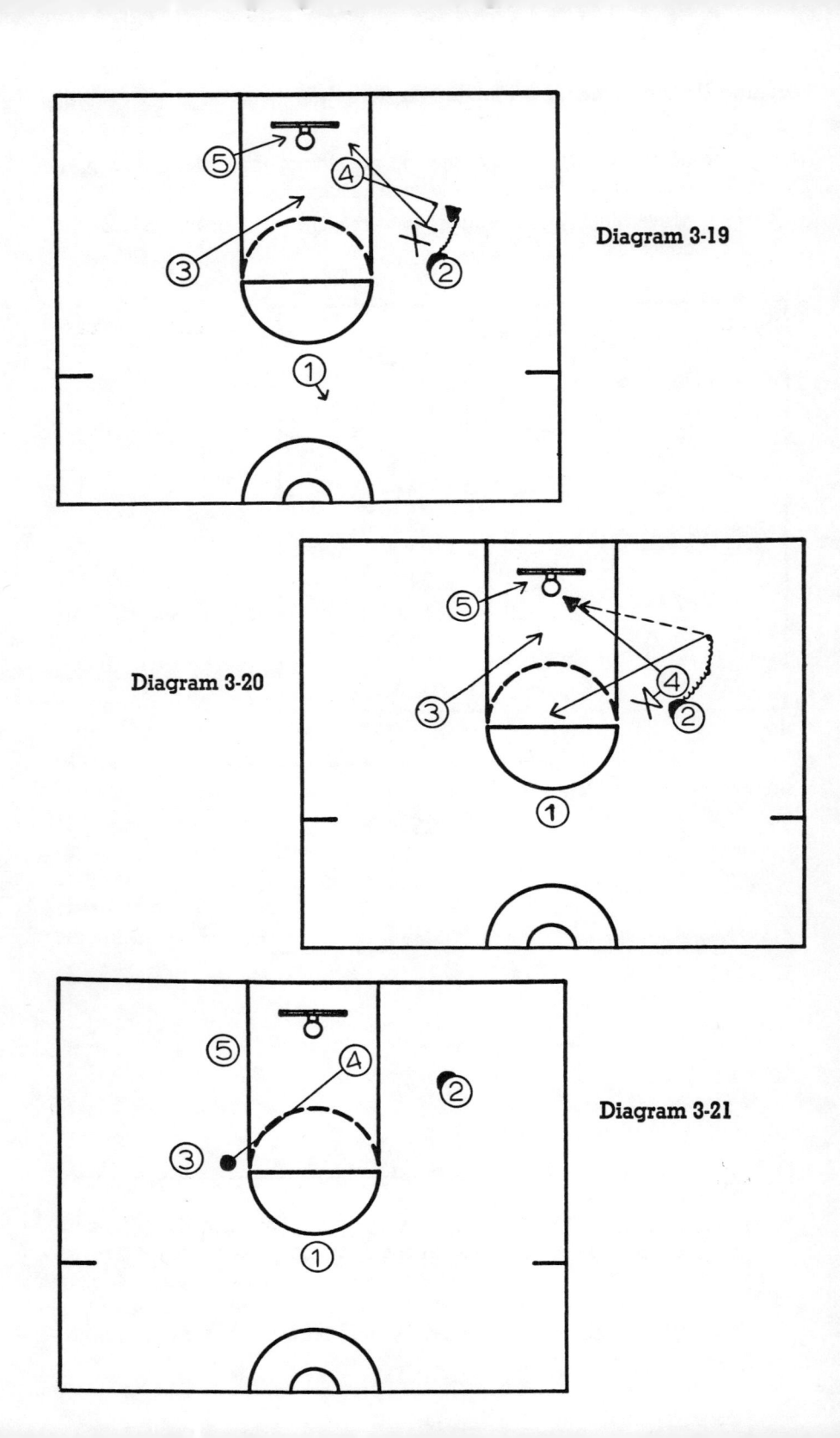

Diagram 3-19

Diagram 3-20

Diagram 3-21

Setting Up the Percentage Man-to-Man Attack 63

is successful, then the low-post man should move to the high-post area on the opposite side of the court, as shown in Diagram 3-21.

These basic, fundamental moves are used to get into the weak-side–strong-side formation of the Five Cutter Offense; they are also used to put immediate offensive pressure on the defense to stop these potentially dangerous offensive maneuvers, that can result in the easy percentage shot if the defense does not remain alert. By keeping the pressure on the defense, it makes it much easier to get into the weak-side–strong-side formation. The defenders are kept so busy defending these simple, but effective offensive moves, that before they have realized what has happened, the offense is into its regular shuffle and backtrap combinations, which make the Five Cutter Offense go. We have found that whenever you want to start any offense, you should put immediate pressure on the defense, combined with decoy moves that can result in the easy basket if not defensed properly; by doing this, it is much easier to get your main offensive attack going. The reason for this is the defense has not had an opportunity to read your plan of attack, because they are too busy with the decoy moves designed to keep the defense busy while the main attack sneaks up on the defense. Many times the defense will ignore the decoy techniques because the main offensive attack is what they are concerned with; they overlook the fundamental moves, and this gives the offense the easy shot without having to go into their main attack.

One other technique the offense can use to get into the weak-side–strong-side formation, especially when facing overplay pressure on the wings, is to have the point man dribble toward one of the wing men. Diagram 3-22 shows the 1 man at the point dribbling toward the

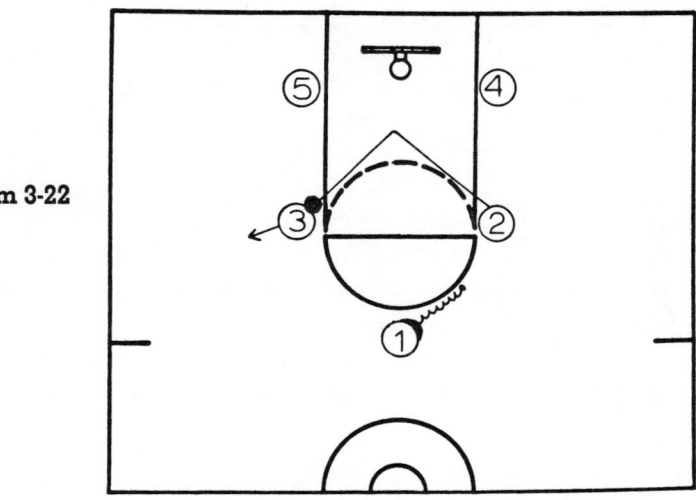

Diagram 3-22

2 man at the right-wing position. As soon as the 2 man sees the 1 man start his dribble toward him, he clears out and cuts through the bucket area, going to the left-side high-post position. Again the weak-side–strong-side formation has been established.

Establishing the Outside and Inside Options

Before going into the options and the plays from each option, we must establish first what an Outside Option is and what an Inside Option is. Diagram 3-23 illustrates these two important moves. An Outside Option is developed any time the wing man passes the ball to

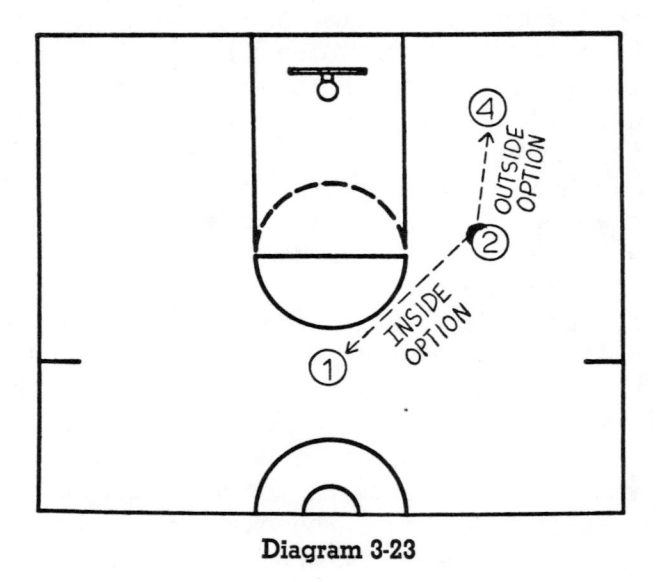

Diagram 3-23

a low-post man in the corner on the side of the ball. An Inside Option is established any time the wing man with the ball passes to the point man.

Diagram 3-24 shows the 2 man passing to the 4 man in the corner, then the 2 man stays put; this is an Outside Option. After passing to 4 in the corner, the 2 man goes through on a cut to the basket. This too is an Outside Option. In Diagram 3-25, the 2 man passes the ball back to the 1 man at the point and then goes through the bucket area; this is an Inside Option. If the 2 man stays after his pass to 1, then this also is an Inside Option, because the opposite-side wing man goes through to start the option.

The names "outside" and "inside" have been determined because when the ball is passed to the corner, it is on the outside of the court,

Setting Up the Percentage Man-to-Man Attack

Diagram 3-24

OUTSIDE OPTION

Diagram 3-25

INSIDE OPTION

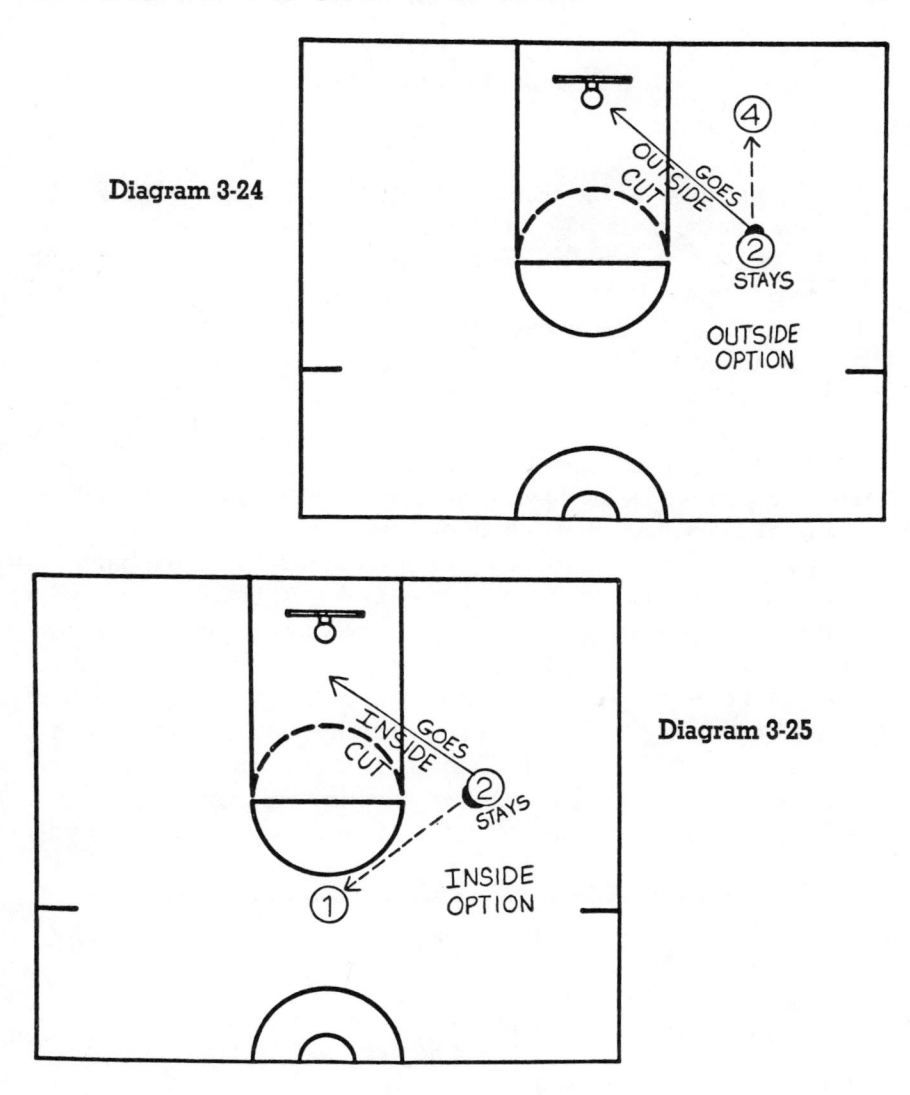

and the wing man who has passed the ball is looking to the outside of the court. When the wing man stays after passing to the corner, then the opposite-side low-post man goes through the bucket, looking to the outside as he cuts. When the ball is returned to the point or the middle of the court, the ball is on the inside of the court and the wing man is looking to the inside of the court. After he makes his pass, and as he cuts through the middle of the bucket area, he is still looking to the inside of the court as he heads for the opposite-side high-post position.

The Outside Options

The 1 Play

The first play of the Outside Option Series is called the 1 play. The 1 man at the point passes to the 2 man at the right-wing position. The 2 man looks to feed the low-post man—in this case, the 4 man in the low-post area. If the 4 man is not open, then he breaks to the corner on the ball side of the court and stops even with the 2 man. The 2 man passes to 4 in the corner, as shown in Diagram 3-26. This pass to the ball-side corner man is the signal that an Outside Option is going to be run. The signal for the 1 play is the 2 man, after passing to 4, stays put; this is the cue for the opposite-side low-post man, the 5 man, to break across the low bucket area in line with the basket, on what is called a flash move, and stop near the basket, as shown in Diagram 3-27. The 5 man should not break across to get the ball until the 4 man has it, because many times if the 5 man breaks too early, at the time he is open the 4 man may not have received the ball yet from 2. The ball actually is still in flight, making it impossible to get it to the 5 man at the instant he is open and in the best possible position to receive the pass. If the 5 man is open, then he should be fed by the 4 man. *Coaching Hint:* When feeding an open man in the power lane, regardless of the option that was used to spring the man free, the two-handed overhead pass should be used to feed the open man. This pass

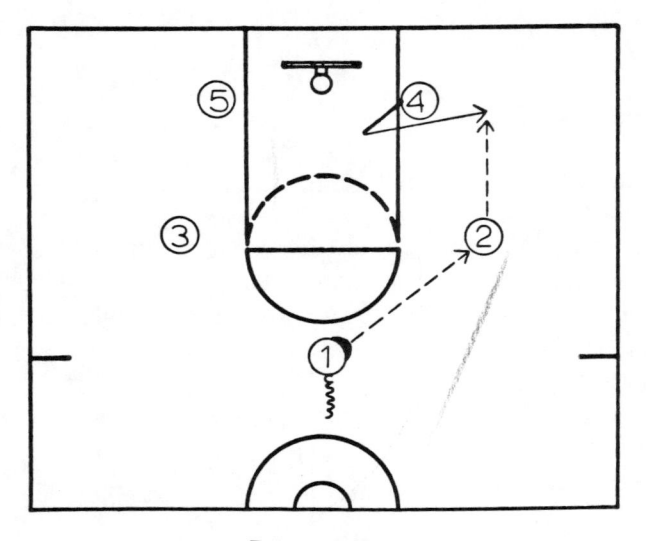

Diagram 3-26

Setting Up the Percentage Man-to-Man Attack

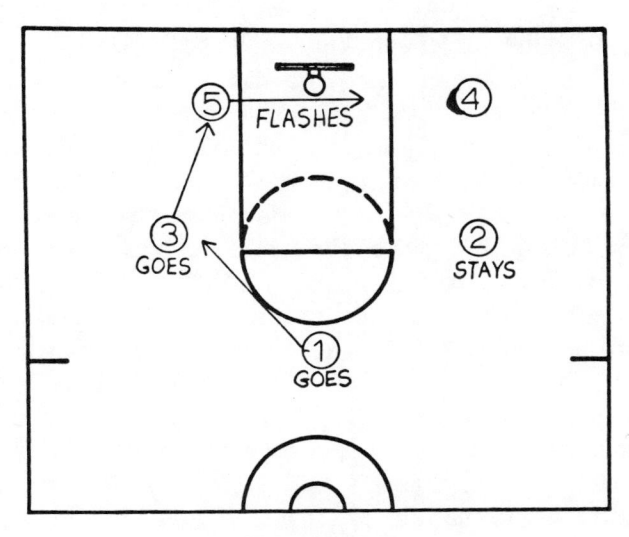

Diagram 3-27

should be used exclusively when feeding into the power lane, because of all the passes that are used in basketball, this is the one that is telegraphed the least. The player should hold the ball over his head immediately after receiving it, with both hands, and just flick his wrists to release the ball. He should not move either foot when executing this pass.

As shown in Diagram 3-28, the 5 man gets the ball in the power

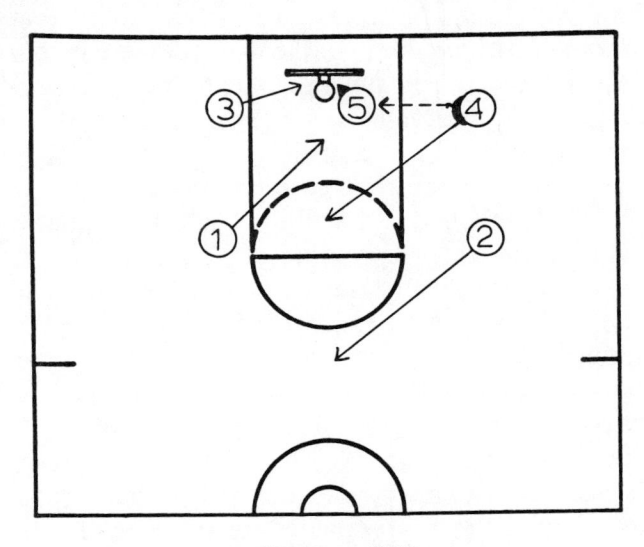

Diagram 3-28

lane close to the basket. As soon as the 5 man receives it, he should square himself to the basket and then use the power shot.

As soon as the 3 man sees that 5 has started his base-line move, he should move down to take the 5 man's original position in the left low-post area and get ready to go to the offensive board on the left side of the basket. The 1 man should move over and take the left-wing position as soon as he sees the 3 man move down to the base line. The 1 man should get in position to rebound in the bucket area in front of the basket on the shot by 5. The 2 man, after seeing the 5 man make his move, heads to the point position to become the player who has defensive responsibility on the shot. The 4 man, after he feeds 5, should wait until 5 shoots, and then he goes to the foul line for the half-and-half responsibility of being in position for any deep rebound, and also to get ready to stop the opponent's fast break. *Coaching Hint:* The reason that the 4 man goes to the foul line after feeding the 5 man is that he must follow the rule that says if you feed a man in the power lane and he shoots, then you go to the foul line. Even though 4 is one of the big men, it must be taken into consideration that if he goes to the offensive board, he may run himself and his man into the area of the 5 man taking the shot. Also, the type of shot that is being taken will not have a long trajectory. This is why the 4 man goes to the foul line and the 1 man goes to the offensive board. At this point it should be explained that these diagrams show the first time through of each play, and that is why the big men, 4 and 5, are usually moving away from the basket on the shot. We do not expect to get the open shot the first time through on each option, regardless of the option that is being run, and after the first time through, the 4 and 5 men are not moving away from the basket, but actually are going to it on the second, third and fourth times through. Again, we do not mind moving the big men away from the hoop on the first time through because the type of shot that develops is the high-percentage type, which means that there should not be a long rebound. It also means that the opponent's defensive big men who are matched up with our big men must also come away from the basket, which takes away some of the defense's rebounding power. We also wish to keep the rule for all options that if you feed a man in the power lane and he shoots, then the man who feeds the shooter must go to the foul line.

The advantages of having the 4 and 5 men move away from the basket on the first time through far outweigh the disadvantages of this offensive maneuver. We have found that forcing our big men to do things that big men are not supposed to do actually helps them

Setting Up the Percentage Man-to-Man Attack 69

become better all-around basketball players, because it makes them more flexible and it gives them the added confidence they need to develop the finer skills of the game.

When using any continuity offensive pattern that moves four or five men each time the pattern is run through, it is very important to keep in mind that the offense usually works best on the third or fourth turns through, because the defense is set up the first and second times through. Four- or five-man continuity patterns are designed to move each player from one position of the offense to another, and it is this technique that more than justifies moving the big men away from the basket in order to take them back to it, using a maneuver that is much more effective than having a big man standing still in the post position resembling a *post*. *Coaching Hint:* Any time a player moves into the power lane to receive a pass, he should put up his inside hand nearest the basket so as to give the feeder as big a target as possible to hit. The cutter should extend his arm as high as possible, and he may even have to jump up to get the pass, come down, square himself to the hoop and go up again. Also, by having the cutter raise his arm, it helps attract the attention of the man who has the ball. The man with the ball has a better chance of seeing a cutter who has his hand in the air than a cutter who does not.

Rules for Defensive Responsibility on an Outside Option

Any time that an Outside Option is run, the following rule must be enforced every time a shot is taken: When the man with the ball feeds a player who is in the power lane, then he should go to the foul line for the half-and-half assignment, and the man who is moving into the point position has the deep defensive responsibility, as shown in Diagram 3-29. When the man with the ball feeds a player outside of the power lane and that player takes a shot, then the feeder must go to the point position for the deep defensive responsibility, Diagram 3-30. If these two simple rules are followed to the letter on every shot taken, then a team should never be "fast broke."

Continuity for the 1 Play

When running the 1 play, if the 5 man is not open in the power lane, then the 4 man dribbles to the right-wing position (Diagram 3-31). The 2 man is now at the point, the 3 man should already be in the left low-post spot, the 1 man should be at the left-wing position and the 5 man moves out of the bucket area to the right low-post spot.

Diagram 3-29

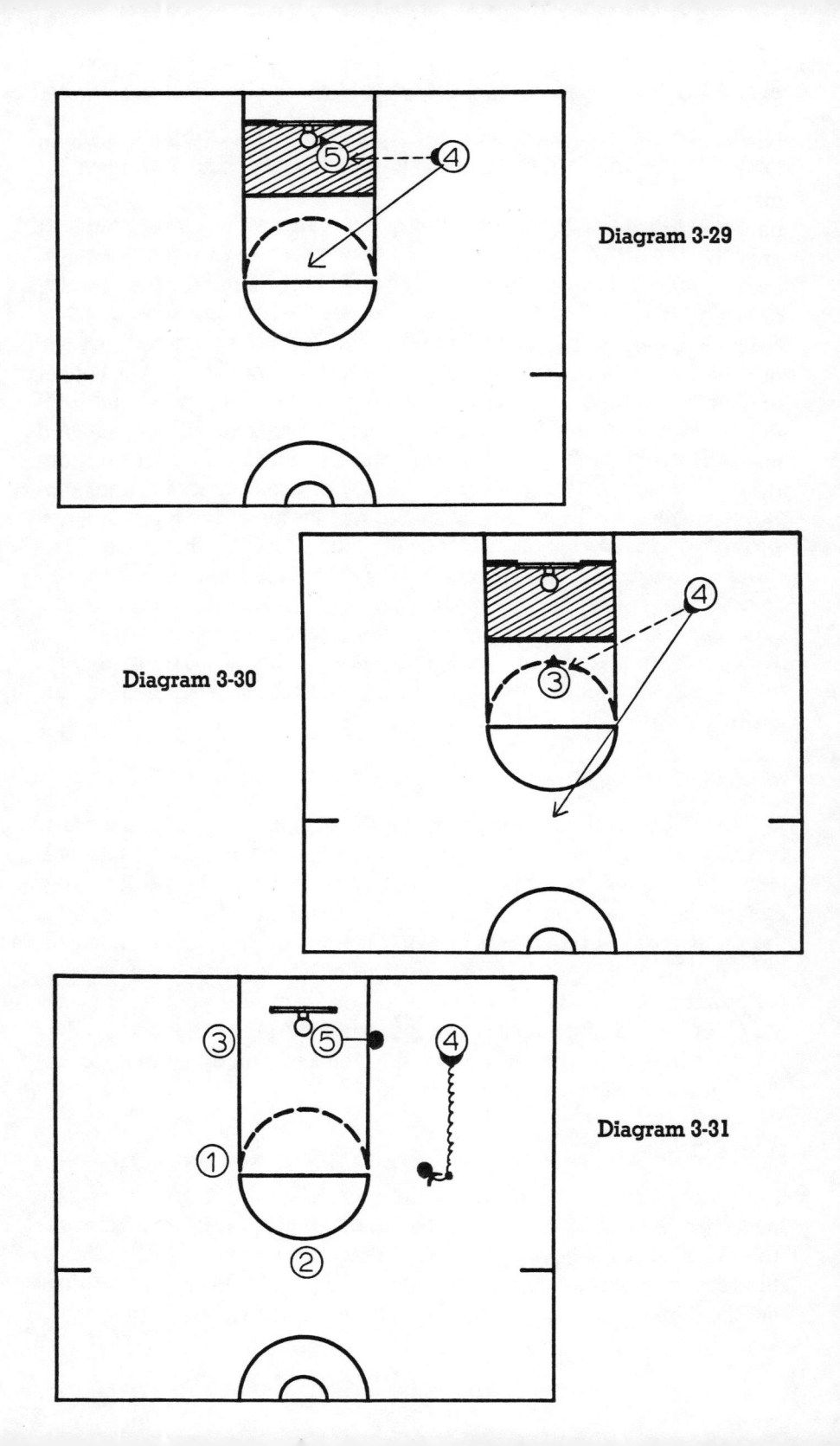

Diagram 3-30

Diagram 3-31

Setting Up the Percentage Man-to-Man Attack 71

Now the offense is still in the Five Cutter Formation, as shown in Diagram 3-31. The man at the right-wing position with the ball, the 4 man, can now immediately start the offense again without getting the ball to the point. He looks inside to feed the 5 man in the low-post area. If 5 is open, he should get the ball. If 5 is not free, then the 4 man can start an Outside Option by passing the ball to 5 in the corner, or he can start an Inside Option by passing the ball to the 2 man at the point position. *Coaching Hint:* The 5 man, after coming across the bucket area in the power lane, should break only to clear the bucket area and then stop. He should stay tight to the key line extended until the 4 man has looked at him to feed him. If 5 is not open for the feed and 4 looks toward the corner, then at this time, and only now, should the 5 man break to the corner, stopping in line with the 4 man to receive the pass (Diagram 3-32). If the 5 man continued on the move to the corner without stopping after he cleared the 3-second area, it

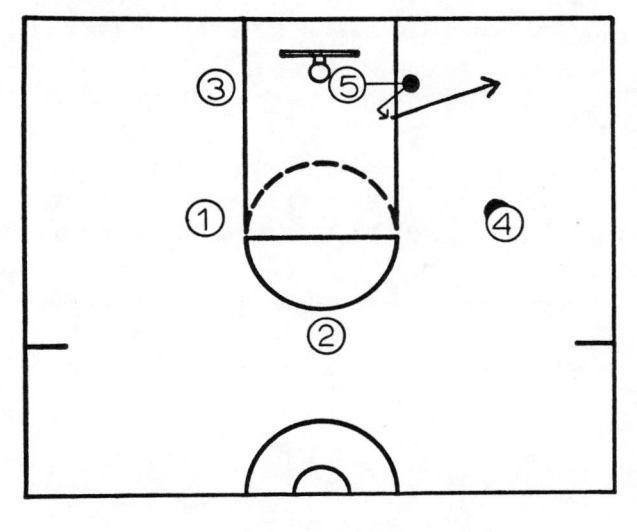

Diagram 3-32

would make his defensive man's job much easier, and also it would take away his threat of getting the pass in the low-post power lane area. By keeping his man busy as he moves into the power lane, it makes it very easy to get the ball from the wing man after he breaks to the corner, because the defensive man cannot overplay his move to the corner without leaving himself very vulnerable to the 5 man when he is in or near the power lane.

This 1 play can be run over and over again as many times as a team desires to run it, in search of the high-percentage power-lane shot. This is an excellent technique to use in setting up a mismatch situation of a short man on a tall man going into the power lane, without allowing the defense to adjust to counteract the disadvantage. If the 1 play was run through four or five times and you have your original left wing man or point man in the power lane, then the offense has a distinct advantage, because the defensive men covering these offensive players are not used to defensing men in this post area in the post position. A man 6′ tall being guarded by a man 5′9″ in height has the same advantage as a 6′6″ man being covered by a 6′3″ player. These mismatches are excellent to take advantage of, by just utilizing the 1 play and running it until you have the man you want in the position you want him in. This is also a fine way of getting a player with four personal fouls into a situation where he must either let the man he is guarding get the ball and allow him to shoot or go for the ball and the man and risk a fifth foul.

Diagram 3-33 shows the complete assignments of each player on the 1 play, on the original signal by the man with the ball at the wing position (as he passes to the corner to signal for an outside option and identify the play to be run by staying put in his position). Diagram 3-34 shows the completed 1 play with no shot developing on the first try. As this diagram depicts, there are five cuts in this pattern. Each player moves by a definite cut during the development of the play, and after the 1 play has been run, each player is in a different position on the floor.

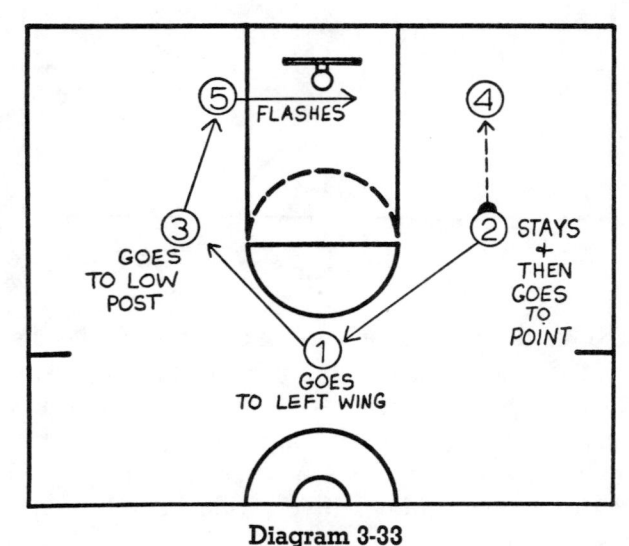

Diagram 3-33

Setting Up the Percentage Man-to-Man Attack

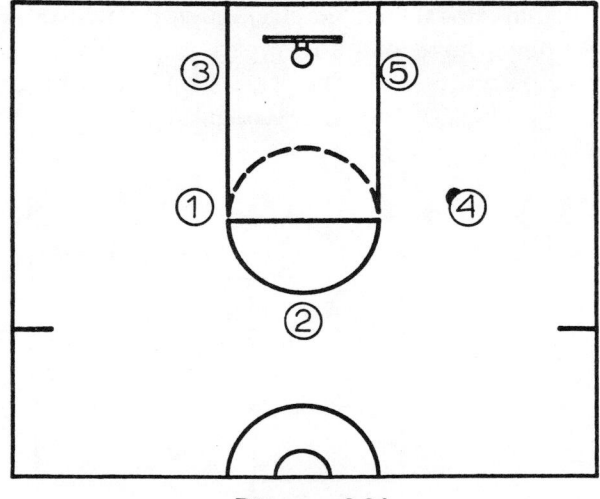

Diagram 3-34

Although this may seem like a very fundamental and simple play, we have found that it has been a very effective option play to use, because it forces the defensive man defending the man cutting or flashing across the low base-line area to defense the player perfectly in order to stop this play. It puts maximum pressure on the defensive player. Many defensive players in this situation do not keep the proper individual triangle of themselves, the ball and the man they are guarding. Many times the defensive player will look at the ball, and this makes it very easy for the offensive player to slip in front of the defender and establish excellent position to receive the ball and get the power shot. The 1 play is extremely effective when it is mixed with the options and plays that will be discussed in this chapter. It is very successful when the offense has been run by moving the defensive players from position to position, by cutting and stopping each time an option has been run and because the defensive players have a tendency to relax after they stop each time. This is an excellent time to run the 1 play. Although very simple and elementary, this play many times results in a high-percentage shot without very much effort on the part of the offense.

The 2 Play

The 2 play is run as an Outside Option. The play is started by a wing man with the ball, the 2 man in Diagram 3-35, who passes to the 4 man in the corner. As soon as the 2 man passes the ball, he immedi-

Setting Up the Percentage Man-to-Man Attack

ately cuts to the basket on a simple give-and-go maneuver. The signal for the 2 play is the 2 man going to the basket after the pass; whereas, in the 1 play, he passed to the corner and stayed. The assignments for the other four players are shown in Diagram 3-36 on the 2 man's signal for the 2 play.

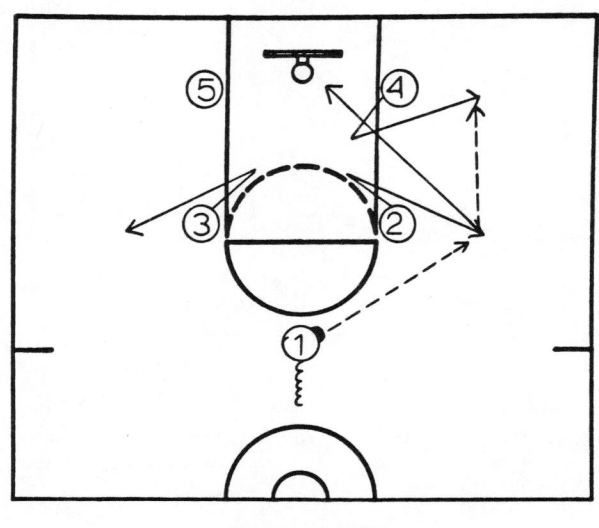

Diagram 3-35

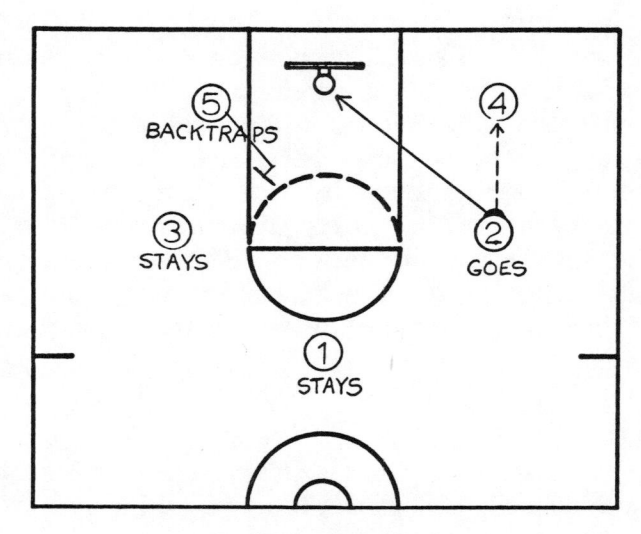

Diagram 3-36

Setting Up the Percentage Man-to-Man Attack 75

If the 2 man is open on his cut to the basket, then he should receive the pass-back from the 4 man. As soon as the 5 man sees that 2 is running a 2 play, he immediately moves up the key line extended to set a backtrap screen for the 3 man. The 3 man stays at his position when he sees the 2 man go. The 1 man stays as he sees the play start. Diagram 3-37 explains what happens when the 2 man gets the ball back from the 4 man. When all the other players see that 2 has received the ball in the power lane, then the following things happen.

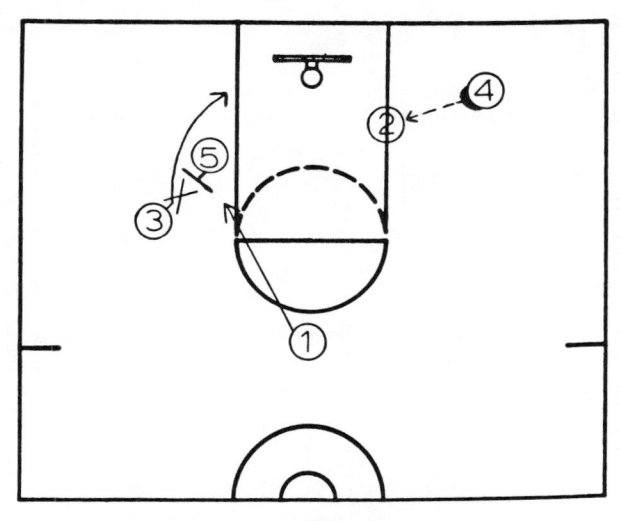

Diagram 3-37

The 3 man starts his cut off the 5 man's backtrap screen. He goes to the outside of the 5 man on his cut. *Coaching Hint:* Whenever we cut a wing man to the power lane off a backtrap screen, he must always go to the outside of the man setting the screen. He will only go to the inside of the screener when running an option as a special offensive adjustment technique, which will be discussed later in this chapter. The 3 man should cut as close to the 5 man as physically possible; he should actually brush the 5 man, if it is possible, as he tries to free himself from his defender.

The 3 man will stop at the left low-post position to get ready to rebound on the left side of the basket. The 1 man starts his move toward the left-wing position in order to set a side screen on the original backtrapper, the 5 man. When the 1 man sees the 2 man get the ball, he stops at the left-wing position and gets ready to rebound in the bucket area in front of the basket. The 5 man, after setting the

Setting Up the Percentage Man-to-Man Attack

backtrap screen, moves to the point position. The 4 man moves to the foul line after the 2 man shoots (follows the rule for a 1-and-2 play: when he feeds a man in the power lane who takes a shot, he must go to the foul line for the half-and-half duty), and the 5 man, who is heading to the point position after coming off the 1 man's side screen by going to the foul circle, has the deep defensive responsibility, because he is moving toward the mid-court area or away from the basket at the time the shot is taken. The action that takes place when the other players see the shot taken is shown in Diagram 3-38. 3 and 1 rebound, 4 has the half-and-half duty at the foul line and 5 has defensive responsibility.

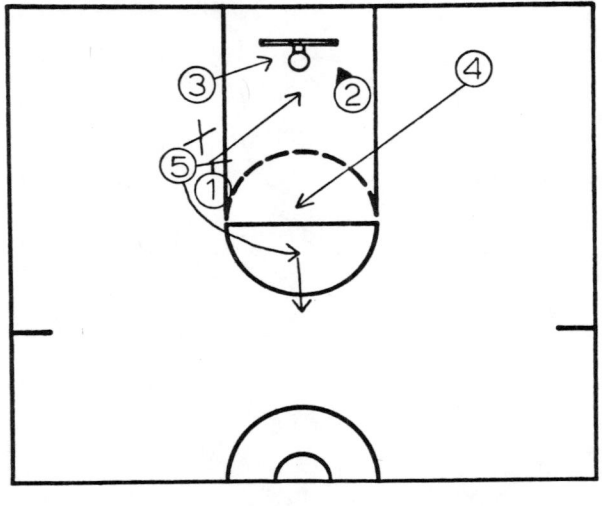

Diagram 3-38

If the 2 man is not open on his cut to the basket, then he quickly cuts up to the high-post position on the left side of the court, as shown in Diagram 3-39. The 5 man should have already set his rear screen on the 3 man's defender (being careful to set a legal backtrap rear screen, which means he must set the screen 2 to 3 feet away from the defensive player so as to allow the man normal body movement as he turns around to go with his man), the 3 man cuts to the outside of the 5 man and moves quickly to the power lane crossing under the basket with his hand extended high, to give the 4 man a good target to hit (Diagram 3-40). If the 3 man is open, then 4 passes the ball to him for the power shot. *Coaching Hint:* It is preferable to hit the man cutting into the power position after he has stopped his cut so that it

Setting Up the Percentage Man-to-Man Attack 77

Diagram 3-39

Diagram 3-40

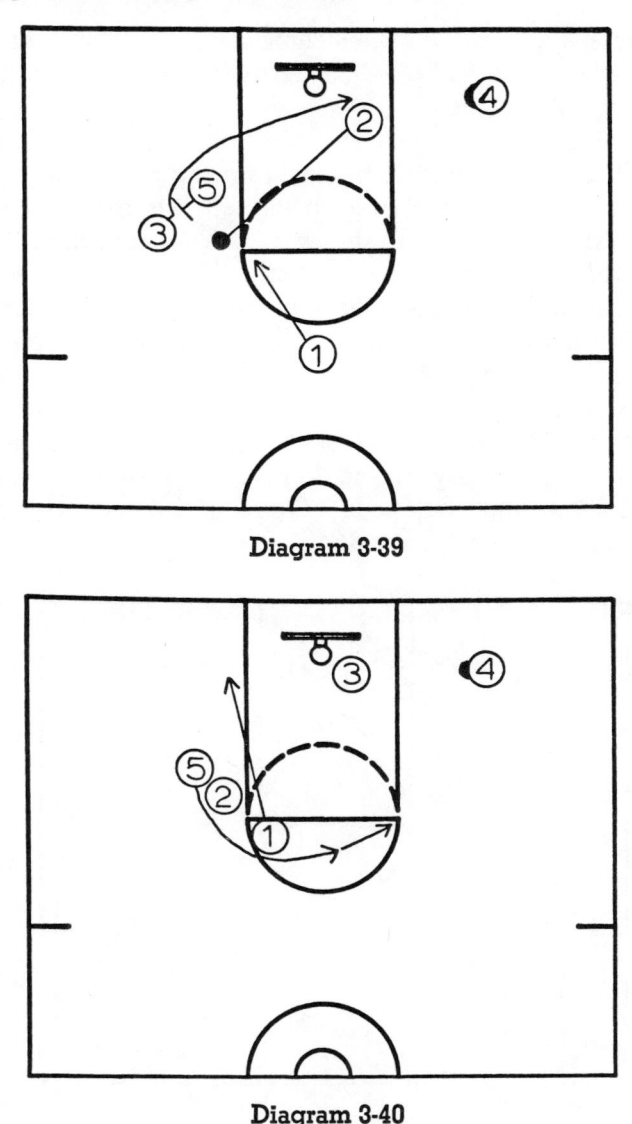

forces him to take the power shot, because if he gets the ball on the move, it is usually too early to stop, and he must continue to move in order to get into position to shoot the moving layup. When a player takes a moving layup shot, his momentum takes him away from the spot on the floor where he took the shot; thus, he is not in position to rebound his own shot if he should miss it. Also, it is easier for the defensive man to block the moving layup shot than the power shot because the player with the ball cannot fake to shake off a tight defender, as he cannot see his defender when he is on the move and concentrating on catching the pass.

If the 3 man takes the power shot, then the 1 man who has moved to the left-wing position to screen for the 5 man moves into the left low-post position to rebound on the left side of the power lane. The 2 man, who cut through to start the 2 play, is now at the left high-post position, and he moves to the middle of the bucket area to rebound in front of the basket. The 4 man goes to the foul line for half-and-half duty because he fed a man who shot from the power lane, and the 5 man coming off the 1 man's side screen to the foul line moves back to the top of the foul circle for defensive responsibility. *Coaching Hint:* When a player moves back to the top of the foul circle for defensive responsibility, he should never turn his back on the play, but instead he should back-pedal. Diagram 3-41 shows the moves when the 3 man takes the power shot.

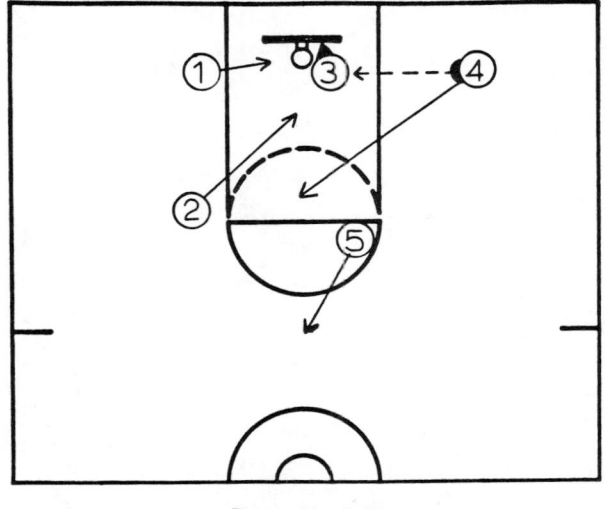

Diagram 3-41

If the 3 man does not get open on his cut to the right side of the power lane, then the 5 man who backtrapped for 3 comes off the 1 man's screen and moves to the foul line, looking to receive the pass at the spot where the foul line meets the key line extended from the 4 man. *Coaching Hint:* The 4 man may have to start his dribble after he sees that 3 is not open, to avoid the 5-second count and the danger of being guarded too closely because of not dribbling soon enough. 4

Setting Up the Percentage Man-to-Man Attack   79

passes to 5 if he is open, and, as shown in Diagram 3-42, 5 takes the shot at the foul line, if he feels he can make it. On the shot, the 1 man who screened for 5 has moved down to the left low-post spot to

Diagram 3-42

rebound to the left of the power lane, the 2 man, who is at the left-wing spot, rebounds to the middle of the power lane and the 3 man, who must clear out of the 3-second area, rebounds to the right side of the power lane. The 4 man follows the rule that when a man passes to a player who is not in the power lane and that player shoots, then the man who fed him the ball, must go to the mid-court area for deep defensive responsibility. The shooter in this situation, the 5 man, has half-and-half duty after he takes his shot. *Coaching Hint:* The player taking the shot should not worry about the half-and-half duty until he has taken his shot and followed through on it. Then, and only then, should he think about the half-and-half duty.

If the 4 man cannot get the ball to the 5 man (or feels that the 5 man will not be open to get the shot even if he did get the ball), he dribbles to the right-wing position. The 3 man takes the right low-post spot, the 1 man takes the left low-post spot, the 2 man takes the left wing and the 5 man becomes the new point man. Now the offense is again in the original Five Cutter Formation and ready to start another play or option, as shown in Diagram 3-43. The beauty of this move is that the ball is now in a wing position, and as soon as the 4 man makes a pass either to the point or to the corner, then another option

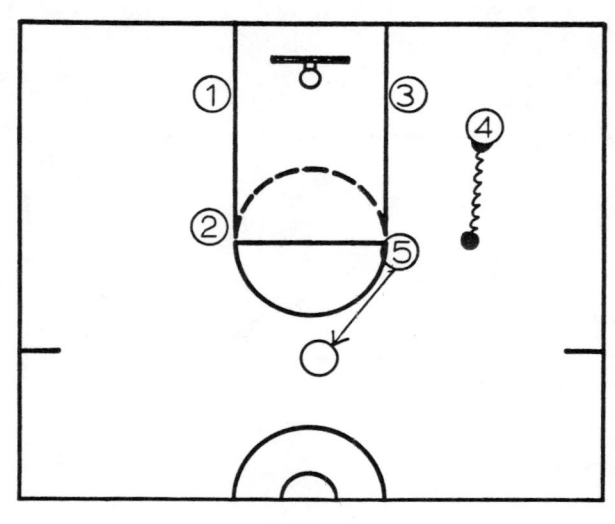

Diagram 3-43

is immediately started before the defense realizes what has developed, because they usually are waiting for the ball to go back to the point to restart the offense, as shown in Diagram 3-44. *Coaching Hint:* Many times, in order to assure that the 5 man will be open coming off the 1

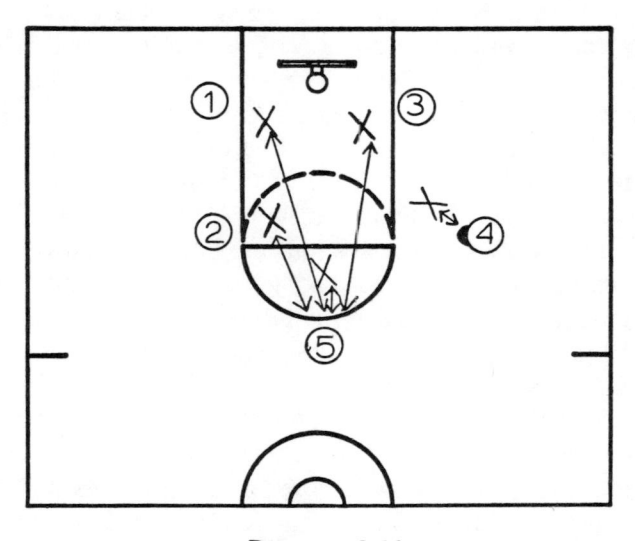

Diagram 3-44

man's side screen, the 2 man should screen the 5 man's defender first as he waits at the left high-post position, waiting to go to the boards on

Setting Up the Percentage Man-to-Man Attack 81

a shot or to go to the left-wing spot if a shot does not develop. The 1 man coming down the left key line extended will also try to screen the 5 man's man in case the 2 man's screen was not successful and the defensive player slips by the screen. By setting two screens on the 5 man's defender, usually the 5 man will be free at the foul line, as shown in Diagram 3-45.

Diagram 3-46 shows what happens if the 5 man gets the ball from the 4 man but cannot get the shot. The 5 man just dribbles the

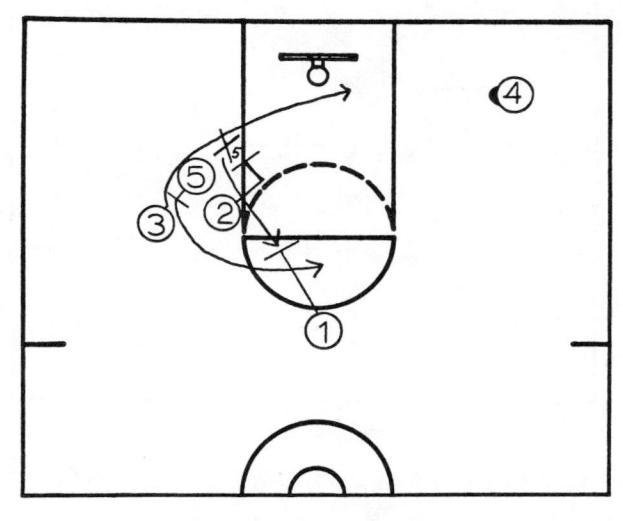

Diagram 3-45

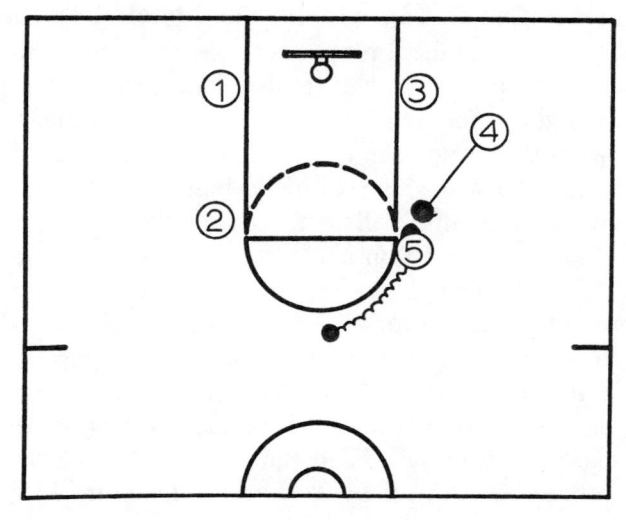

Diagram 3-46

ball back to the point and the 4 man moves into the tight right-wing spot. The 2 man moves into the tight left-wing spot, with 1 and 3 taking the low-post positions.

Diagram 3-47 shows the cuts of the five players as the 2 play is run. Again the Five Cutter Attack moves each player to a different spot on the floor each time a play is run.

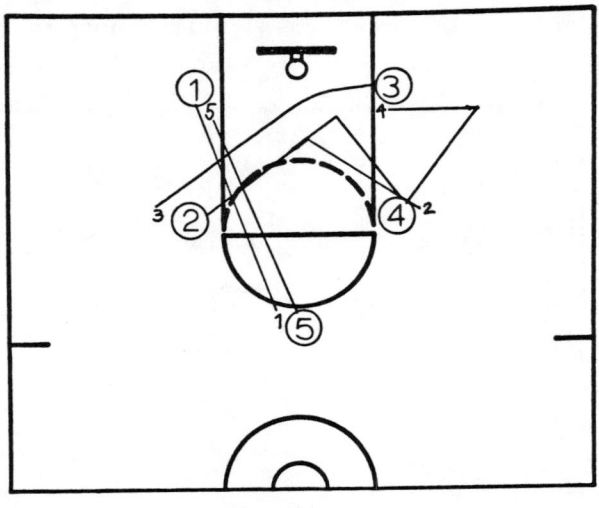

Diagram 3-47

Alternating the 1 Play and the 2 Play

So far we have covered just the Outside Options Series by describing the 1 play and the 2 play. Any time either the 1 play or the 2 play has been run and a shot has not developed, the ball is at the wing spot, unless it got to the point position on the 2 play and the shot did not develop; in that event, the offense is now reset in the Five Cutter Formation and the wing man with the ball is ready to run another play. When he passes the ball to the corner, after looking inside to feed the new low-post man on his side of the court, he can run either the 1 play or the 2 play. These two plays can be run alternately with some degree of success, even though the offense if going to start on and be run on the same side of the court as the play that was run before. The reason that it can be run effectively is that if the wing man with the ball passes to the corner and stays, then the opposite-side low-post man flashes, and because his man is trying to pick up the signal, he may take his eyes off his man, as shown in Diagram 3-48, making it

Setting Up the Percentage Man-to-Man Attack

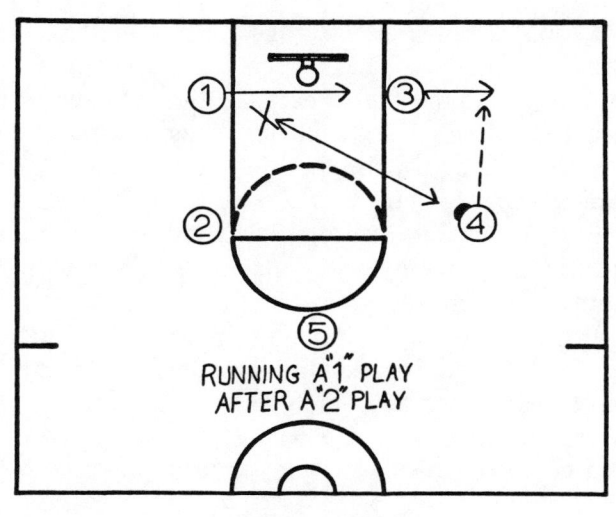

Diagram 3-48

RUNNING A "1" PLAY AFTER A "2" PLAY

easy for the 1 man in the left low-post spot to be open as he beats his man across the lane. Any combination of plays can be alternated. This will be discussed thoroughly in this chapter in the section, Interchanging the Outside Options and the Inside Option. This maneuver of mixing the 1 and 2 play is very effective when the defense starts to anticipate the option, if the 1 or 2 play has been run several times in a row without changing the play. Diagram 3-49 shows how the defense

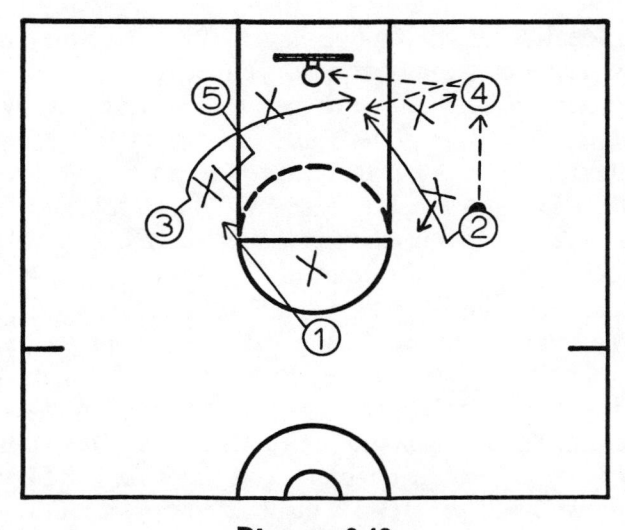

Diagram 3-49

has a tendency to lean with the offense if several 1 plays have been run in succession; then the offense runs a 2 play. The defensive player guarding the wing man will have a tendency to want to move to the point after 2 passes to the 4 man because that is the way the offensive player in that position has been moving, thus making it easy for 2 to get through to the hoop for the shot on a 2 play; also, the 5 man will have an easier time setting the rear screen on the 3 man's man because he will anticipate 3 going just to the left low-post spot, and he may become a little lazy, making it easier for the 5 man to set the screen more effectively. These two plays complement each other and make each option more effective by running the other option first in order to set the defense up. The defense must play the first "play run" honestly in order to stop the actual play which follows successfully. This sets up the defense for the second play to be run. Again, the defense can be decoyed with one play and then burned with the next play.

Of course the outside options can be run on the opposite side of the court, by having the wing man pass the ball back to the point man and the point man pass the ball to the other wing. However, this can only be done if a team is running the Outside Options. Why this can only be done when running just the Outside Options will be fully understood when the Inside Option is explained in the next section of this chapter.

The Identical Inside Option

The Identical Inside Option is actually a dual play. It is called the 3 play. The 3 play can be run from either side of the court, and the side that it is started on is determined by the wing man who has the ball. Diagram 3-50 shows the 2 man, who is in the right-wing spot, starting the play by passing the ball to the point or the 1 man. The pass to the point shows that an Inside Option is going to be run. The move that the 2 man makes after he passes the ball to the 1 man determines which side of the court the 3 play is going to be started on. If the 2 man stays put, then the 3 play will be started on the opposite side of the court from the 2 man. If the 2 man passes and goes through, then the 3 play will start on the right side of the court. The key to this play is that the only person on the court who knows which option or which play is going to be run is the wing man with the ball. All eyes must be focused on him—especially on the 3 play. The 2 man, as shown in Diagram 3-51, passes to the 1 man at the point and

Setting Up the Percentage Man-to-Man Attack

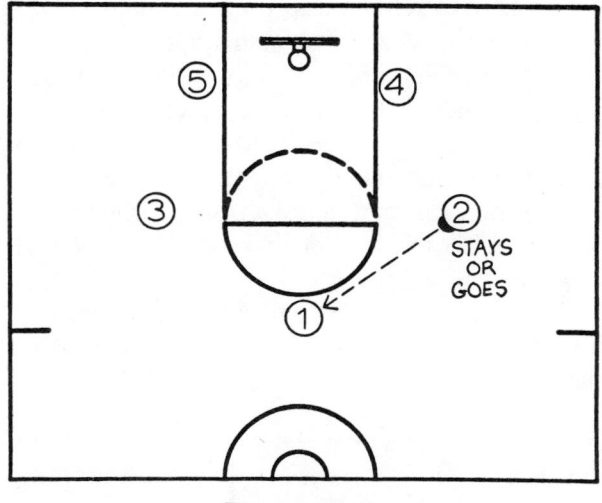

Diagram 3-50

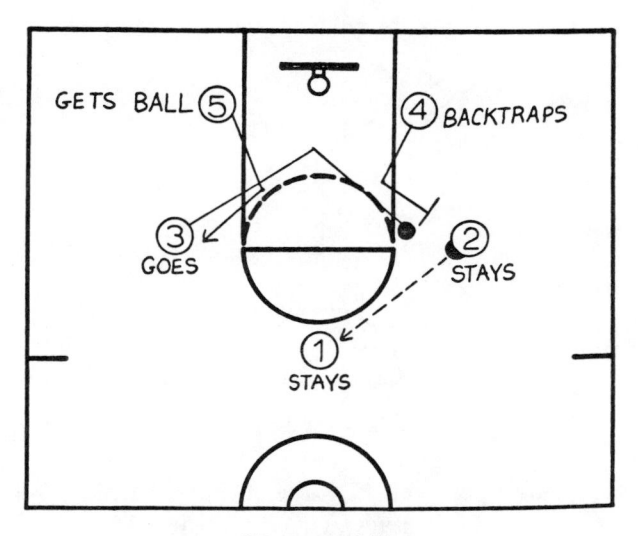

Diagram 3-51

stays. This is the cue for the 3 man to go through the bucket area and then to the right-side high-post position. The 5 man, as soon as he sees the 3 man start through, breaks up the key line into the bucket area and forces his man to be brushed off the cutting 3 man. The 5 man must make a deep V into the bucket area in maneuvering to clear his man off 3 in order to receive the pass from 1. The 5 man should get the ball even with the foul line and about 5 feet from the key line. The

4 man moves up to set the backtrap on the 2 man, who stayed after making the pass to the 1 man. The 1 man stays put to receive the passback from the 2 man. Diagram 3-52 shows the identical play started on the right side when the 2 man passes back to 1 at the point and goes through. The assignments now read that the 3 man, upon seeing 2 go, stays, and the 5 man sets the backtrap for the 3 man, who has stayed. The 4 man runs his man into 2, cutting through to the left high-post spot by V'ing into the bucket and breaking out to get the ball from 1 at a point even with the foul line about 5 feet from the key line. 1's job is the same: Get the ball back from the wing man and then move it to the side of the court that the wing man leaves on to cut through to the opposite-side high-post spot.

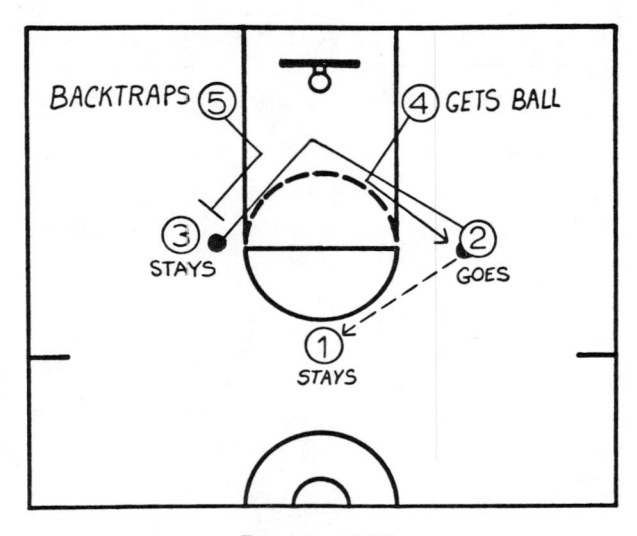

Diagram 3-52

Diagrams 3-53 and 3-54 show the complete 3 play. Wing man 2 passes to 1 at the point and stays. This is the signal for the 3 play. He stays after his pass, and this is the signal that the 3 play will start on the left side of the court. 3 sees that 2 stays, so he goes through the bucket area by moving on an angle directly to the basket, but after he gets three steps into the key area, he quickly changes direction and heads on a straight line from there to the opposite-side high-post position. It is at this point that the 1 man can hit the 3 man as he moves to the high-post position, if he should be open. The 5 man, seeing that 2 stayed, quickly moves into the bucket area by making a V to run his man into the cutting 3. 5 breaks off 3 to receive the pass from 1. 4

Setting Up the Percentage Man-to-Man Attack   87

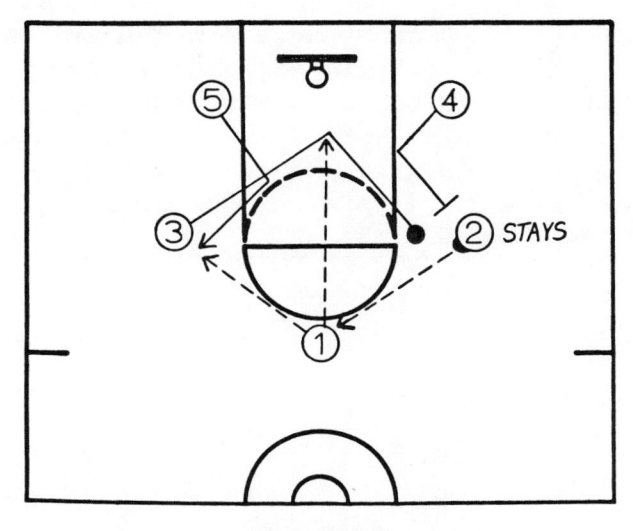

Diagram 3-53

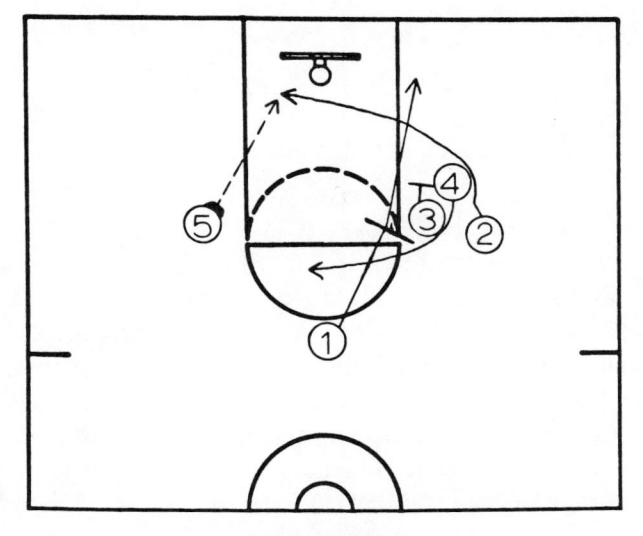

Diagram 3-54

moves up to set the backtrap screen on 2. 2 should not cut through off 4's screen until he sees that 5 has the ball. The reason for this is, of course, that if he starts too soon when he is open, 5 may not have the ball in position to feed him. 2 always cuts to the outside off the backtrap screener, and, as was explained in the 2 play, he should try to make slight contact with the 4 man when executing this cut. Also, 2 should try to go as fast as possible when cutting off the backtrap screen in order to free himself when he reaches the left side of the power lane. At the same time this is going on, the 3 man sets a screen on the backtrapper, 4, and the 1 man starts moving toward the 3 man, picking up the 5 man's man to screen if 3 has not been successful. Diagram 3-55 shows what occurs when 5 hits 2, using the two-hand overhead pass, and 2 takes the power shot. 3, after screening 5's man,

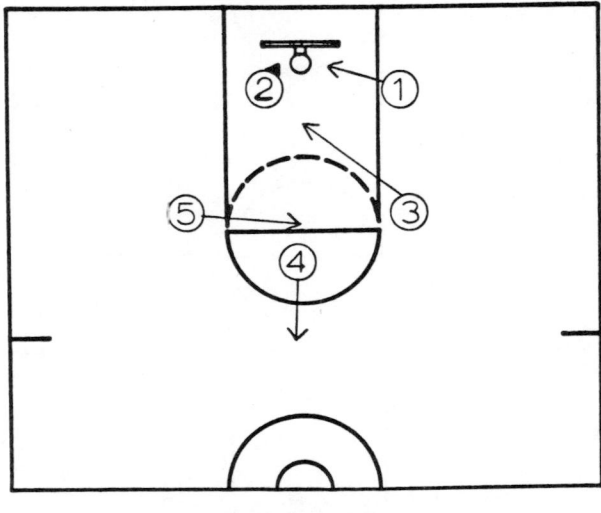

Diagram 3-55

stays at the right-wing position, and 1 moves down the key line after screening 5's man to the right low-post position. 4 comes off the screens set by 3 and 1 and moves into the foul circle area as close to the foul line as possible. 1 rebounds on the right side of the power lane, while 3 rebounds to the middle of the power lane. 4 has the deep defensive responsibility because he is moving toward the mid-court area, and the 5 man, who feeds a man in the power lane, the 2 man, moves to the foul circle for half-and-half duty. *Coaching Hint:* The rule the 1 and 2 plays have concerning where to go if you feed a player inside or outside the power lane and that player takes the shot, apply for the 3 play also. So regardless of the play run, the half-and-half and defensive responsibility assignments will be the same. Feed a man who shoots in the power lane and you go to the foul line; feed a man who shoots outside the power lane and you go to the mid-court or top of the foul circle area for defensive responsibility.

Diagram 3-56 shows that 5 cannot feed 2 in the power lane, so

Setting Up the Percentage Man-to-Man Attack

Diagram 3-56

Diagram 3-57

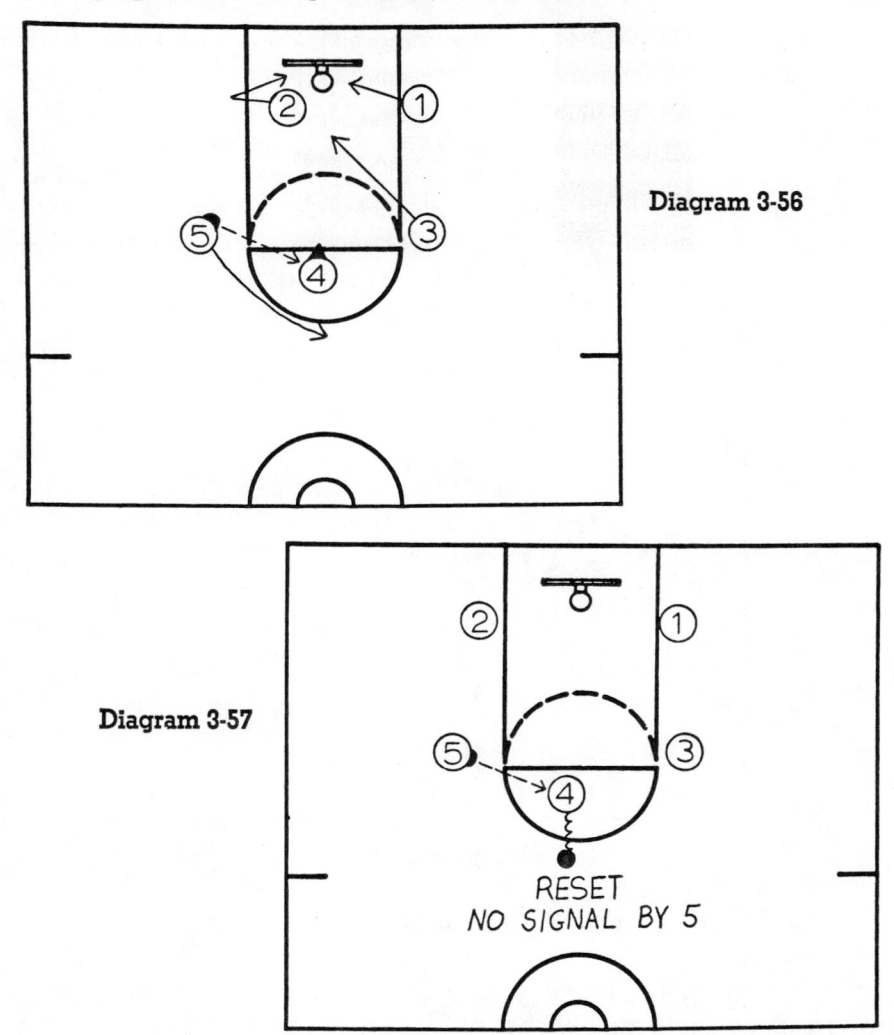

RESET
NO SIGNAL BY 5

he looks for his secondary choice, the 4 man at the foul line. He passes to 4 who takes the shot at the foul line. 2 clears the 3-second area as soon as he sees that he is not going to get the ball. 1 and 3 rebound as in Diagram 3-55. 5, however, following the rule about feeding a player who shoots outside of the power lane, moves to the top of the foul circle for the deep defensive responsibility, while the shooter, 4, has the half-and-half assignment after he has completed his shot.

Diagram 3-57 illustrates what happens when 4 gets the pass from 5 but cannot shoot. 4 dribbles back to the top of the circle to become the new point man, while 2 and 1 have become the new low-post men and 5 and 3 have become the new wing men. *Coaching Hint:* When the 4 man has to dribble back to reset the offense, this automatically occurs off 5's pass to the point and staying to signal the play, for the 3 play. The offensive players should ignore this pass and stay if the man at the point has to dribble back in order to set up the formation. However, if he does not get the shot and also does not dribble back out, then the signal is on as shown in Diagram 3-58. 5 passes to 4 in the circle. If 4 does get the shot, but does not go out of the dribble to

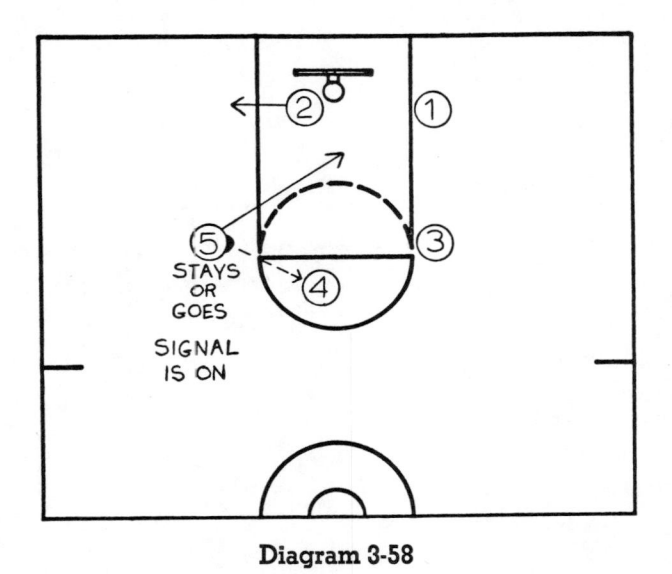

Diagram 3-58

the top of the circle, then the 3 man should go through to the left-side high-post spot as soon as he sees that 4 does not shoot, because 5 has passed to the point and stayed, and many times the 4 man or the backtrapper coming up will be forced outside the circle anyway by his defender; thus, the offense wants to keep its continuity, so the players must watch the wing man with the ball to see if he stays or goes so that they can react correctly. After a team has gotten used to running this play, they will be able to tell without too much trouble when the player moving to the foul line is going to be able to get a shot off. This technique is shown in Diagrams 3-58 and 3-59. However, if a mixup occurs and no player goes through, then the 4 man can do one of two things: pass to either wing man and let him start the option and the play or dribble toward one of the wings and initiate an automatic 3 play. When one of the wings sees the point man dribble toward him, he should clear out by moving toward the basket and then up the

Setting Up the Percentage Man-to-Man Attack 91

Diagram 3-59

GOES OR STAYS

SIGNAL IS ON BY 5

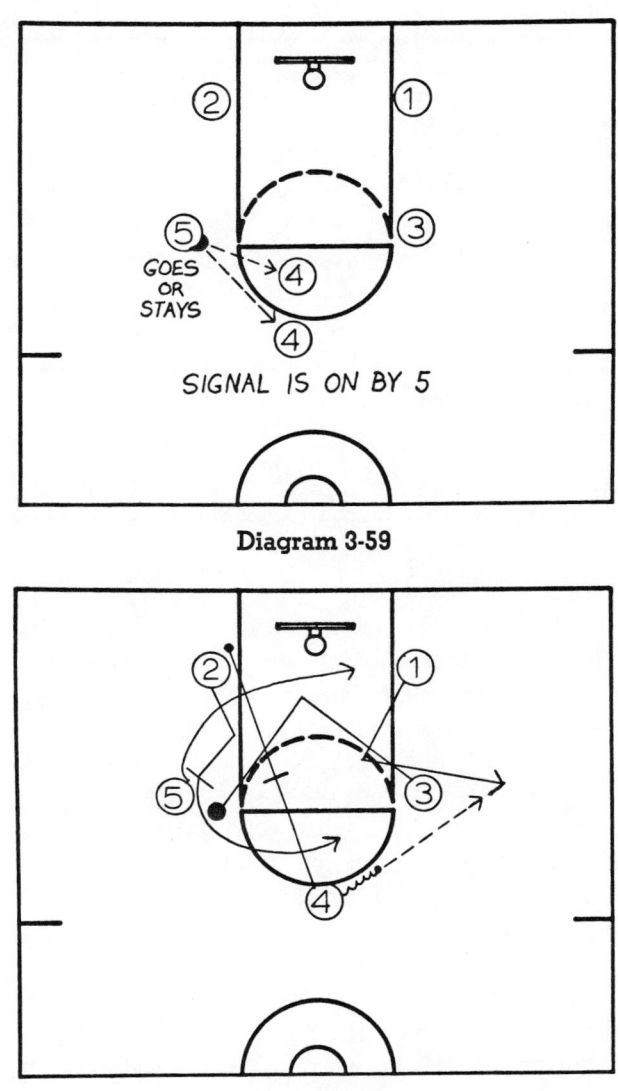

Diagram 3-60

bucket area to the high-post spot. After the wing man's cut, the 3 play is run as it is at any other time. This maneuver is shown in Diagram 3-60.

Diagram 3-61 shows all five cuts of the 3 play of the Identical Inside Option of the Five Cutter Offense. Every time the 3 play is run, each player again is moved to a different spot on the floor by a specially designed cut that makes the offense go. Through continuous

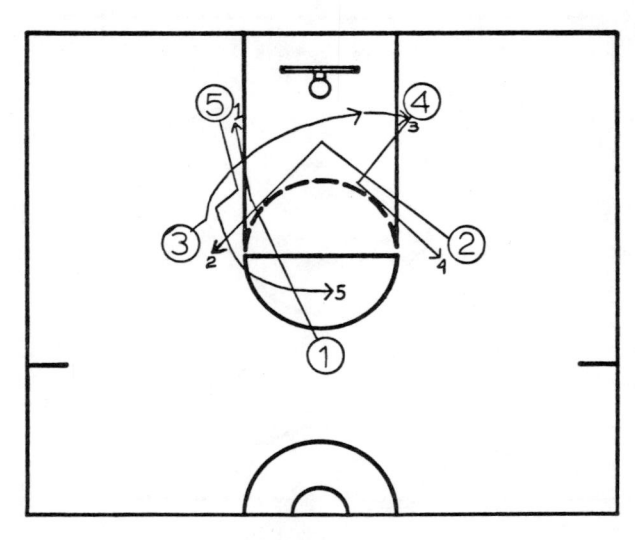

Diagram 3-61

running of the 3 play from side to side, by either having the wing man with the ball stay or go after he passes the ball to the point man, you have an offensive attack that can be used by itself exclusively and which can be powerful and devastating.

Each time the 3 play is run through or turned over, the offense is always in the original Five Cutter Formation and the ball is at the wing position. Here the wing man can start the Identical Inside Option again by passing to the point and determining which wing man is going to get backtrapped, as well as dictate the side of the court the play is going to originate on, by either staying or going. One of the best features of the Five Cutter Offense is that the offense is ready to go immediately after one play has been run and the ball is in such a position that it does not have to be passed more than once to start another play or option. Also the 3 play has the unique value of having the signal given by a wing man for both the option to be run and the play that will be used.

The Identical Inside Option got its name from the fact that the 3 play can be run the same way from either side of the court. The only thing that is not identical on this play is which side of the court the play is going to start on. But once it has started the play is exactly the same, regardless of which side of the court it is run from. We have run just this 3 play as our complete man-to-man attack in many games, never using the 1 or 2 play. The 3 play offers so much movement and so much flexibility to change the start of the play, and also it creates so

Setting Up the Percentage Man-to-Man Attack

many problems for the defense, that it is not necessary to run any other play. *Coaching Hint:* It should not be overlooked that after the 3 play has been turned over once, the wing man should always look inside to the low-post man on his side of the court to see if he is open to be fed in the power lane before the wing man starts another option, regardless of whether it is an Inside Option or an Outside Option. Every time the 1, 2 or 3 plays have been turned over, the wing man with the ball should keep the defense honest by looking inside to feed the low-post man on his side. Many easy 2 pointers will result if this is done, because the defense is so busy trying to follow the intricate moves of the Five Cutter Offense that they overlook the simplest of offensive maneuvers.

Rotating to the Outside Options

An effective technique that can be combined with the Five Cutter Offense against the man-to-man defenses to give the offense a different look, is the rotation of the players before going into the Five Cutter Attack. The point man is usually the man who starts the rotation, as he is the man with the ball 90% of the time before the offense begins. The man with the ball is the only man who can start a rotation move. The wing men can start a rotation when they have the ball at the wing position. The signal for the rotation can be done two ways by the wing men and only one way by the point man. The signal by the wing men is either the wing man dribbling directly to the point position or his yelling "Rotate" and then dribbling directly to the point position. The point man can only signal for the rotation by yelling "rotate" and then dribbling to either wing position.

Point Man's Rotation

Diagram 3-62 shows the rotation being started by the point man. He can go to either side. 1 dribbles toward the 2 man after yelling "Rotate." The 2 man moves to the right low-post spot, the 4 man moves across the bucket to become the new left low-post man, the 5 man moves up to the left-wing spot and the 3 man becomes the new point man. The 1 man should look to feed the 2 man in the low-post area and the 2 man should move into the power lane on the right side of the basket and post himself to get the ball. If he does not get the ball, then he should move out to the corner to receive the pass from 1 in order to start a 1 or 2 play of the Outside Options Series (Diagram 3-63).

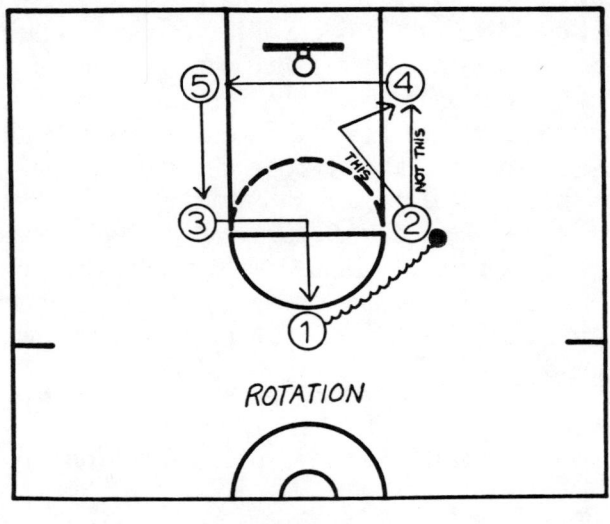

Diagram 3-62

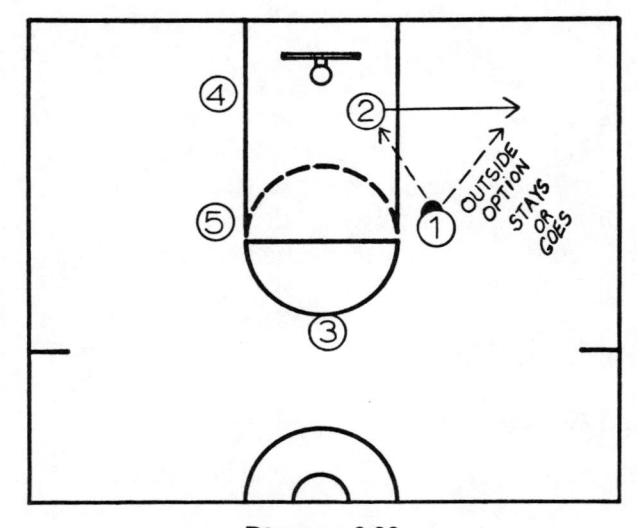

Diagram 3-63

Wing Man's Rotation

The wing man who receives the ball from 1, as shown in Diagram 3-64, is the 2 man. He can start a rotation to the point only by either yelling "Rotate" or dribbling directly to the point. As soon as the other four players see this move, they rotate. The 1 man moves to the left-wing spot, but he must make a sharp V into the bucket and

Setting Up the Percentage Man-to-Man Attack

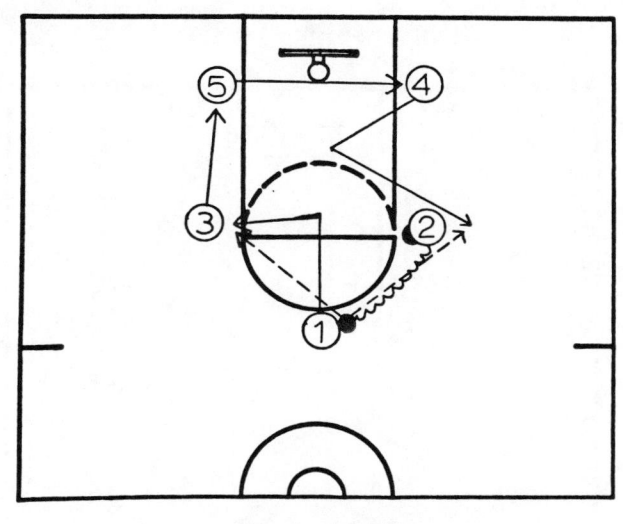

Diagram 3-64

then to the wing in order to free himself to get a pass from the point. The 3 man moves to the left low-post spot, the 5 man moves across to become the right low-post man and the 4 man makes a V into the bucket area to become a potential wing-man receiver. The 2 man can pass to either new wing man, who in turn will start the option to be used and the play that will be run from the desired option.

Rotating to the Identical Inside Option

The rotation to the Identical Inside Option is done the same way as the rotation to the Outside Options. The point man yells "Rotate" and dribbles toward one of the wings. Diagram 3-65 has the 1 man dribbling toward the 2 man. The 3 man makes a good V into the bucket area before breaking to the top of the circle to become the new point man. The 1 man now passes the ball to the 3 man and an Inside Option is on. The 1 man either stays or goes, to determine which side the 3 play is going to start from and which wing man is going to go through to initiate the play.

The rotation by the wing man is the same for the Inside Option as it is for the Outside Options, as was shown in Diagram 3-63. By rotating to these options, it gives the offense another look that the defense has not experienced. Again it puts good pressure on the defense by keeping it moving, and it allows a team to get into the regular

Five Cutter Offense by using a decoy because it keeps the defense busy defending a simple offensive maneuver.

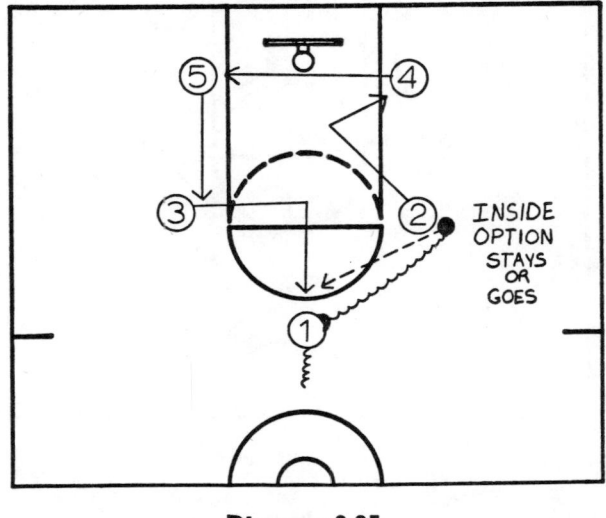

Diagram 3-65

Interchanging the Outside Options and the Identical Inside Option

Although the Outside Options and the Identical Inside Option are excellent offensive maneuvers by themselves, the technique of combining them offers the offense unlimited resources in attacking any type of man-to-man defense. The Five Cutter Options offer just three basic plays:

> The 1 play
> The 2 play
> The 3 play

However, when these options are run interchangeably, they are very difficult to defense, because the man at the wing with the ball in his possession is the only man in the gym who knows what option he is going to run, when the players are allowed to run any of the three plays on their own. When mixing assigned options, we do it in the following manner: We run the options by the play numbers. If we say we want to run the 3 play and if it does not get us the percentage shot we are running, then the man with the ball in the wing position should run the 1 play after the 3 play has been run through. We call this

Setting Up the Percentage Man-to-Man Attack 97

running a 31—the 3 play followed by the 1 play. The following numbers show the combinations that can be used:

	2 Play Sequences	
11	21	31
12	22	32
13	23	33

	3 Play Sequences	
111	211	311
112	212	312
113	213	313
121	221	321
122	222	322
123	223	323
131	231	331
132	232	332
133	233	333

We never use more than three sequences of assigned plays. We may tell the players to keep running a 2 play sequence over and over again (*example:* keep running 31's until the percentage shot is attained). If we run through a 3 sequence play and we do not get the desired shot, then the players are on their own to run whatever option they feel will be most effective, depending on how the defense is playing us on the individual plays. Again, the beauty of this offense is that after each play is run, the ball is immediately in the wing position to start the next option without the ball having to go to the point. Also, the 3 play can be run from either side of the court, and this gives the offense even more flexibility because the attack can be shifted from one side of the court to the other and still be just as effective, without interrupting the rhythm of the movement. The 3 play can be started on either side of the court depending upon the move of the wing with the ball after the pass to the point, and this is very difficult for the defense to react to. Because the Outside Options or the Identical Inside Option can be started by just one pass by the wing with the ball, if the offense has run a couple of 33's and then goes to a 1 play, it is hard for the defense to adjust, because the 1 play is started so quickly by the wing man's pass. This will catch the defense going the wrong way many times. By just using the 1, 2 and 3 play sequences, there are 39 combinations of plays that can be run together by just interchanging the Outside Options' Plays, 1 and 2, with the Identical Inside Option's two-way 3 play.

The amount of movement in the Five Cutter Offense (every man moving from one position to another each and every time a play is run) creates many confusing problems for the defense, and if a team is patient enough, eventually it will get the high-percentage shot it is seeking.

We have also found that when we are running assigned 2 or 3 play sequences, if the wing man with the ball cannot get it to the desired position, either the point or the corner, then usually if he goes to the opposite position from which he was supposed to go, he has little trouble starting another option and play.

Also, when the players are allowed to run any of the three plays in any order they wish, it really amounts to organized, free-lance, disciplined plays, because the options can be gotten into so quickly. The wing man with the ball starts the option, and after he has designated what option he wants run, he still determines what play is going to be used. All the players have an opportunity to run the ball club for at least one play, and this makes for good team morale, as every player gets an opportunity to play "quarterback."

The challenge that this offense offers the players is unique in itself because each player must know everything there is to know about each and every position, from start to finish, and also the execution of each play for each option. Players pride themselves on being able to execute this intricate and interesting offense to perfection under game conditions. This Five Cutter Attack builds unbelievable team pride and morale.

Developing the Individual Special Offensive Adjustment Techniques

The four individual special adjustment techniques are:

(1) Going over the top or topping the defense.
(2) Double screening the defense.
(3) Screen rolling the defense.
(4) Circling the defense.

These simple but highly flexible offensive adjustment maneuvers can be blended into the regular offensive 1, 2 and 3 plays to give the attack all the diversified maneuvers it will need when facing defenses that sag, switch or anticipate the play. Each of these adjustments are automatic, and individual players can use them at any time. Also, after each of these special adjustment techniques have been used and a percentage shot is not obtained, the offense is still in the basic 1-2-2 setup of the Five Cutter Attack.

Setting Up the Percentage Man-to-Man Attack

The most difficult part of using these adjustment techniques is that a great deal of time must be spent on practicing them, because each player must know how to recognize and when to use each technique in different situations. However, because the basic offense of the Five Cutter Attack only has three plays, after these plays have been learned, a coach can spend a great deal of his offensive man-to-man practice time working on the special adjustment techniques. Players like to employ these maneuvers, and they enjoy working on them in practice because it forces them to really know the offense, how it works and what has to be done in order to assure that it will function, regardless of what the defense may use against it.

Players now will be responsible for knowing the following material, to be used in the man-to-man attack on an individual basis:

(1) Signals for the Outside Options:
    (a) Signals for the 1 play and the 2 play.
(2) Signal for the Identical Inside Option:
    (a) Signal for the 3 play.
(3) Each individual position of the formation and the assignments for each position for the 1, 2 and 3 plays, from start to finish.
(4) The four special individual adjustment techniques and how to use them, and also how to react to them when teammates use these techniques.

Using the Special Adjustment Techniques Against the Sagging, Switching and Anticipating Defenses

The special offensive adjustment techniques that are to be used against the sagging, switching and anticipating defenses are basically the same for all the different defensive man-to-man tactics. Once the adjustments are learned to combat the sagging defense, the same adjustments can be used against the switching and anticipating defenses, and vice versa. Because the tactics of the sagging, switching and anticipating defenses are basically the same in their objective of stopping the Five Cutter Offense, the special adjustment techniques will work against all of these kinds of defensive maneuvers. Each player must be able to recognize these defensive tactics and know what special adjustment technique he should use in the given situation at hand. The main objective of the sagging, switching and anticipating defenses is that of "playing" the play that is to be run. When a team sags, they usually have the defensive man play off the man who is supposed to cut into the power lane, and when the defense is switching, then the man who is guarding the backtrapper usually switches and picks up the cutter going through to the power lane. Diagram 3-66 shows the sagging technique and Diagram 3-67 illustrates the switching techniques that are used by the defense. When a team plays an anticipating defense, we mean that the defenders are trying to guess the option that is to be run, so that each and every player can beat the offensive man he is guarding to the position the offensive player is supposed to go to, on any given play. Diagram 3-68 shows this type of defense.

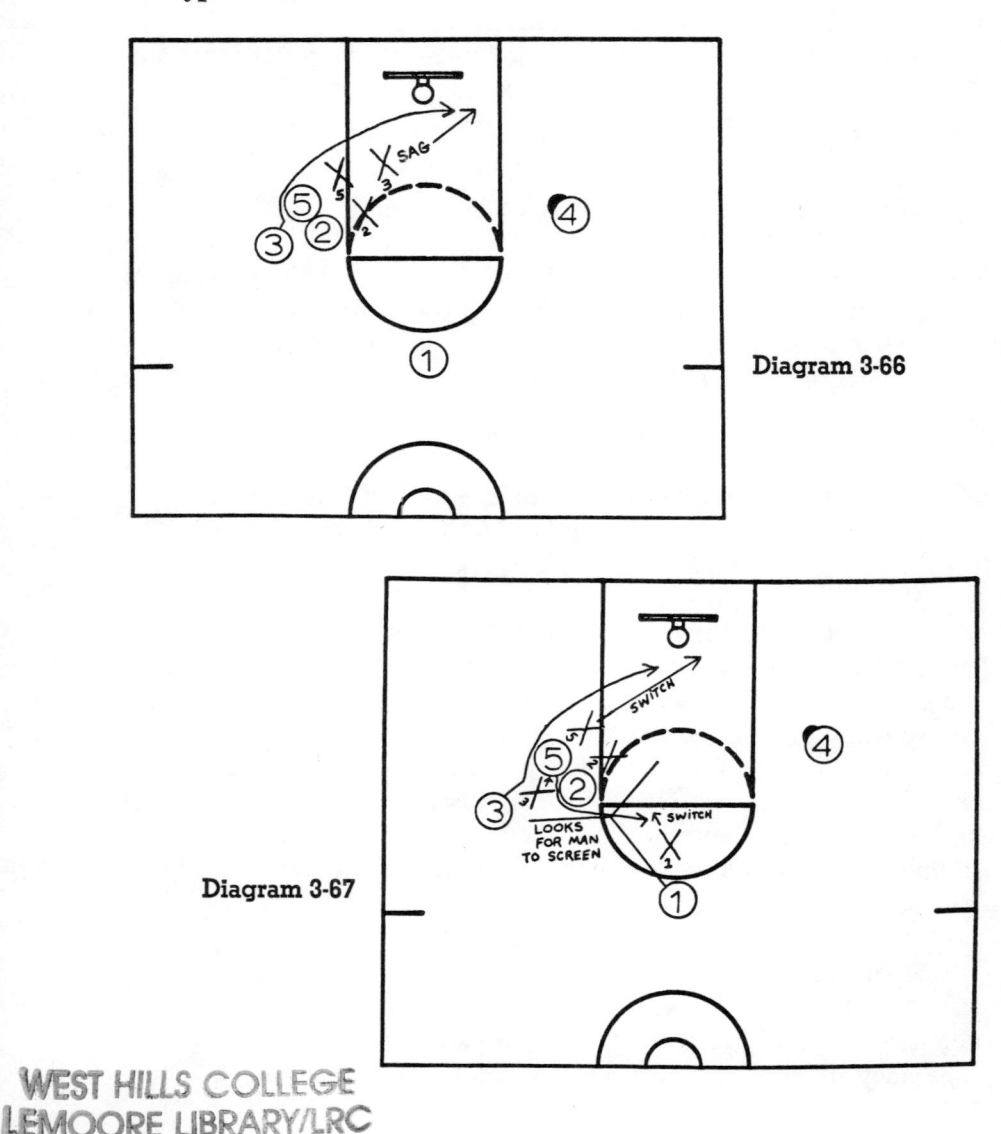

Diagram 3-66

Diagram 3-67

Setting Up the Percentage Man-to-Man Attack 101

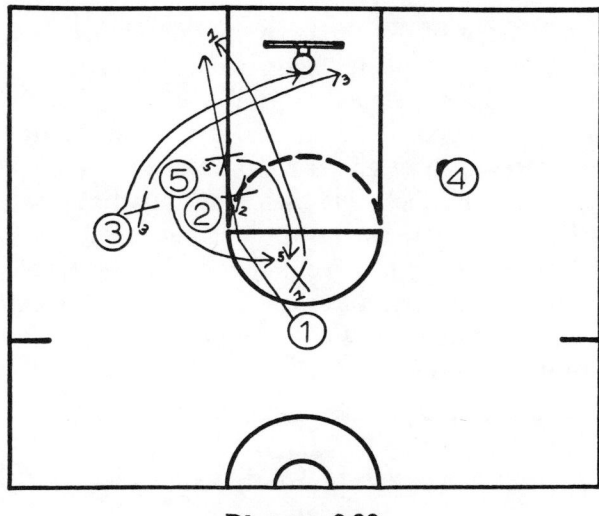

Diagram 3-68

Going over the Top of the Defensive Adjustments

One of the most effective special adjustment techniques that the Five Cutter Offense has in its arsenal of surprises for the defense is that of going over the top of these defensive maneuvers. This is done by having the strong-side wing man, the 3 man in Diagram 3-69, start to go off the 5 man's backtrap screen (he actually should go one or two steps beyond the 5 man), then he stops and suddenly comes back

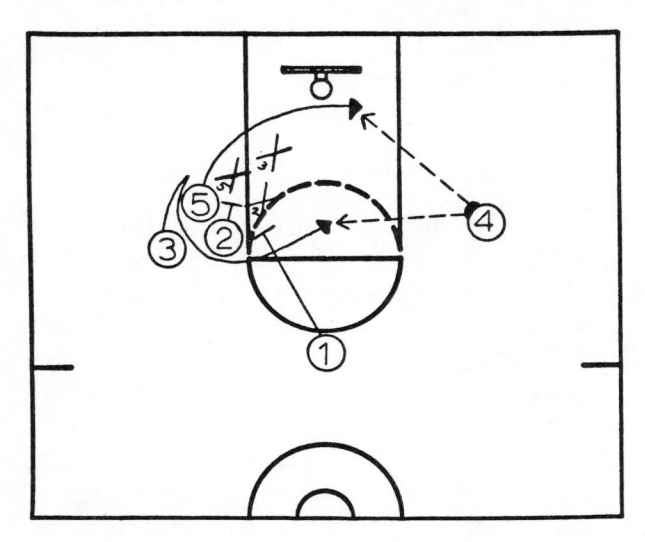

Diagram 3-69

around the 5 man and heads to the foul line. The 5 man, after seeing the 3 man go in front of him, rolls to the power lane. Actually the 3 man and the 5 man just change assignments. This is especially effective against the sagging defense, as the 3 man usually beats his defender to the foul line and can get the shot there. Many times as the 3 man's man starts to react and tries to move up the bucket to get to the 3 man, he actually picks his own man guarding the 5 man as 5 moves across the bucket, as shown in Diagram 3-70. This special adjustment is run, of course, from the 2 play or the 3 play. This maneuver keeps the defense guessing, and it is very difficult for them to react quickly enough to recover in time to stop the play. This special adjustment technique is called "topping the defense."

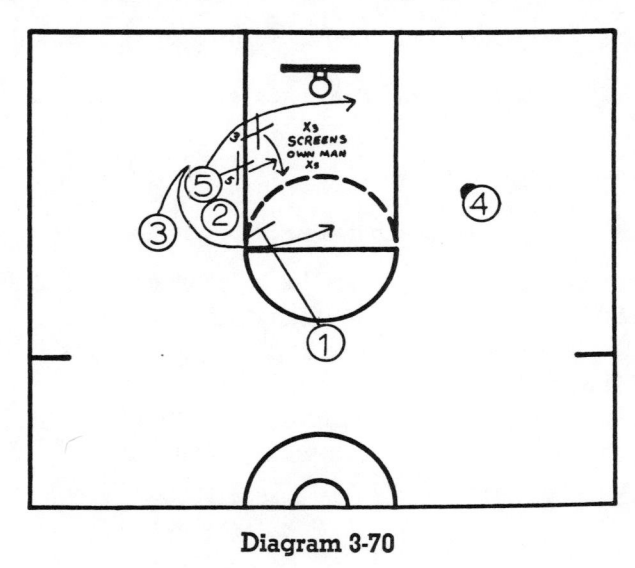

Diagram 3-70

Double Screening the Defensive Adjustments

The second special adjustment technique that can be used against the sagging, switching or anticipatory defensive adjustments is the double-screen play. The strong-side wing man in Diagram 3-71, the 3 man, yells "Sag" and he starts to go to the outside of the 5 man, who has set the backtrap. Then the 3 man quickly pops back in front of the 5 and 2 men, who have formed a double screen, and 4 passes the ball back to 1, who in turn feeds 3 coming in front of the double screen for the shot. If 3 does not get the shot, then he just dribbles the ball to the point like a wing rotation move, with the 4 man moving to the right low-post spot and 1 going to the right wing. 5 returns to the

Setting Up the Percentage Man-to-Man Attack

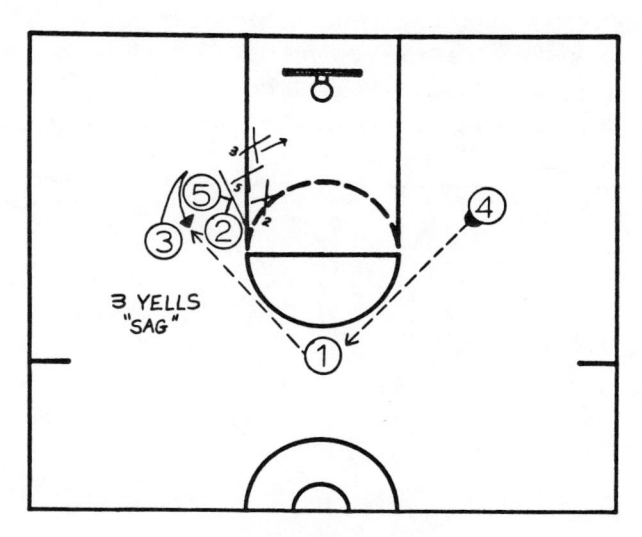

Diagram 3-71

left low-post spot and 2 stays at the left-wing position. The offense is now in the Five Cutter Offensive Formation, ready to start another option without any delay, as shown in Diagram 3-72.

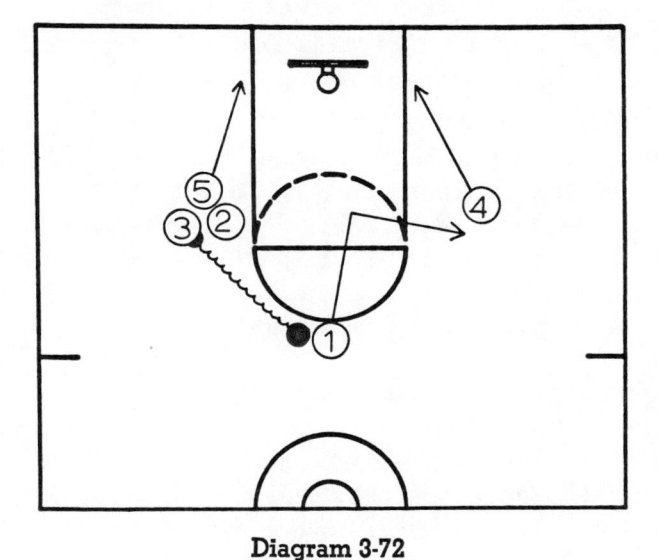

Diagram 3-72

Screen Rolling the Defensive Adjustments

The next special offensive adjustment technique is tne screen roll. This technique is employed whenever the 2 play or 3 play is in use. The backtrap man, after seeing the strong-side wing man clear out of the low-post area, rolls off his screen and moves over to the right side of the power lane, as shown in Diagram 3-73. If the 5 man is open, then he should get the pass. The point man's assignment is the

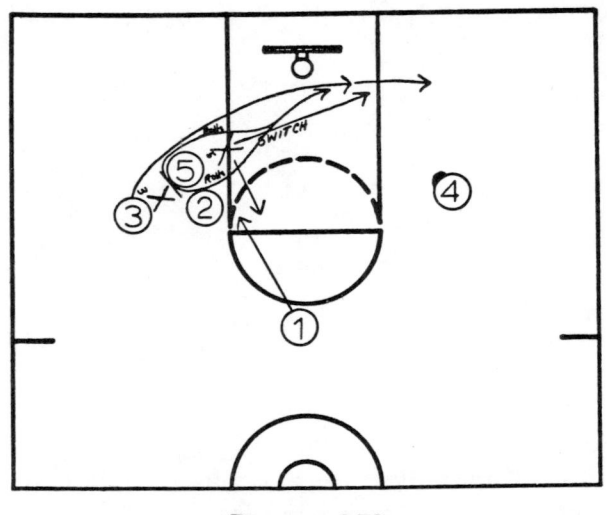

Diagram 3-73

same, except that he does not screen 5's man and he goes to the left low-post spot while the 2 man remains at the left wing. This adjustment move is very effective because the man guarding 5 usually is anticipating that 5 will head for the point. Also, when a team is switching on the backtrap maneuver, the 5 man has inside position on the defensive man who was guarding 3, if 5's man picks up the 3 man on the cut to the power lane. The 5 man must be alert to the switching technique of the defense so that he will roll at the right time. He can make this move any time he feels his man is trying to beat him to the foul line, after 3 has cleared the power lane. Diagram 3-74 shows what happens when the 5 man is not open on the screen-roll move. 4 dribbles to the point, the 3 man moves up to the right wing and the 5 man takes the right low-post spot. Again, the Five Cutter Offense is ready to go into another option and play.

Another screen-roll technique that can be used when the 2 or 3 play is being run is the following: The 1 man starts his move to screen the 5 man, but he quickly rolls to the basket (Diagram 3-75) when he sees that the defense is going to switch on the screen he is about to set on the 5 man's defender, or if he sees that the defense is trying to beat

Setting Up the Percentage Man-to-Man Attack 105

Diagram 3-74

Diagram 3-75

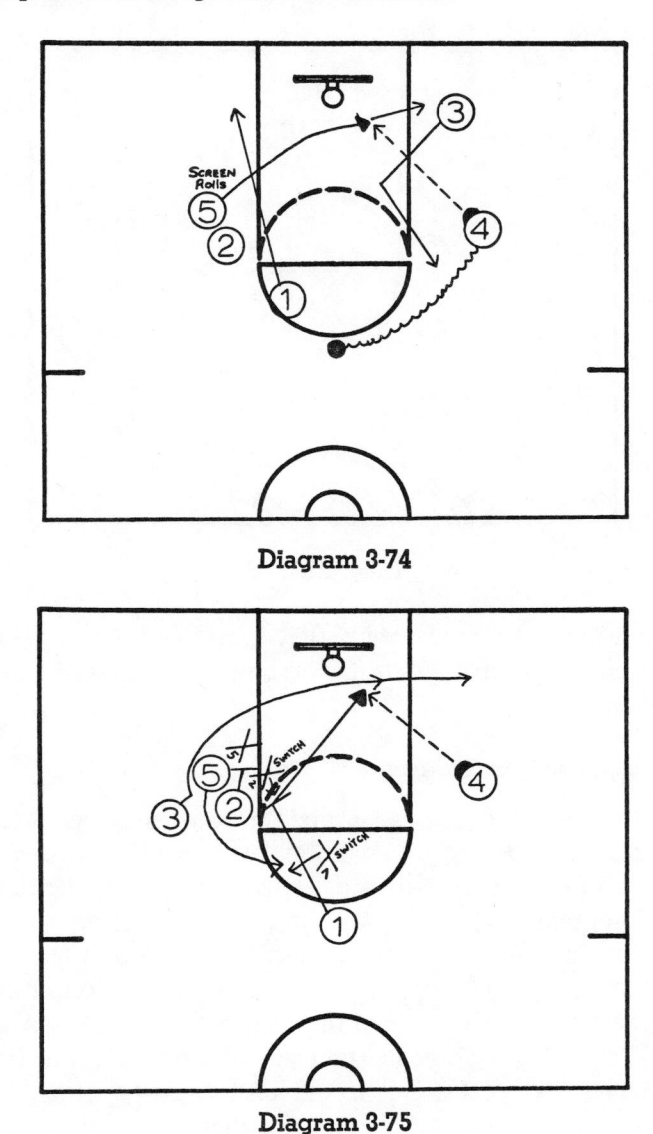

him to his position at the left low post and 5's man is anticipating the move to the foul line. 1 quickly rolls to the right side of the power lane. 3 clears the power lane, 2 screens for 5 and 4 looks to feed 1. If 1 is not open, then he quickly heads for the left low-post spot where he originally was supposed to go when running a normal 2 or 3 play. The offense is now reset and ready to go, as shown in Diagram 3-76.

These screen-roll adjustment techniques are automatic, and the

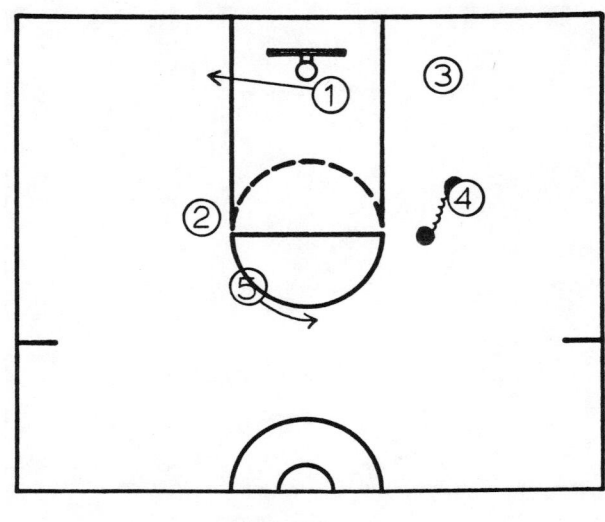

Diagram 3-76

players may use them whenever they feel the time is right. These moves catch the defense going the wrong way and will result in the easy percentage shot.

Circling the Defensive Adjustments

The last of the individual special offensive adjustment techniques is the circle adjustment. This adjustment maneuver can be used against any type of man-to-man defensive adjustment the defense can employ. Diagram 3-77 shows the strong-side wing man, 3, utilizing the top move by faking the cut to the power lane and going over the top of 5, but instead of stopping at the foul line, he continues on in a circular pattern to go directly to the man with the ball—in this situation, the 4 man. 5 moves to the right side of the power lane because he saw 3 go over the top. 1 moves to the left low-post spot and 2 remains at the left wing. 4 has the choice of either giving the ball to 3 or keeping the ball himself and driving to the hoop. If 4 gives the ball to 3, then 3 looks for the shot. If 3 shoots, then 4 has deep defensive responsibility. If 3 cannot shoot, then 4 goes to the point and the 3 man becomes the new right-wing man. Diagram 3-78 shows the Five Cutter Formation if the shot does not develop off this special move. Also, if 4 kept the ball but could not drive, then he would dribble the ball to the point. Regardless of what the 4 man does, the offense is still ready to go into another option and play.

Setting Up the Percentage Man-to-Man Attack

Diagram 3-77

Diagram 3-78

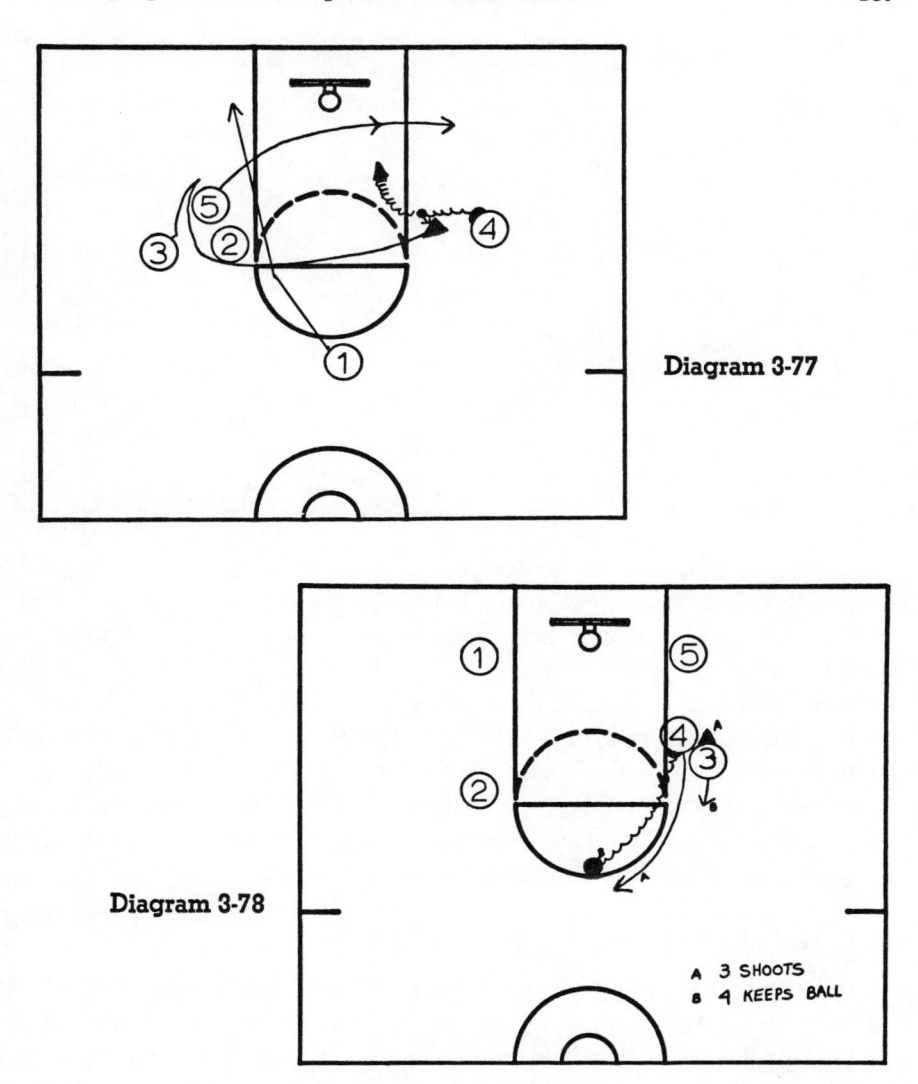

A 3 SHOOTS
B 4 KEEPS BALL

The 1 man can use the circle move to get himself and the offense into a new situation that the defense has not seen. As shown in Diagram 3-79, the 1 man passes to 4 and takes two steps toward the left-wing spot, giving the defense the idea that he is running a normal pattern for a 2 or 3 play. But instead he quickly stops and circles to his right, going toward the 4 man and to the outside of him. The 4 man should keep the ball, and as soon as the 1 man is even with him, 4 should pass the ball quickly to the 5 man, who has come off 2's screen after 5 has backtrapped for 3. 5, upon receiving the pass from

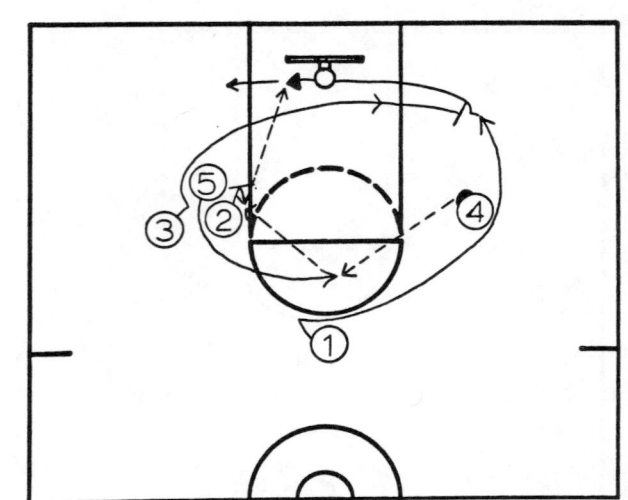

Diagram 3-79

4, must pass the ball immediately to 2 at the left-wing spot because 3 is going to backtrap the 1 man's man, and 2 should look to feed 1 at the left of the power lane. If 1 is not open, then he continues on out of the power lane and takes the left low-post spot as he would have in a normal 2 or 3 play. 3 takes the right low-post spot, 4 is still at the right wing, 5 is the new point man and 2 is now the "quarterback" with the ball at the left wing. Each player is in the same position he would have been in if a normal 2 or 3 play had been run and a shot had not developed. This special adjustment technique can be used against the sag, switch or anticipating move with equal results.

The Team Special Offensive Adjustment Techniques

When the defenders are sagging off the strong-side wing man (the 3 man), the 5 man, in anticipation of the 3 man's cut off his backtrap to the right power lane side, must set his backtrap screen extremely low along the key line extended. If the man playing 3 continually sags off, or any man guarding a strong-side wing cutter does the same, then we may have to change our formation to counteract the sag. Diagram 3-80 shows this slight adjustment in the Five Cutter Formation. 5 has to set the backtrap lower than he would like to because of the deep sag of 3's man. The 2 man, as he cuts through, looks for the 5 man as soon as he starts his move across the halfway point of the 3-second area. 2 has to make his adjustment quickly. 2 should move over and post himself to the inside or to the left of 5. This means, as shown in Diagram 3-80, that the 5 man and the 2 man stand side-by-side, and they are lower than they have been shown in

Setting Up the Percentage Man-to-Man Attack

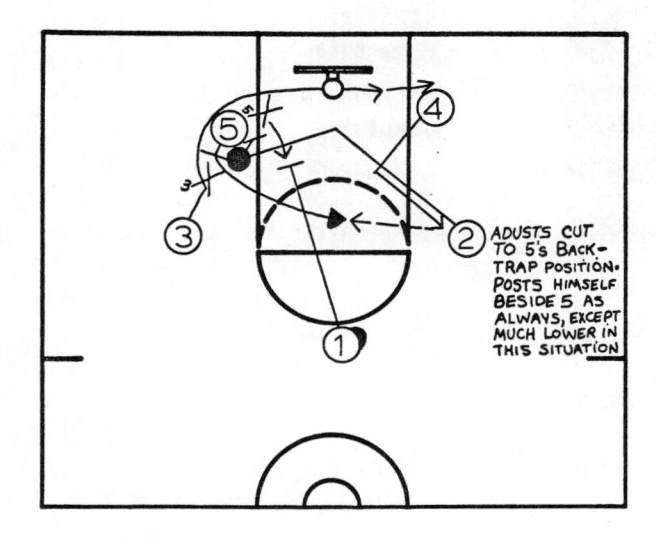

2 ADJUSTS CUT TO 5's BACK-TRAP POSITION. POSTS HIMSELF BESIDE 5 AS ALWAYS, EXCEPT MUCH LOWER IN THIS SITUATION

Diagram 3-80

the other diagrams. 2's cut through the 3-second area occurs on the 2 or 3 play.

Just exactly where 5 will set his backtrap depends upon the position of 3's man. Regardless of where 5 has to set the backtrap (so long as it is not in the 3-second area), 2 must get to 5's side as soon as possible to get ready to screen for 5 after 3 moves off 5's backtrap. The offensive patterns of the 2 or 3 play are exactly the same, no matter where the backtrap is set along the key line extended.

2 is responsible for finding 5, going directly to 5's inside and standing directly beside him, as 5's main job is to headhunt the defensive man sagging off 3 and set a good legal backtrap screen on him, regardless of where 5 has to set it.

We have found through experience that the higher the backtrap screen by 5 can be set, the more effective it is in freeing 3 in the power lane to the right of the basket. This is true because the lower the 3 man has to cut toward the base line, the easier it is for him to be beaten to the power lane. We do have to concede a little when the screen is set lower; however, this definitely opens up the foul circle area for the 5 man after he moves off 2 and 1's screens. Usually if 5 and 2 are forced into forming the double barrier low, 5 will get his shot nearer the basket, and without too much difficulty, because it gives the 1 man more time to pick up 5's man to screen if the defensive man has slipped by 2's side screen, low on the key line. Also, it allows 1 to screen 5's man much lower than if the backtrap was set in the normal position. The sag may take away the power shot some, but it is an open invitation to take the shot in the lower half of the foul circle.

110　　　　　　　　　　　Setting Up the Percentage Man-to-Man Attack

There is one special team play that should be employed against the sagging, switching or anticipatory defenses. This play will work against any of these defensive techniques. The one play that should be used is the 31 play—running the 3 play and then going to the 1 play if the 3 play is not successful. Diagram 3-81 shows how the defense sags to stop the 3 play. Because the defense has been told to sag, it has a tendency to do this after the 3 play has been run through unsuccessfully. It is at this time that going to the 1 play is effective. Diagram 3-82 shows 4 passing to 3 in the corner. *Coaching Hint:* When facing teams that sag, switch or anticipate the play, the strong-side wing man cutter should not stop in the power lane, but instead cut quickly to a spot about 4 to 5 feet from the key line. The cutter should not stop for he knows that he will not be open in the power lane because of the defensive maneuvers designed to take away that shot. Usually when the defense is doing this they have a tendency to release the cutter when he goes to the corner, especially if he does not stop in the power lane. It is at this point that the ball should be gotten to the cutter. The cutter should make sure that he squares himself to the basket before he receives the pass so that he can shoot immediately after he receives the pass from the wing man. If the cutter does not square himself after he cuts through, then by the time he does he will have lost the opportunity to shoot, because the defender will move out in time to stop him.

If 3 is open, as shown in Diagram 3-83, then he should shoot. If he is not open, then he looks for 1 coming across the base line on a 1

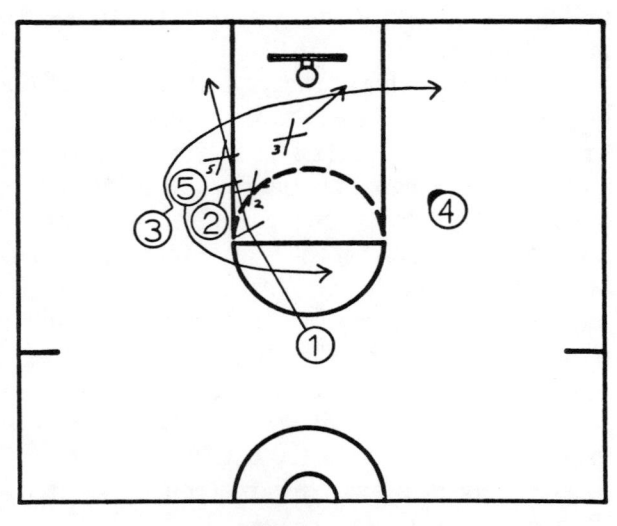

Diagram 3-81

Setting Up the Percentage Man-to-Man Attack

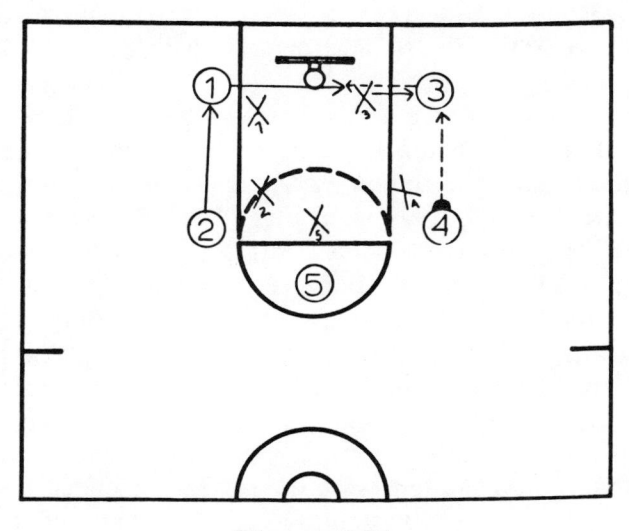

Diagram 3-82

play because 4 passed to the corner and stayed, which is the signal for the 1 play. *Coaching Hint:* An important point to remember when a defense is sagging, switching or anticipating is that the ball should be gotten to the corner, because the defense is so anxious to stop the power lane game and the foul line game that it forgets about the corners. This is why we like to use the 31 combination because it forces us to put the ball into the corner without having to think about it. Another very important coaching technique that must be mentioned

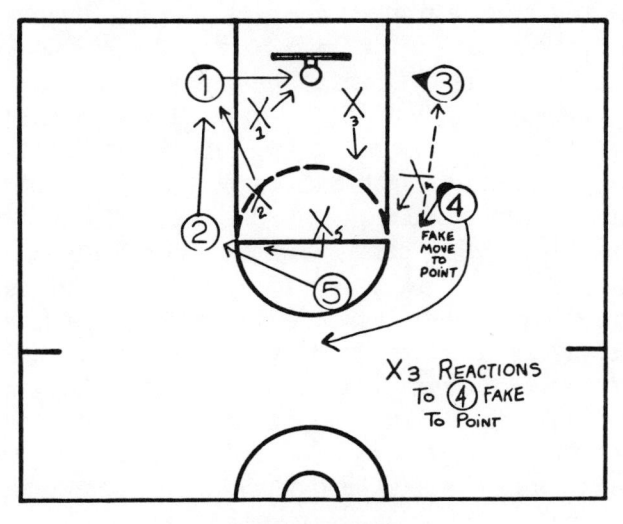

Diagram 3-83

at this time is the technique that the 4 man or the wing man with the ball should use in setting up the strong-side wing cutter in the corner. After the 3 man has gotten to the spot in the power lane that he normally would stop at, the 4 man looks immediately to the foul line. (He actually should square himself to the foul line because if 5 is open, then 4 should pass to him, and even if 5 is not going to be free enough to get the shot, the 4 man wants the defensive players to feel that the ball is going to the point position.) The 4 man must set the defense up by giving the indication that he wants to get the ball to the point. This usually will cause the defensive man guarding the 3 man in the corner to anticipate enough to sag off 3, believing that if the ball goes to the point then he will have to do one of two things: (1) if 4 passes and stays, 3 will move up to set the backtrap or (2) if 4 passes and goes, then 3 will move up to get the ball. Because he knows this, he starts to move up and in toward the key line extended to get ahead of 3's move. Now if 4 pivots and passes to 3 in the corner, 3 should be able to get the shot so long as he is no more than 5 or 6 feet from the key line extended, making it about an 11- or 12-foot shot. This offensive team adjustment is shown in Diagram 3-83. This maneuver is extremely effective and has a tendency to really keep the defense more honest than the individual special adjustment techniques, because in order for the defense to really stop the Five Cutter Offense, it must sag and switch, and to sag or switch a team must anticipate, if they are going to sag or switch effectively enough to interfere with the offensive patterns.

Actually any combination of the 1, 2 or 3 play sequences can be used to counteract these troublesome defensive adjustments so long as an outside option is run after a 3 play because the ball has to go into a corner in order to start an Outside Option. However, the most important things to remember with regard to this team special adjustment are the two techniques the wing man with the ball must use in order to have the defense feel that the ball is going to the point. The wing executes one of these techniques by facing the point position squarely, pivoting quickly and then passing to the man on the base line, who is no more than 5 or 6 feet away from the key line. The strong-side wing employs the other technique when he cuts into the power lane. He can see that he will not be open so he does not stop, but continues right on to the 5- or 6-foot distance from the key line, and then he stops and squares himself to the basket as 4 is setting the defense up by looking to the point. In this way, the strong-side wing man can shoot the ball as soon as he gets it from 4, and his man will not be able to react in time to prevent the shot. Time must be taken to work on these two impor-

Setting Up the Percentage Man-to-Man Attack 113

tant techniques. Diagram 3-84 shows a good drill to use to simulate game conditions for these two important team special offensive adjustments.

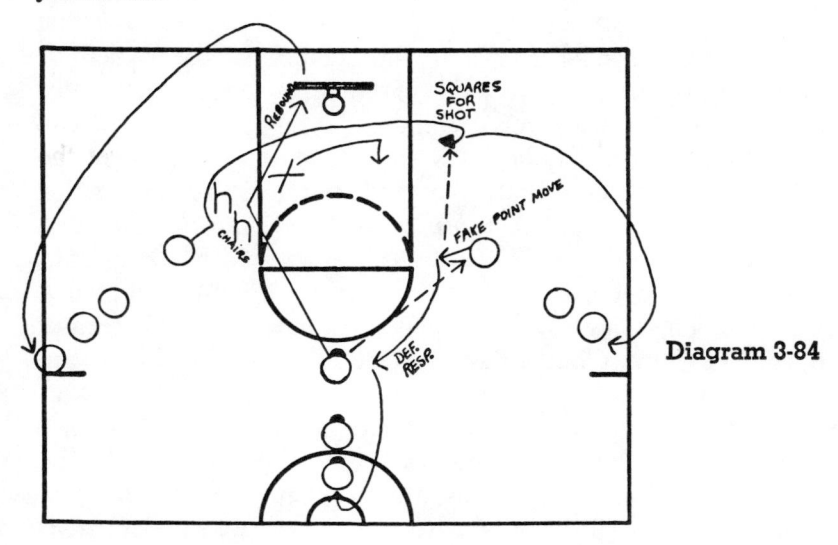

Diagram 3-84

It is important to note that when a shot is taken from the corner, the rule which governs defensive responsibility is in effect. The man who feeds another man who is not in the power lane has deep responsibility. Diagram 3-85 shows that 4, after seeing 3 shoot in the base line area outside of the power lane, moves to the top of the foul circle for deep defensive responsibility. 1 moves across the power lane to get the ball because 4 passed to 3 and stayed to signal the 1 play. 2, who has moved to the left low-post area, rebounds to the left of the power lane. The 5 man, who has moved to the left wing, rebounds to the front of the power lane. 3, after following his shot, has half-and-half duty.

Coaching Hint: Players must be reminded that any time the ball is passed to the low-post area and is not in the power lane, this is considered the corner of the court, indicating a signal for an Outside Option. Therefore, they must expect and react to the signal for the 1 play or the 2 play.

Handling the Tight Man-to-Man Front-Court Pressure

Any team that uses the ball-control or percentage-control offense must expect to be pressured in the front court if sagging or switching tactics do not affect the offensive attack. No team is going to play a percentage- or ball-controlled offense with a passive man-to-man defense that will allow the offense to do as it pleases. Therefore, a team that employs this control type of play must have patterns that will work effectively against half-court tight-denial defense. When we refer to denial type defense, we mean the overplay type that has the defensive man playing between his man and the ball at all times. Man-to-man front-court pressure that is used against the percentage-controlled offense is not usually the wild and reckless desperation type, but instead is designed to force the offense away from its ball-control patterns and cause confusion on the part of the offense. Usually this type of defense will try to pick up the offense as it crosses the center line. There are several effective maneuvers the Percentage-Controlled Five Cutter Offense has available to bypass this front-court pressure and get into the Outside Options and Identical Inside Option. We have found that the most difficult factor to be contended with is the initial pressure, because once the Percentage-Controlled Five Cutter Offense gets into its options, the pressure does not seem to bother the pattern at all. In fact, there is an increase in the effectiveness of the Five Cutter Offense when teams put pressure on, instead of sagging or switching in an attempt to defense the attack successfully.

Verbal Release Call

The verbal release call has been described in this chapter as one of the ways to get into the Five Cutter Offensive Formation of the weak-side–strong-side floor balance. We will review it quickly here. Diagram 3-86 shows the 1 man bringing the ball up; he is met at midcourt by his man. Seeing this pressure and the pressure that is being put on the wings, the point man simply calls a wing man's last name and the wing man cuts through to the opposite-side high-post position. The offense is then ready to run the 3 play. 4 must make sure that he rubs his man off the 3 man as 3 cuts through the bucket area.

Dribble Release Move

The dribble release move is exactly like the verbal release call, except that it is initiated by the 1 man dribbling toward one of the wings. In Diagram 3-87 he dribbles toward the 2 man, who moves just

Diagram 3-85

Diagram 3-86

①'s VERBAL
RELEASE CALL
TO ②

Diagram 3-87

①'s
DRIBBLE
RELEASE
MOVE
TO
②

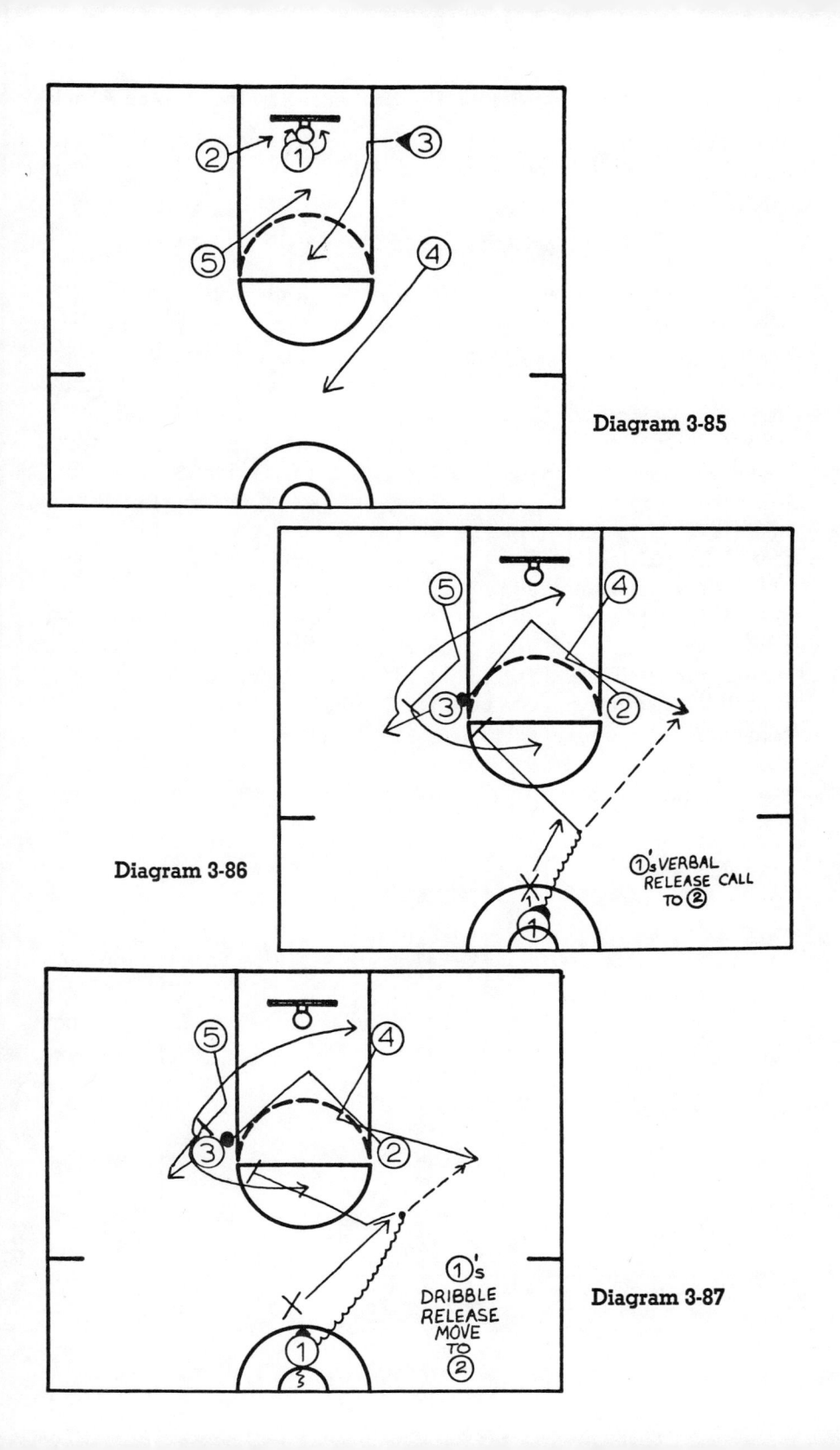

like he did in Diagram 3-86. The dribble release move goes right into the 3 play just like the verbal release call did.

The Stack to the Identical Inside Option

The stack formation, as shown in Diagram 3-88, is used only when the Five Cutter Offense is having difficulty in handling the pressure that the defense is putting on against the regular 1-2-2 formation. The low-post men on each side just move up and stand directly behind the wing men on their side of the court. They should stand with their toes touching the heels of the wing men. Actually, from here the movement is exactly like the dribble release move, except that when the point man starts to dribble to the side of the court to have a man clear out, the low-post man behind the wing man is the man who clears out. He does this by stepping around in front of the wing man, and the wing man should break off the low-post man to a point on the floor as near to the foul line extended as possible. After the low-post man clears out, he goes to the opposite-side high-post spot. The wing man on the opposite side should break out 4 or 5 feet as the point man dribbles toward the other wing man. The left-side low-post man sets a backtrap on the 3 man's defender and the offense is ready to go into the 3 play. Diagram 3-88 shows 3 and 5 together on the left side of the key line and the 2 and 4 men together on the right side of the key line.

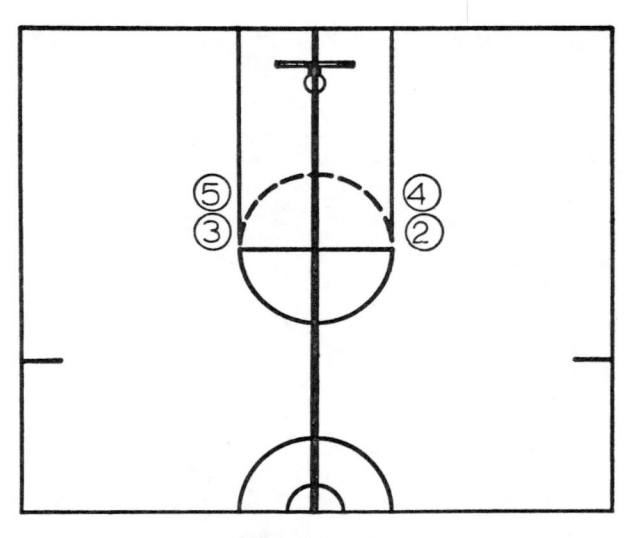

Diagram 3-88

Setting Up the Percentage Man-to-Man Attack   117

The 1 man dribbles toward the 2 and 4 men, so 4 moves around 2 and 2 breaks off 4 to get the ball. 4 goes to the left-side high-post spot. 3 moves back off and away from 5 so that 5 can backtrap 3's man. 1 passes to 2 at the point where 2 is open, the nearer the foul line the better, and the offense is now into the Identical Inside Option by initiating the 3 play. (See Diagram 3-89.)

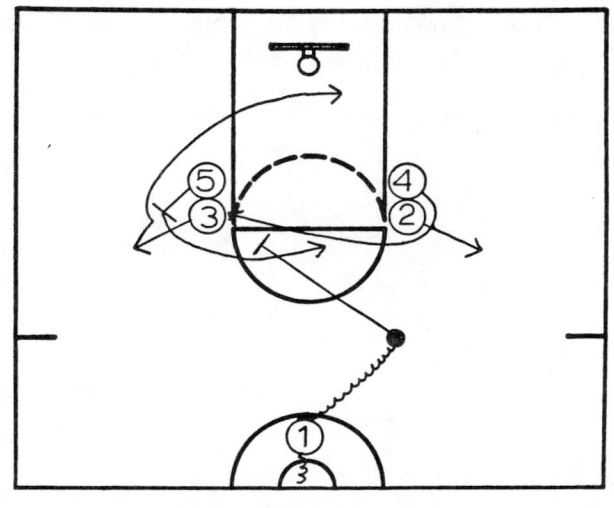

Diagram 3-89

The Strong-Side Safety Valve

Usually most shuffle or backtrap weak-side–strong-side offenses employ a strong-side option or play with their regular normal half-court attack. In the percentage-controlled offense, we use the strong-side situation only when we are facing pressure defenses. The reasoning behind this is that we want to be able to give the strong side the ball without any difficulty when facing the pressure defense, and if we use the strong-side play with our regular Five Cutter Options, the defense will know what to expect when we run the strong-side play. Not only that, but when the defense expects the ball to go to the weak side, it becomes a very simple maneuver to get the ball to the strong side, even against pressure.

We use the strong-side play much like a quarterback uses his halfback who has delayed in the backfield on a pass play. The primary and secondary receivers are covered, so he throws a short pass to the halfback who is acting as a safety valve.

We only use the strong-side play as a safety valve when we cannot get the ball to the weak side. However, after we get the ball to the strong side, we do run a play that runs one man into the power lane and another into the foul line circle. If neither of these men are open, then the offense is in the Five Cutter 1-2-2 formation, with the ball at the wing spot, ready to run another option and play. We call this strong-side play the Strong-Side Safety Valve.

Diagram 3-90 shows the 1 man trying to pass to the weak side after the 2 man has cut through to the opposite-side high-post posi-

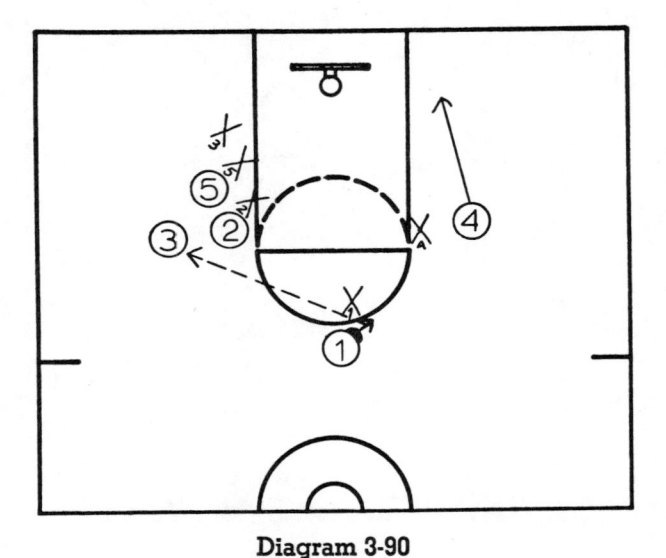

Diagram 3-90

tion, but he cannot get the ball to 4 because of the defensive pressure being put on both the 1 man and the 4 man. 1 immediately pivots and looks to pass to the strong side of the court. One reason why 3 is usually open on the strong-side wing position is that 3's man is usually anticipating that he is going to cut through to the power lane as soon as 4 gets the ball, so 3's man plays off or sags in front of 3 to pick him up or beat 3 to the right side of the power lane. This, of course, is the reason why 3 is open when 1 passes to him because 3's man is too deep to react in time to put any pressure at all on the wing, let alone interfere with 1 passing to 3. The 4 man, as soon as he sees that 1 has released the ball to 3, moves back down to his original low-post position, but instead of going tight to the key line, he stays about 3 feet away from it. The reason for 4 doing this will be shown in Diagram 3-91.

Setting Up the Percentage Man-to-Man Attack

Diagram 3-91

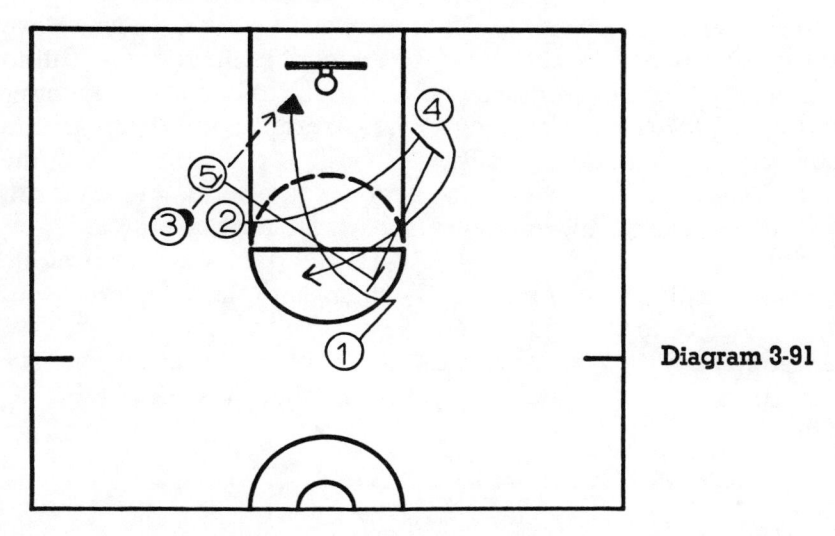

As soon as 5 and 2 see that the ball is going to the strong side, they must react quickly. 2 immediately goes back across the lane and sets a screen on 4's man. 5 moves up the foul circle and sets a backtrap screen on 1's man. 1 can help set this backtrap up by taking a step or two to his right, and this makes 5's job a little easier and much more effective. 1 cuts to the left of 5's screen and goes to the left side of the power lane. 3 feeds 1 if he is open for the power shot. 5, after 1 cuts off his screen, moves down to his left and sets a double screen with 2 on 4's man. 4 breaks into the foul line circle area off the double screen of 2 and 5. Diagram 3-92 shows what happens when 1 takes

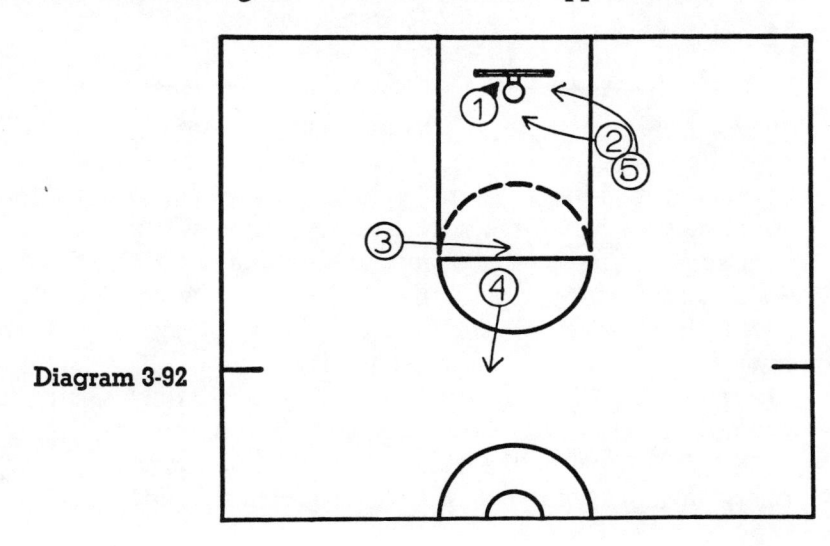

Diagram 3-92

the power shot in the power lane. 2 rebounds to the right of the power lane while 5 rebounds to the middle of the power lane. Because 3 fed a man in the power lane who shot, he goes to the foul line for half-and-half duty, and 4, who is heading toward the mid-court area off the double screen, has the deep defensive responsibility.

In Diagram 3-93, the 1 man is not open to receive the pass from 3, so 3 then looks for his secondary man, the 4 man coming into the foul circle area off the double screen. 4 should take the shot if he is open and feels that he can make it. 1 rebounds to the left power lane area, 2 rebounds to the right power lane area and 5 goes to the middle of the power lane. 3, who fed a man outside the power lane who shot, has the deep defensive responsibility, and the shooter, 4, has half-and-half duty.

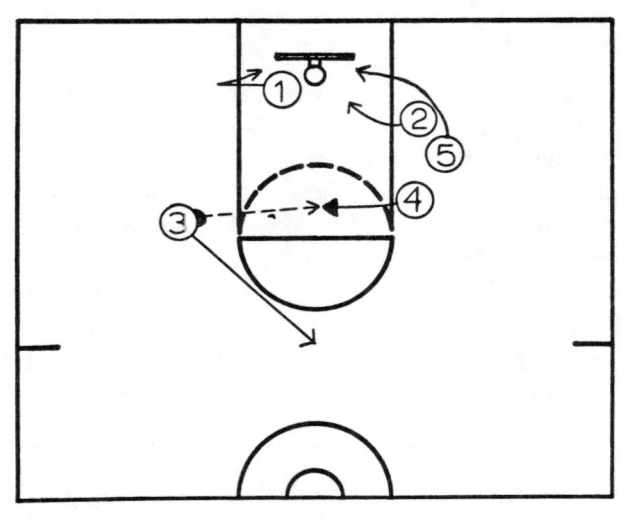

Diagram 3-93

Diagram 3-94 shows that neither 1 nor 4 is open to get the shot, so 3 keeps the ball. 1 takes the left low-post spot, 2 goes to the right-wing spot, 5 takes the right low-post position and goes to the point and 3 stays at the left-wing position with the ball. Now the offense is in the Five Cutter Formation with the ball at the signal position, all set to go immediately into another option and play.

Coaching Hint: Remember, this play should only be used against pressure defenses, and it should only be run when the point man cannot get the ball to the weak side of the floor. Also this strong-side safety valve can only be used on an Identical-Inside-Option 3 play.

Setting Up the Percentage Man-to-Man Attack 121

This is an excellent play to run from the stack formation, as well as from the regular basic 1-2-2 setup of the Five Cutter Offense.

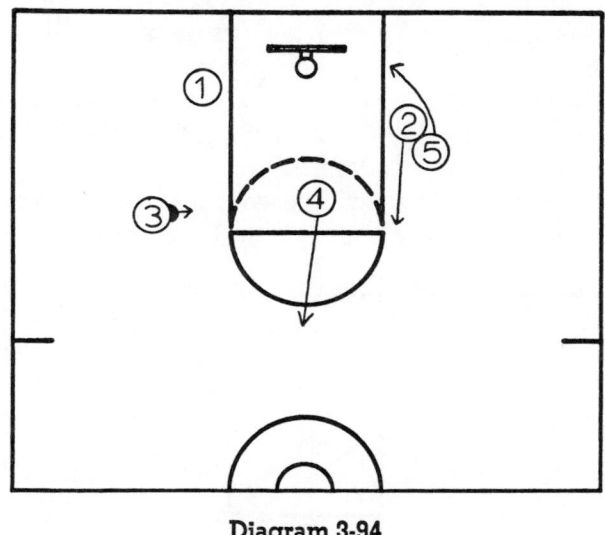

Diagram 3-94

The Auxiliary Offense to the Five Cutter Attack

The Auxiliary Offense is used only when the Five Cutter Attack is having difficulty getting into its offensive patterns. The Auxiliary Offensive setup is shown in Diagram 3-95. It is basically a 2-3 forma-

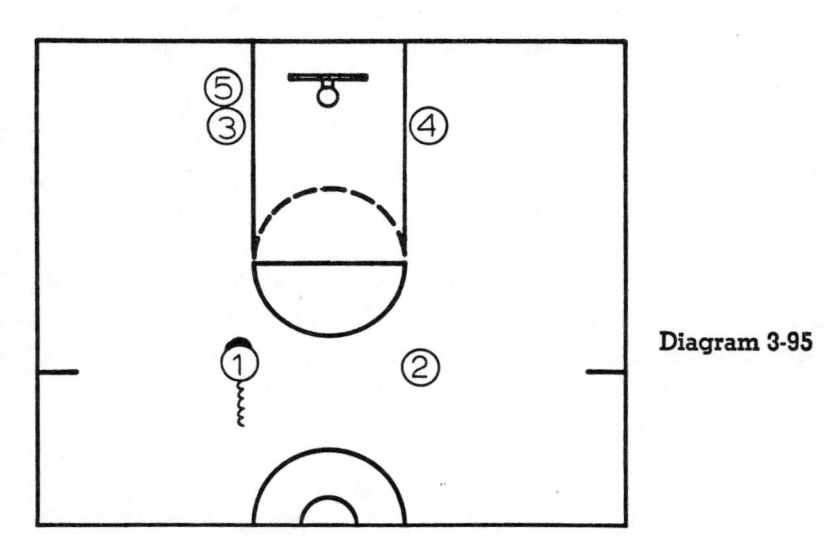

Diagram 3-95

tion. The guards try to stay even with the key line extended, the forwards line up in the low-post positions and the center stays on the same side of the court that the ball is on, behind the low-post man on that side of the court. 1 and 2 are shown as the guards and 3 and 4 are the forwards, with 5 being the post man or center. Notice that 1 and 3 are on the same side of the court and 2 and 4 are on the right side. The 5 man must try to stay on the same side as the ball, behind the low-post man on that side at all times.

1 and 2 bring the ball up the court, and in Diagram 3-96, 1 brings it up on the left side. As soon as 1 gets to the mid-court area

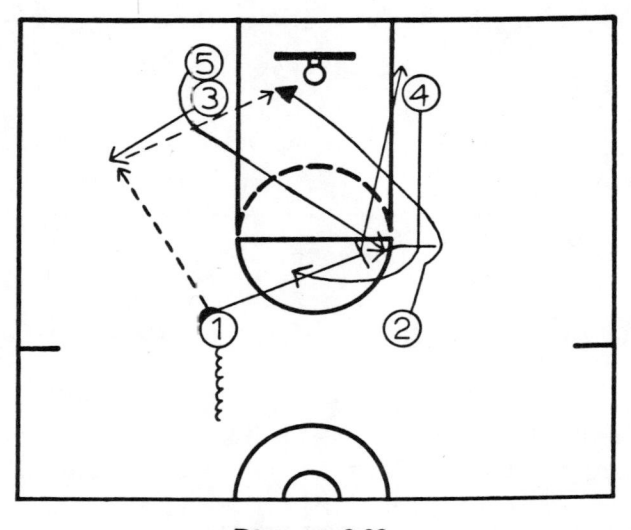

Diagram 3-96

marker, the 5 man moves around in front of the 3 man, the same way as in the stack formation, and the 3 man breaks directly off 5 to get in position to receive the pass from 1. 3 should try to get the ball as tight to the key line as possible. The 5 man continues on to the high-post spot on the right side of the court. The 4 man, as soon as he sees 1 release the pass to 3, moves up the key line and sets a backtrap screen on the defensive player guarding 2. 2 breaks to the right of the screen set by 4 and moves into the power lane at full speed. The 1 man, after passing to 3, moves to his right and sets a side screen on 4, who set the original backtrap on 2. 3 feeds 2 if he is open. 4 comes off 1's screen and moves into the foul circle area. Diagram 3-97 shows 2 shooting the power shot, so 1 and 5 rebound to the right and middle of the power lane. 3 follows the same rules about where to go if he feeds

Setting Up the Percentage Man-to-Man Attack 123

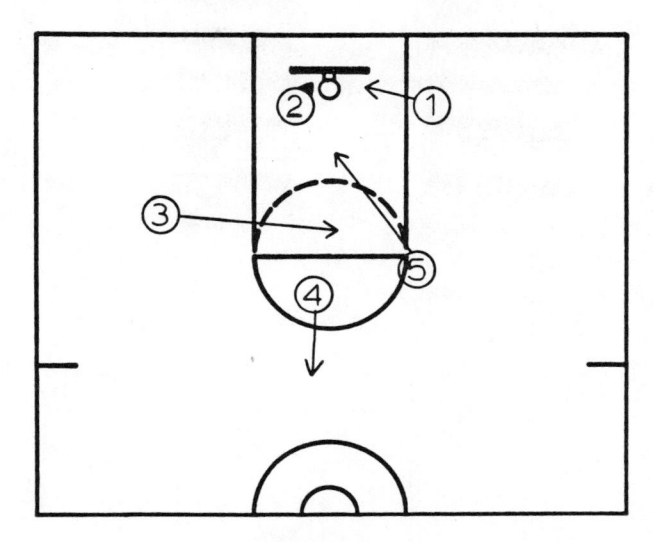

Diagram 3-97

a man in the power lane who shoots, by going to the foul line for half-and-half duty. The 4 man has defensive responsibility because he was moving away from the basket and heading to the mid-court area above the top of the foul circle when the shot was taken.

Diagram 3-98 has 4 receiving the pass from 3 because 2 was not open for the shot. If 4 shoots, then 2 rebounds to the left of the power

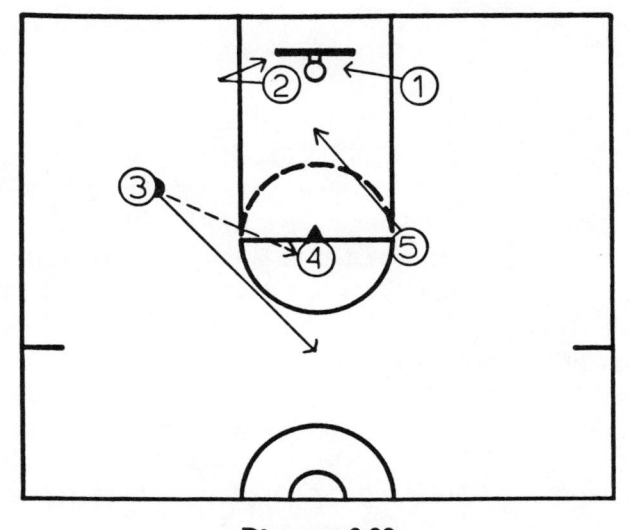

Diagram 3-98

lane, 1 rebounds to the right and 5 goes to the middle. 3 follows this rule: If you feed a man outside of the power lane who shoots, then you have deep defensive responsibility; the shooter, 4, has half-and-half duty after he follows through on his shot. If 3 cannot hit either 2 or 4, then Diagram 3-99 shows the offense reset into the Five Cutter Formation. 2 takes the left low-post spot, 1 takes the right low-post position, 5 takes the right wing, 4 goes to the point and 3 stays at the left-wing position with the ball. Again the Five Cutter Attack is ready to begin from the wing position.

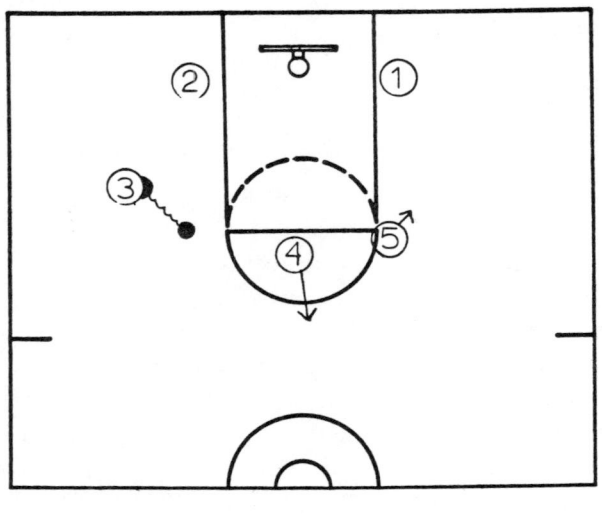

Diagram 3-99

If 1 cannot get the pass to 3, or if he just passes to 2, then the play is run from the right instead of the left. If the pass is thrown to the 2 man from 1, the 5 man should try to get across the bucket to make his move around the 4 man so as to free 4. If 5 gets halfway across the bucket area and sees that he is not going to be able to get to 4 in time, then he just moves up to the left-wing spot as quickly and directly as possible. Diagram 3-100 shows the Auxiliary Option being run to the right after 1 passed to 2.

If the 1 man cannot pass to either 3 or 2, and if he can still keep his dribble, the play shown in Diagram 3-101 is very effective. 1 just dribbles toward 2 and 2 moves toward 1 as he dribbles. 1 then gives 2 the ball. 5 moves around 3 and 2 passes to 3. 4 backtraps for 1, who moves to the base-line power spot, and 5 continues on to the right high-post spot. 2 now screens for 4 and 4 goes to the foul circle area.

Setting Up the Percentage Man-to-Man Attack 125

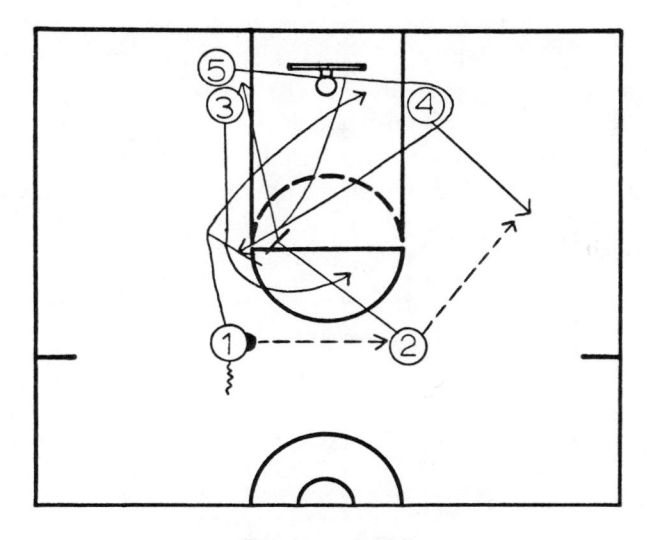

Diagram 3-100

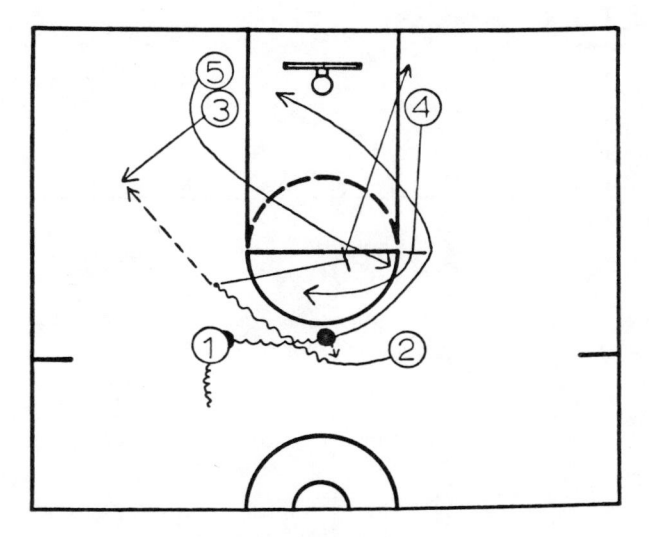

Diagram 3-101

Diagram 3-102 shows 1 dribbling toward 2, but instead of giving the ball to 2, 1 keeps it and passes to 4. 5 breaks directly to the left high-post spot and 3 sets a backtrap screen for 2. 2 moves to the power lane as fast as he can, 1 screens for 3 and 3 moves to the foul circle area.

These dribble-weave and dribble-weave-keep techniques are excellent plays to use against pressure defense (which makes it very difficult for the 1 or 2 man to get the ball to the 3 or 4 man on the straight pass). Because these techniques create so much circular movement, it is very difficult for the defense to stop the backtrap on the guards as they cross over and change positions on the floor. If nobody is open on these two maneuvers, then the offense is now in the Five Cutter Formation, with the ball in the starting position at the wing position, ready to have the wing man start an Outside or an Inside Option.

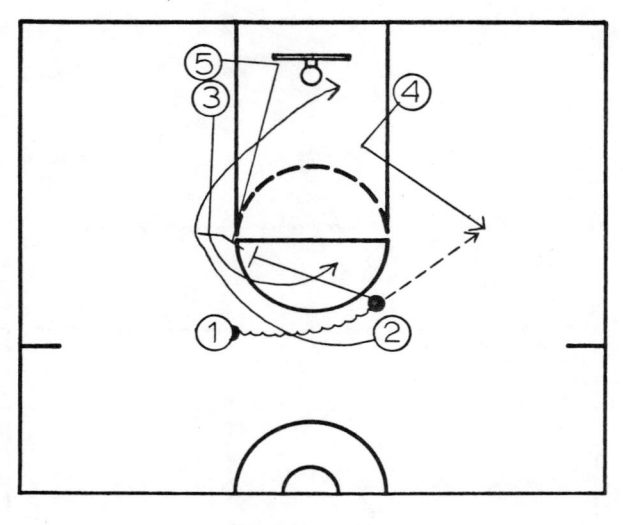

Diagram 3-102

CHAPTER 4

Breaking Man-to-Man Pressure Defenses with the All-Purpose Offense

Meeting Pressure Defenses

Percentage ball-controlled teams must accept the fact that they are going to face a large number of full-court man-to-man and full-court zone presses. They will face many different variations of these; therefore, they must be able to handle them with a high degree of success.

These full-court presses are designed not only to harass the offensive team into turnovers, but also to confuse and force the offense into changing its method of attack. This change may mean only that the offense is forced to bring the ball up court with some form of resistance instead of being allowed to do exactly as it pleases.

Just forcing a change in the method of offensive attack can cause a great deal of confusion and trouble for the disciplined, set-pattern attack team. Because our basic style of play over the years has been the deliberate percentage-controlled type, we have faced many types of presses designed to force us away from the set attack.

Aims of Pressure Defenses

Many of these presses were not aimed at stealing the ball or forcing offensive turnovers, but were used instead to keep us from setting up our percentage-controlled offense and not allowing us to determine the tempo of the game.

The first thing that must be done when facing any full-court pressure defense is to determine if the pressure defense is going to be: (1) an active press or (2) a passive press. The active press is designed to force turnovers or to steal the ball, while the function of the passive press is primarily to force the offense away from its predetermined percentage-controlled patterns and speed up the tempo of the game. After determining the aim of the press, either active or passive, the offense should then go into its preplanned patterns for the type of press that is being applied.

Active Presses

When facing the active press, the best way to handle it or any other man-to-man full-court pressure tactic, is to give the ball to your best ball handler, then get out of his way and let him bring it up on the dribble. However, the type of player that can do this effectively is not found on every high school team.

Therefore, it is very important to have disciplined controlled-percentage patterns that the team can use. Usually when facing the active press, we bring just two guards into the back court and let them try to beat the defense up the court, going into our regular patterns; however, if we have too much difficulty, then we use our regular percentage-controlled Identical Inside Option full-court and run it out of the regular 1-2-2 setup or the stack formation. We also have some special plays that can be run from the 1-2-2 setup of the Five Cutter Formation.

We have found that when a team is applying strong active pressure, unless our guards are quick enough to beat the defense in the back court, we have had more success running the 3 play of the Inside Option full-court, because it puts more pressure on the individual defensive players and gives us an opportunity to score very quickly if the defense commits a mental or physical error. The active press is a gambling type of defense. We want to have the entire court available to our offense because this puts great pressure on the defense

Breaking Man-to-Man Pressure Defenses

to cover the whole court. Also, the defenders have to move backwards. Moving backwards at a high rate of speed may be easy for the defensive team's guards and small men, but it is another story for the defense's big men.

We allow the defensive team to set up its defense; this enables our own players to get to their assigned spots on the floor when facing any type of full-court man-to-man pressure.

Passive Presses

When facing the passive man-to-man full-court presses, designed to force us away from our set plan of attack, the first thing we attempt to do is give the ball to our best ball handler and see if he can handle the pressure by himself by dribbling the ball up. If we find that we cannot get into our regular Outside or Inside Options by having just the guard bring the ball up on his own, then we usually have both guards bring it up together. Usually having the two guards bring the ball up by screening for each other is effective enough to allow us to dribble into the Outside Options and the Identical Inside Option.

Dribbling into the Outside Options

When employing the use of both guards in the back court against any man-to-man full-court pressure, we have the guard who is not taking the ball out position himself on the foul line even with the basket. Usually the man taking the ball out-of-bounds is the best ball handler of the two wing men in the Five Cutter Formation, and the point man is the player stationed at the foul line. The low-post men station themselves in their normal low-post areas, and the remaining wing man positions himself at mid-court. Diagram 4-1 shows the offensive setup. 2 takes the ball out-of-bounds, the 1 man is at the foul line, 3 is at mid-court and 4 and 5 are at their low-post positions. The reason 3 is at the center line is that he can go to the rescue of 2 if he cannot get the ball into 1 because 1 is being double teamed. The man at the foul line should make hard V moves in order to get the ball; if the 1 man is right-handed, then he should try to get the ball to his right as he stands facing the opponent's basket. This gives him the whole side of the court and more to use his right hand to bring the ball up, as shown in Diagram 4-2. The man at the foul line may have to fake V's in order to get open for the pass from the man out-of-bounds, but he

Breaking Man-to-Man Pressure Defenses

Diagram 4-1

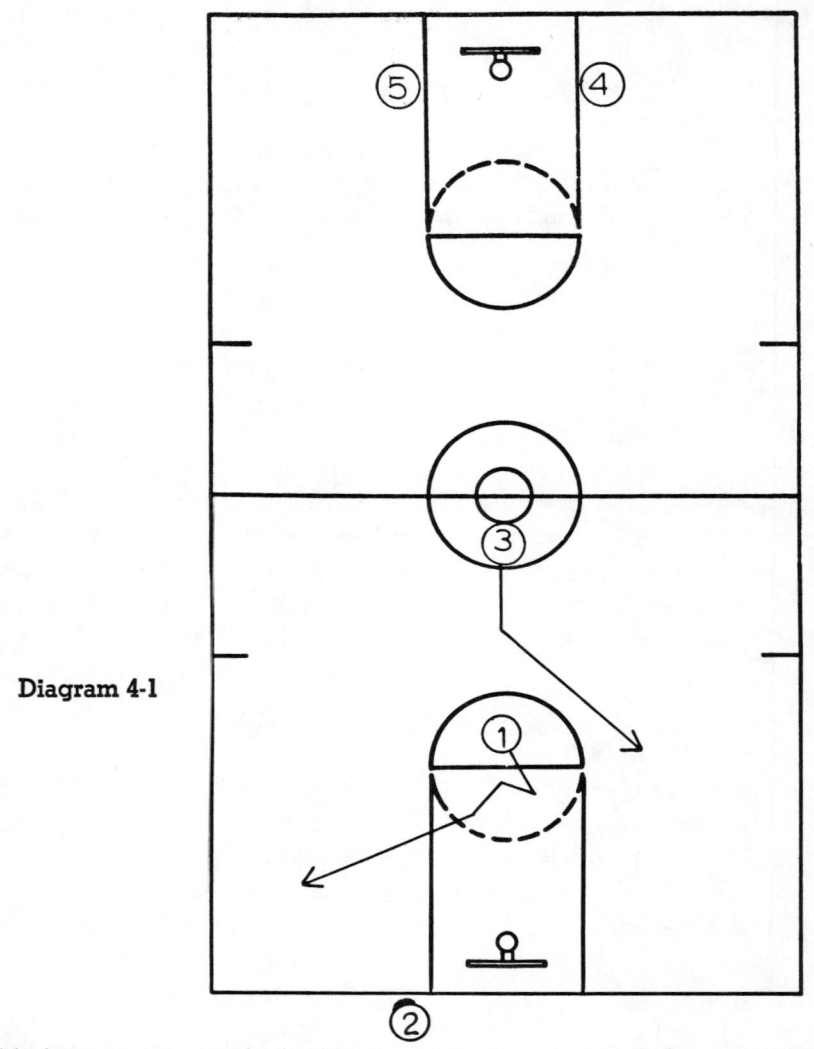

should always try to get the ball in the pocket or corner of the court so that he can use his strong hand to bring the ball up on the dribble. As soon as the 3 man at the center circle sees that 1 has received the pass in-bounds, then he heads to his left-wing position; however, he should back-pedal to this area or look over his shoulder so that he can come back to help out if the 1 and 2 men get in trouble.

After 2 passes to 1, the 2 man has two choices of cuts. He may cut to the outside of the 1 man, and this allows 1 the choice of keeping the ball himself or handing the ball off to 2. If one of the guards happens to be left-handed, this can really make this two-guard attack in the back court unbeatable in bringing the ball up court. We shall

Breaking Man-to-Man Pressure Defenses 131

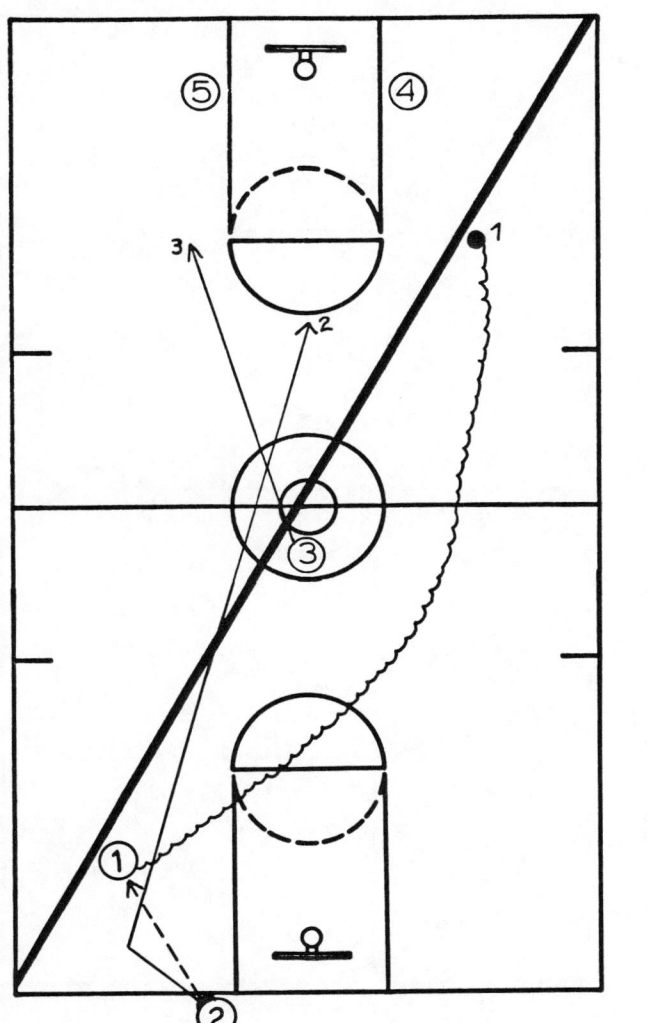

Diagram 4-2

assume though that in these plays both guards are right-handed. This forces the guard with the ball, the 1 man, to keep the ball more times than giving it to 2 cutting by, because 2 can only use his weak (left) hand. Diagram 4-3 shows 1 keeping the ball, pivoting and looking up court. After this, he dribbles with his right hand up the middle of the court and then to an angle, heading to the right-wing position. 1 dribbles toward the right-wing position and 2 moves to the point position. 2, after taking several steps beyond 1, should stop and look back to see if 1 got double teamed. Usually if 2 does not have a man with him at the point, he notices this and immediately hooks so that 1 can pass to him and let him bring the ball up. This technique will be

Diagram 4-3

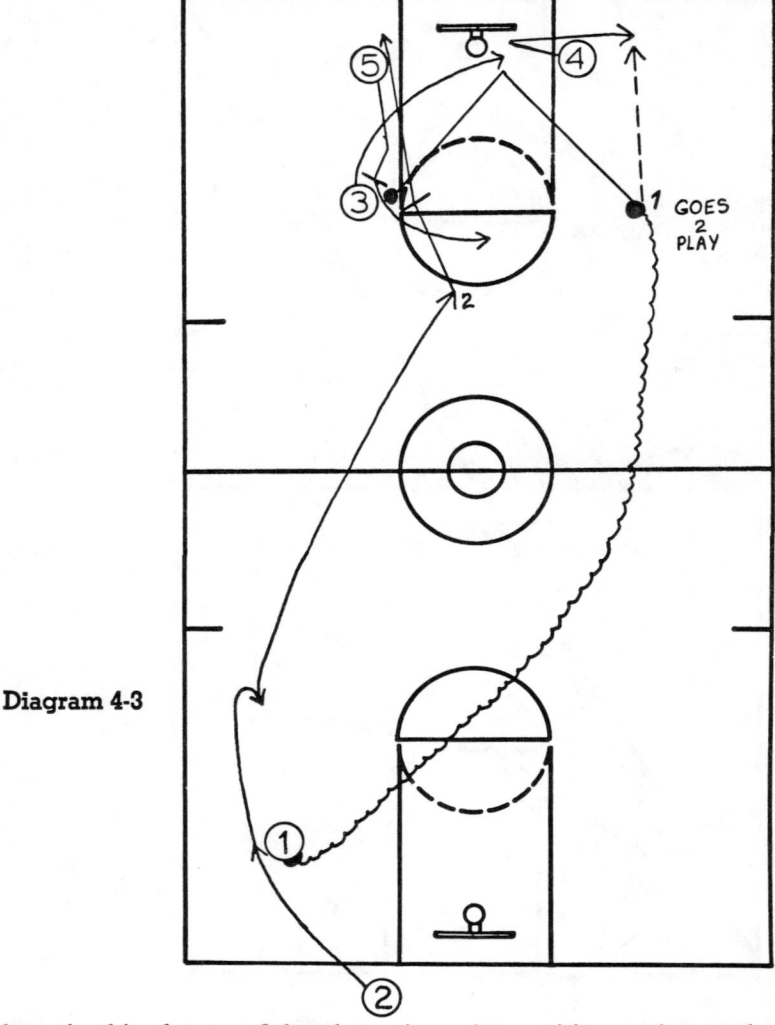

shown later in this chapter. 2 heads to the point position and now the offense is in the regular Five Cutter Formation. 1 should start either a 1 or 2 play after he passes to 4. Usually the 2 play is more effective because the 1 man is on the move. Also, he has taken his man a long way on defense and the defensive man may relax for a second; this will allow 1 to beat him to the hoop on the give-and-go maneuver of the 2 play. Of course if 1 is open, he should get the return pass. If 1 does not get the ball, then the offense goes into the regular 2 play of the Outside Option, as shown in Diagram 4-3.

Diagram 4-4 shows 1 handing off to 2, and 2 brings the ball up and takes it to the left-wing spot; 3 moves over to the right wing as soon as he sees 1 get the ball. 1 comes up court and becomes the point

Breaking Man-to-Man Pressure Defenses

Diagram 4-4

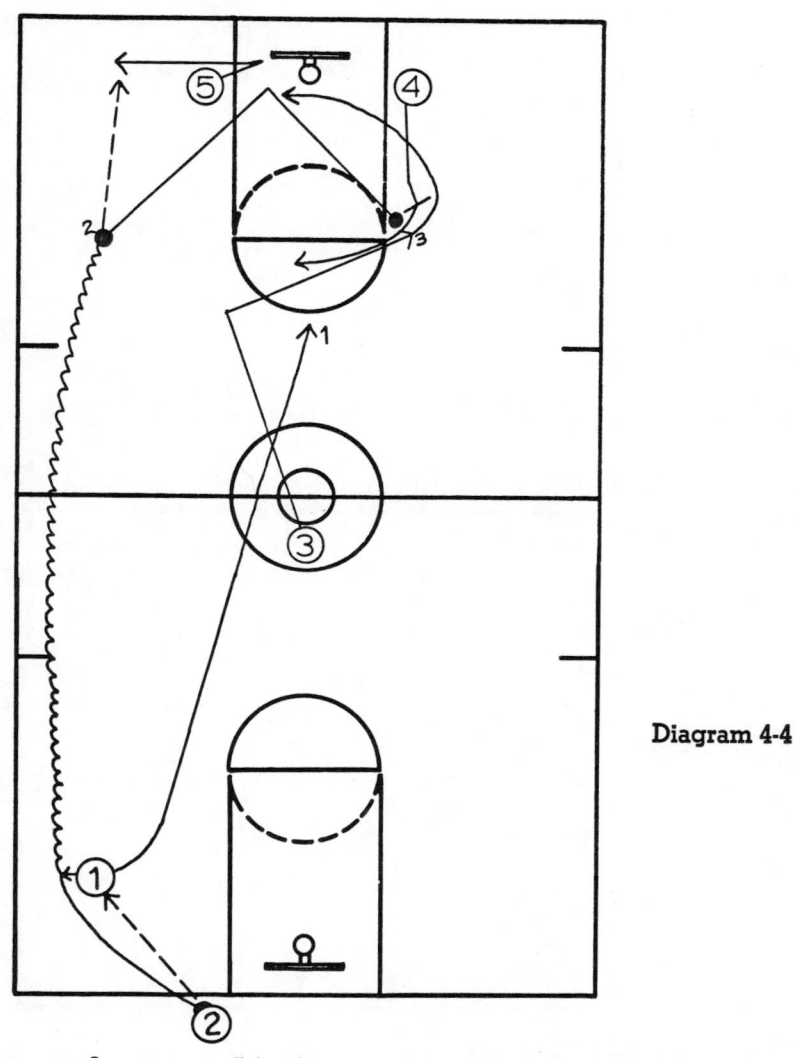

man; 2 passes to 5 in the corner and goes through to signal for the 2 play.

Diagram 4-5 shows 2 hooking back as soon as he realizes that his man is not with him, because he has moved over to double team 1. 1 passes over the double team to 2 and 2 brings the ball up, looking for a 4-on-3 situation. If the 4-on-3 situation does not get the desired high-percentage shot the offense is seeking, then 2 dribbles toward the right-wing spot and runs a 1 play by passing to 4 and staying. 1 moves up court to become the point man.

Diagram 4-6 shows the other choice of cuts the 2 man can make after he passes to 1. 1, upon receiving the ball, pivots and faces up court as he waits for 2 to run to the inside of him to set a running

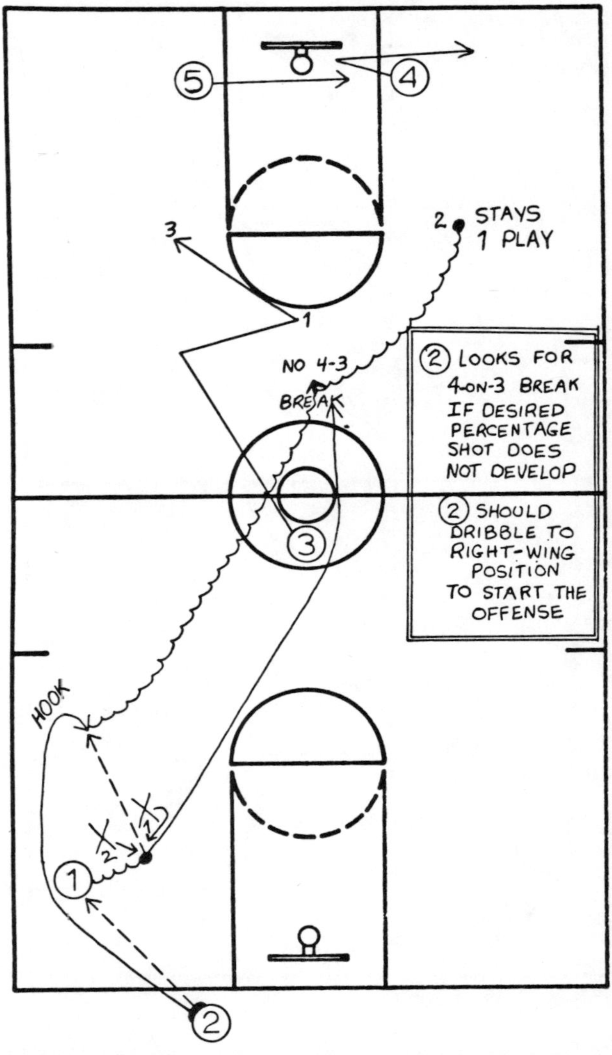
5
4
3
2 STAYS 1 PLAY
1
NO 4-3 BREAK
② LOOKS FOR 4-ON-3 BREAK IF DESIRED PERCENTAGE SHOT DOES NOT DEVELOP
② SHOULD DRIBBLE TO RIGHT-WING POSITION TO START THE OFFENSE
3
HOOK
X2
X1
1
2

Diagram 4-5

screen. 1 should dribble right off 2 as he passes by him in order to run his defensive man into 2. 2 must be especially keen to the double-team situation on this move because both defensive players are close together when 2 passes in front of 1, or if the defense should jump switch on the cross.

Dribbling into the Identical Inside Option

When the man with the ball, who is bringing it up on a dribble, wants to run an Identical Inside Option, then all he does is bring the ball up the middle to the point position. This is harder to do than getting the ball to the wing positions. However, if he does get the ball

Breaking Man-to-Man Pressure Defenses

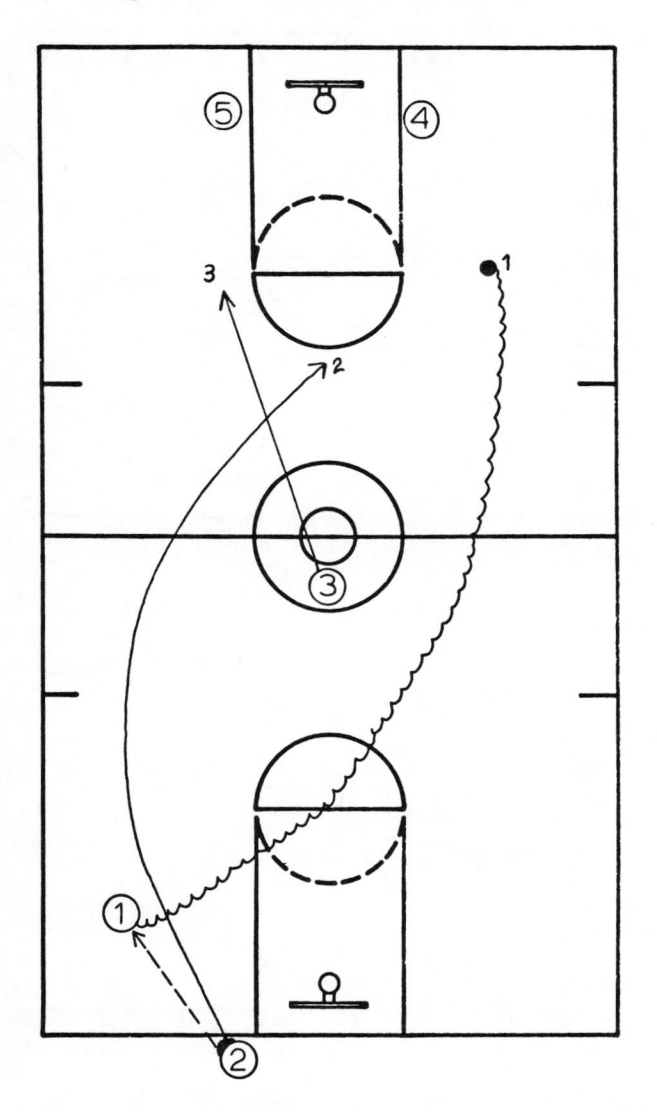

Diagram 4-6

to the point position, he just dribbles toward the wing spot he wants to go through and automatically starts the 3 play. This is shown in Diagram 4-7. 2 passes to 1 and cuts to the inside. 1 starts to rub his man off 2 as he cuts by. However, 2's man stays to double team 1. 2 hooks back as soon as he notices that his man is not with him. 1 passes back to 2. 2 this time decides to take the ball to the middle of the floor to the point position. 3 moves across to the right-wing position as soon as he sees that 2 has the ball, because 3 does not know if 2 is going to the left-wing spot or the point. 1, after seeing where 2 is going, just moves up court to the left-wing position. 2 dribbles toward 3 and the 3 play of the Identical Inside Option is on.

Diagram 4-7

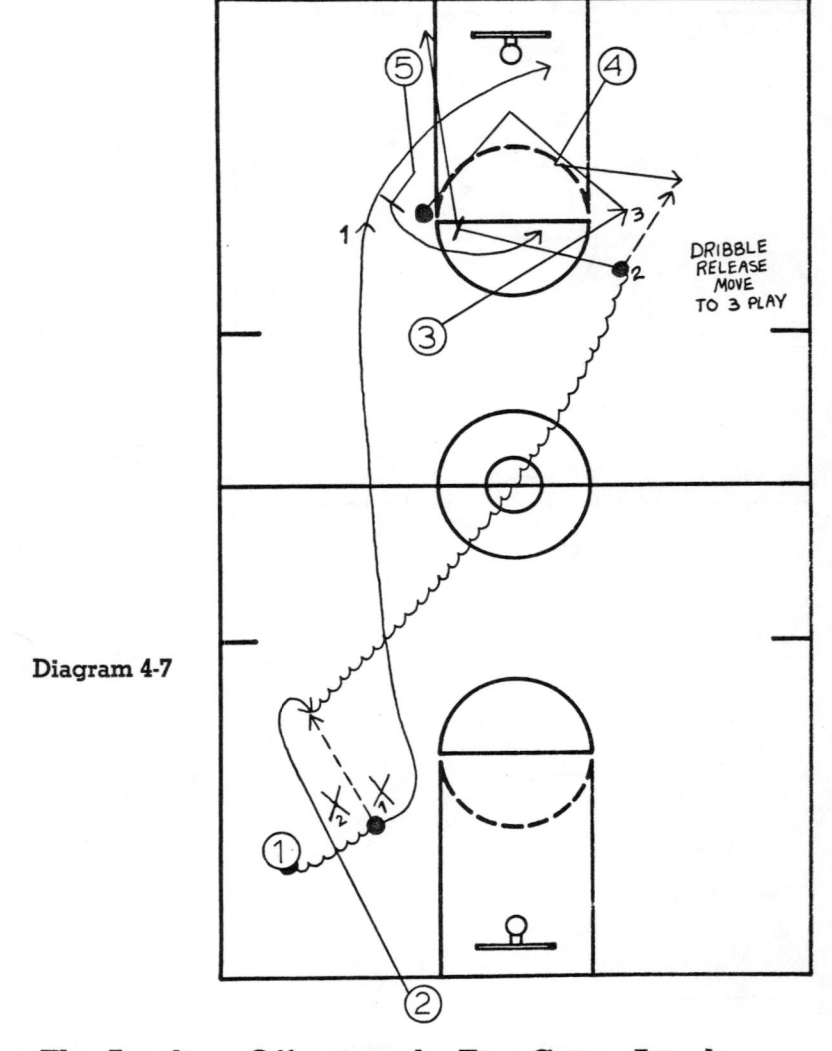

DRIBBLE RELEASE MOVE TO 3 PLAY

The Auxiliary Offense to the Five Cutter Attack

If we are encountering difficulty in getting into the Outside Options of the Five Cutter Offense, but we are having success in getting the ball up court by just using the 1 and 2 men, then we will run the Auxiliary Offense to get into the Five Cutter Offense. This allows the guards a better angle to get the ball to the low-post men because they do not have to go so wide to the sideline to start the play or option. Diagram 4-8 shows 1 bringing the ball up. His angle is changed a little from Diagram 4-2, so that he has a little more room to bring the ball up to get it to the 4 man, because 1 can go closer to the

Breaking Man-to-Man Pressure Defenses 137

Diagram 4-8

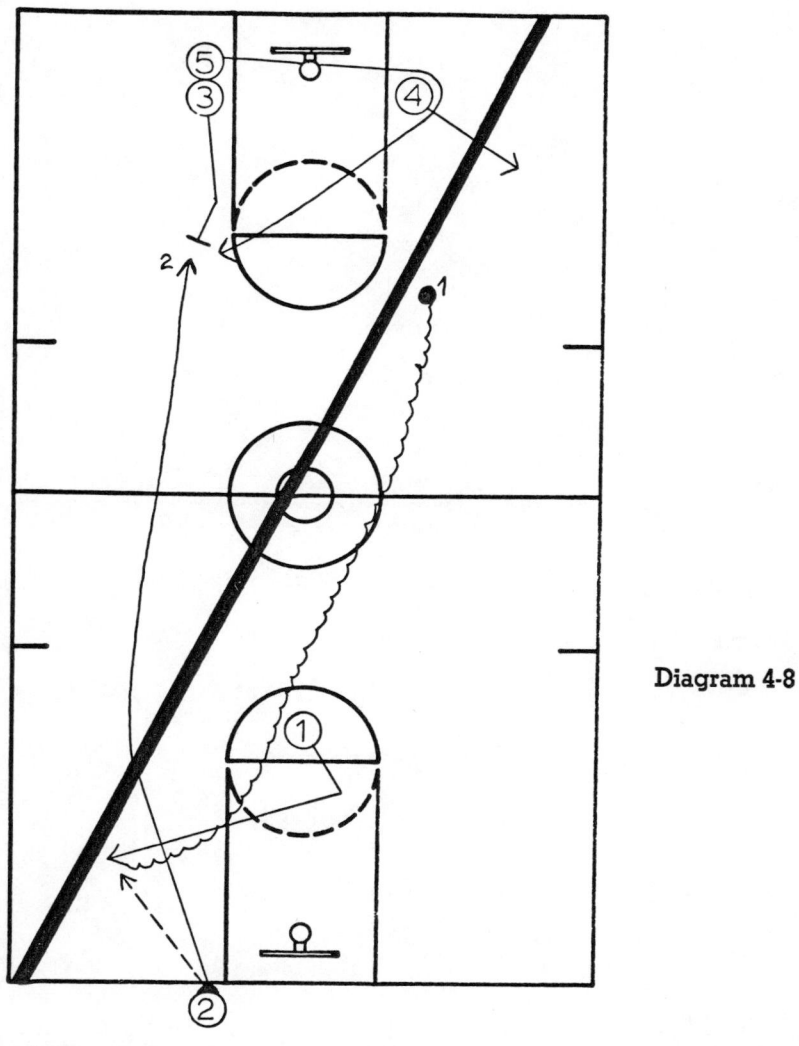

middle of the court. 1 brings the ball up on the dribble and feeds 4, who has made a good V to get into position to receive 1's pass. 4 must be careful in timing his move so that he will be open at the instant 1 wants to release the ball. 4's cut will be higher than when we are running the Outside Option of the Five Cutter Attack because we do not want the ball in the corner when we are running the Auxiliary Offense. 4 should make his move so that he is free between the foul-line extended and the first foul-line divider from the foul line. 2 moves up court in line or just ahead of 1, and he should be in line with 1 when 1 makes his pass to 4. 5, who was behind 3, sees that 1 is going to go to the other side of the court, so he gets behind 4 and moves

Diagram 4-9

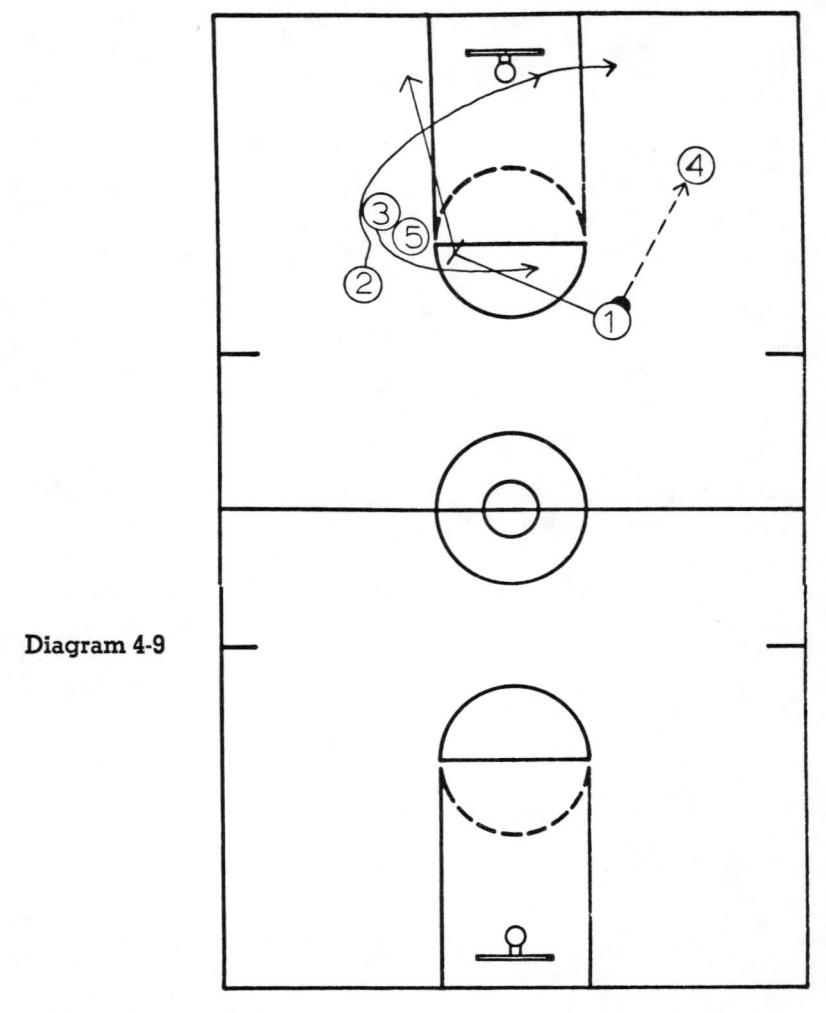

around him while 4 breaks off 5 to get the ball. 3 moves up to backtrap 2's man and 4 looks to feed 2 at the right low-post area in the power lane. 1 moves over to screen for 3, and if neither 2 nor 3 are open, then the offense is now in the Five Cutter Formation with the ball at the wing position, ready to start an Outside or Inside Option (Diagram 4-9). This play has been very effective in freeing the 2 man because the man guarding him does not expect to be backtrapped from the rear after coming all the way with 2 from the back court, and again he may have a tendency to relax for just a second. If 2 times his cut right, he should be free for the easy moving layup or power shot.
Coaching Hint: Remember that the moves of the 1 and 2 men in the

Breaking Man-to-Man Pressure Defenses 139

Diagram 4-10

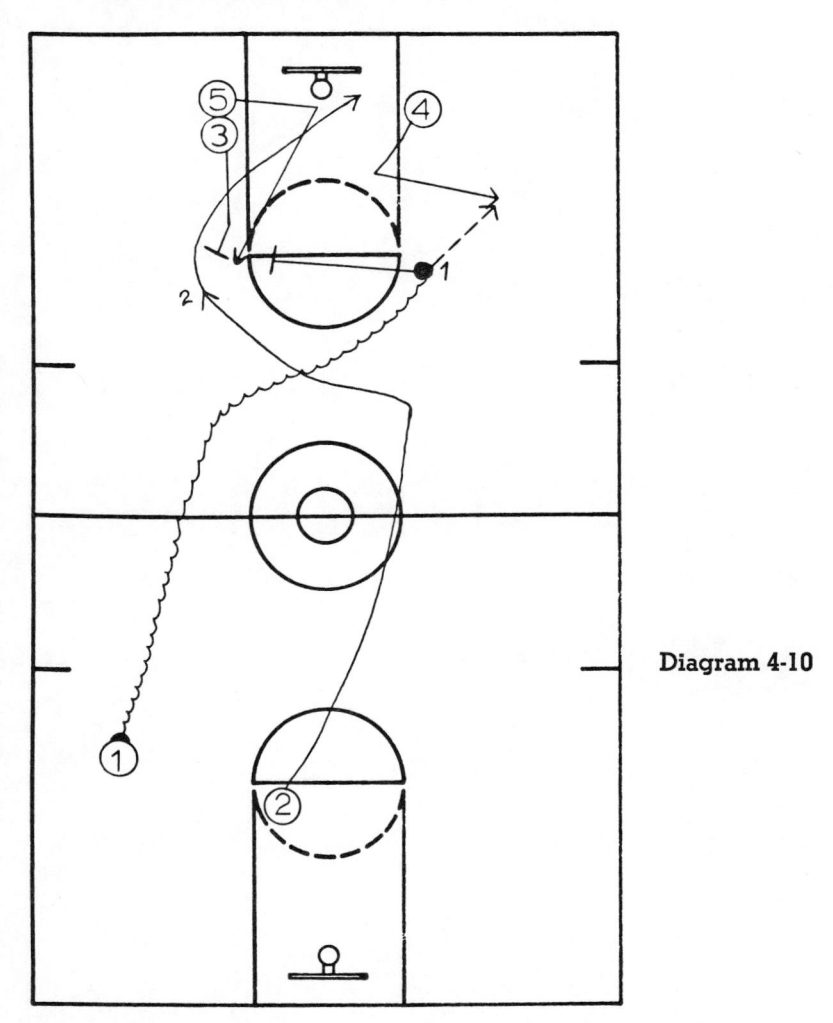

back court are the same as they were when they were bringing the ball up court to get into the Five Cutter Offense.

Diagram 4-10 shows the crossing technique that the 1 and 2 men can use if they are having difficulty getting the ball to the wing positions. The 1 man, as he brings the ball up the left side of the court, makes a move to the middle because his man is overplaying him and he can see that he is going to have difficulty getting the ball to 3. 1 dribbles toward the middle and heads for the mid-court area in the front court. The 2 man at the opposite guard position, when he sees 1 make his move to the middle, heads toward 1 to meet him. 1 dribbles and crosses in front of 2. In this play, 1 keeps the ball and 1 and 2

Diagram 4-11

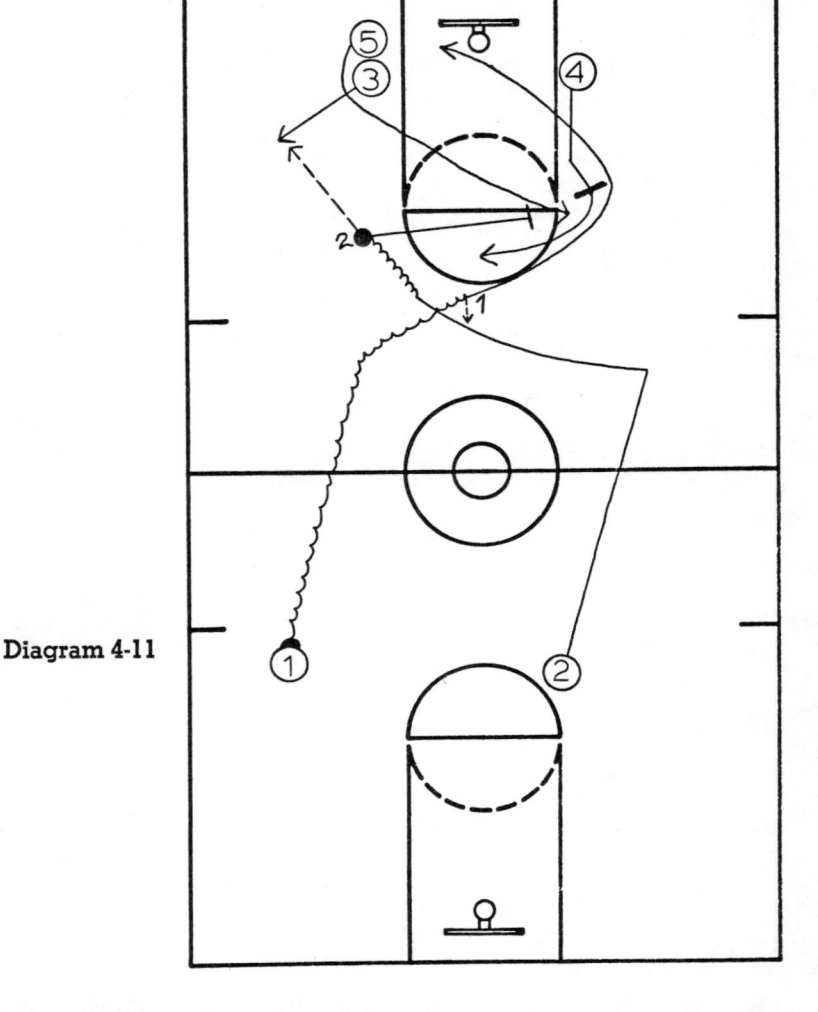

swap guard positions. 1 continues his dribble and gets a good angle to pass to 4 near the right-wing spot. 2 moves over and gets his man ready to be backtrapped by the 3 man. At this point, we are now in the regular Auxiliary Offense. Diagram 4-11 shows 1 giving the ball to 2 as they cross, and thus the same play (Diagram 4-10) is now run on the opposite side.

Using the Identical Inside Option Full-Court

The Identical Inside Option is such an effective pattern run front court that we use this same option full-court when facing man-to-man

Breaking Man-to-Man Pressure Defenses 141

Diagram 4-12

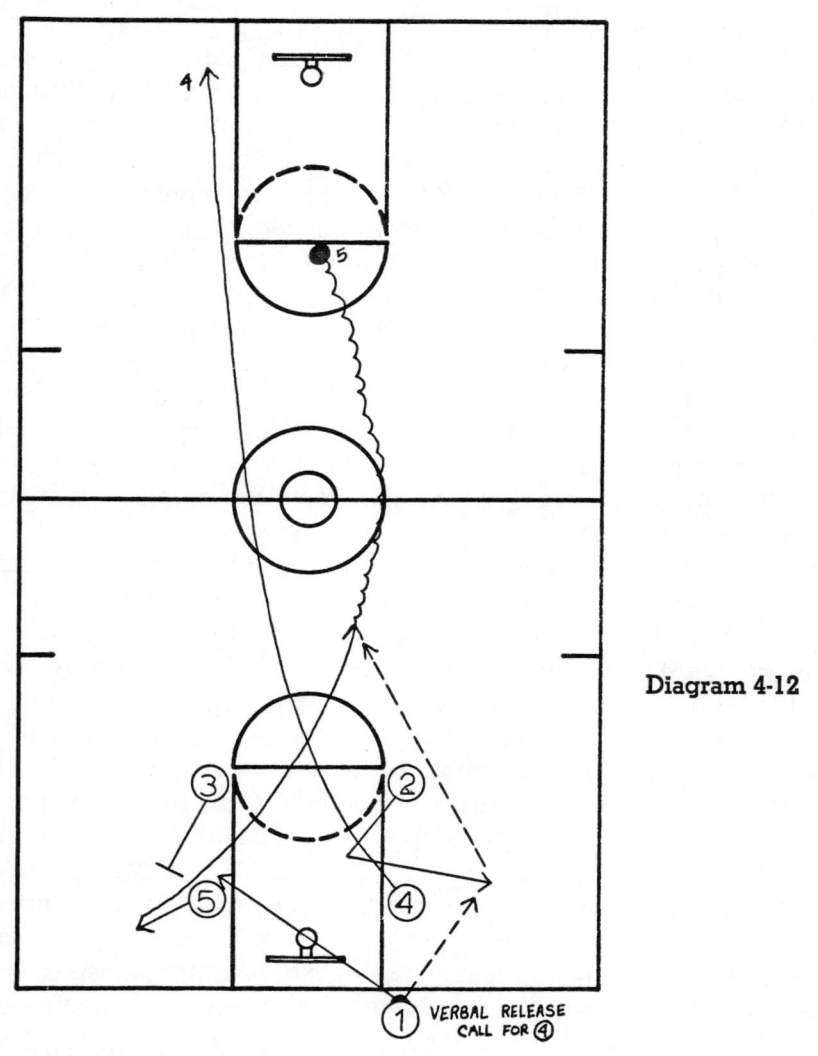

full-court presses, especially if the press is a tough, active press. By utilizing this pattern full-court, we find that we do not have to teach another special press offense. The players know the assignments half-court, so we just have to stress a few special adjustment moves. Also, we have a good press offense designed to spread the defense out and get the 2-on-1 or 3-on-2 fast-break situation. When using the Identical-Inside-Option 3 play full-court, we are much more willing to go for the quick basket if we can shake the first two cutters free than we are if we cannot get the ball to the first two cutters. Diagram 4-12 shows the 3 play run full-court. The 1 man takes the ball out-of-bounds to either side of the key line extended, so that the backboard will not interfere with either his vision or his passing ability. The wing men line up at the foul-line and key-line meeting point, with 2 lining up on the left and 3 lining up on the right. The 4 and 5 men line up in the low-post area like they would if they were in their own front court.

1 uses the verbal release call and signals one of the 4 or 5 men to clear out. In Diagram 4-12, 1 calls the 4 man to go. 4 cuts toward the opponent's foul line and takes off to go to the left low-post position in his own front court. If 4 should be open, then 1 will throw the long bomb to him. 2 breaks off 4 by making a strong V to the basket. 2 tries to get the ball as close to the key line as possible. 3 moves up to set a rear backtrap screen on 5's man as 5 takes several steps to the outside when 1 calls 4 to go. 1 passes to 2. As soon as 5 sees that 2 has the ball, he cuts off 3's backtrap. Note that 5 can cut either left or right in running the 3 play full-court. He has this option because he is not going to use a special adjustment technique in this situation against full-court pressure. The side 5 goes on to make his cut off 3 depends on how his man is guarding him. Regardless of the side he goes to, 2 tries to feed 5 at some point between the opponent's foul line and the center line. In this situation, 2 passes to 5 at the halfway point between the foul line and the center line. If 5 is free enough to get the pass, then usually he and 4, who is deep, have a 2-on-1 situation as 5 dribbles to the foul line at his basket. 5 tries to stay in the middle of the court on the dribble to the foul line. *Coaching Hint:* Even though 5 is a big man, we are willing to let him bring the ball up court on a dribble because if he is open to get the ball off 3's backtrap screen, then he usually is wide open with no defender on him. Usually, after we have done this once or twice, he is no longer open as his man sags through. 5 then just moves up court without the ball, and we continue the pattern by positioning our big men, 4 and 5, down court and having our three ball handlers bring the ball to them. Actually we are really trying to set the defense up, but we shall take advantage if 5 is open on his cut off 3's backtrap. The 1 man, after passing to 2, moves to his left and sets a side screen for the original backtrapper, the 3 man. 3 cuts off 1's screen and moves into the opponent's 3-second area in front of the basket. If 2 cannot hit 5, then 5 continues up court and goes to the right low-post position. At this point, as is shown in Diagram 4-13, 4 and 5 should swap positions on the floor to get into their normal Five Cutter Offensive Positions. However, this is not absolutely necessary if they do not have time to swap or forget to do so. 2 looks for 3 coming off 1's screen and he passes to him if he is free in front of the basket. After 2 passes to 3, he runs diagonally

Breaking Man-to-Man Pressure Defenses 143

Diagram 4-13

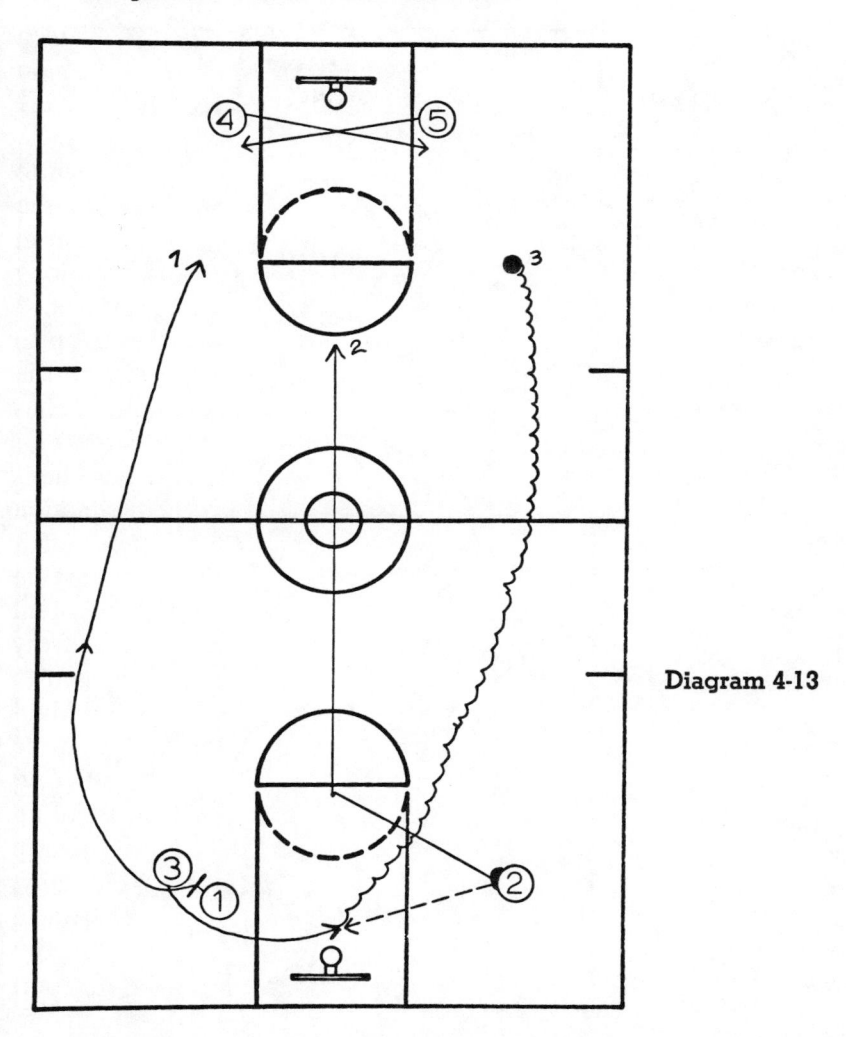

across the court and 3 dribbles off him heading up court. 1, after setting the screen for 3, goes to the mid-court area at the left sideline to act as a safety valve should 2 or 3 be in any kind of trouble. 3 brings the ball up the right-hand side of the court to the right-wing position. 1 takes the left-wing position and 2 takes the point. 2 should be alert for a possible double team on 3 after their crossing maneuver. The offense is now in the Five Cutter 1-2-2 Formation and ready to go. In this situation, 3 should run an Outside Option.

Diagram 4-14 shows 2 cannot pass to 3 off 1's screen, so 3 moves over and crosses in front of 2; 2 takes the ball to the middle. 1, who is in the mid-court area on the left, takes a look to see if 2 can handle

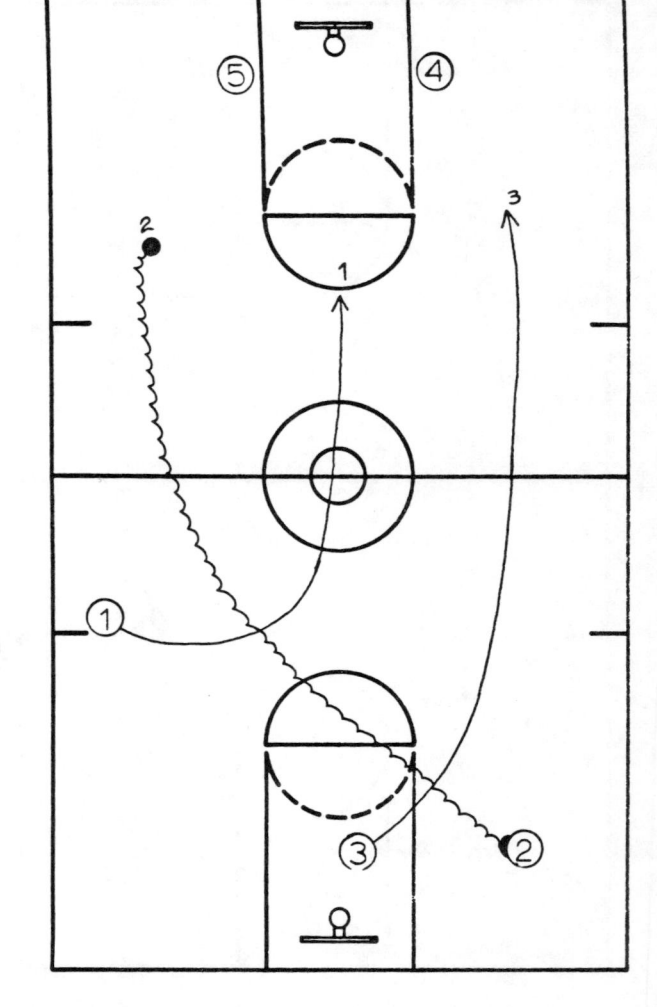

Diagram 4-14

the situation or if he needs help. If 2 needs help, then 1 moves over to cross in front of 2. 2 dribbles to the left wing, 3 takes the right wing and 1 goes to the point. 1 should again be alert for a double team on 2.

Of course, this pattern can be run to the other side if 1 calls the 5 man to clear out. Diagram 4-15 shows the strong-side safety valve that 1 has if he cannot get the ball to 2. 5's man has a tendency to cheat over into the key area, anticipating 5's move to the middle of 3's backtrap. 1 fakes the pass to 2, even though he knows he cannot get it to 2. This tends to force the defense to lean even more to the ball. Very quickly, 1 should pivot and pass to 5. 4, of course, has cleared

Breaking Man-to-Man Pressure Defenses   145

Diagram 4-15

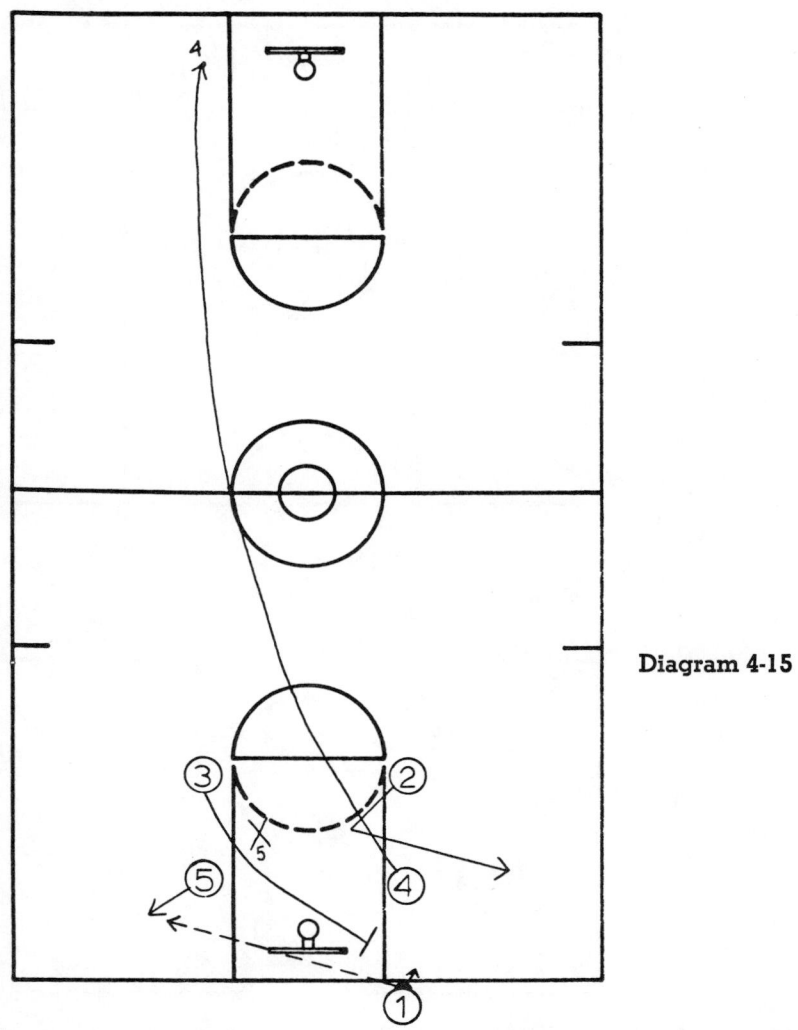

deep, and 3, upon seeing the pass to 5, moves up and sets a backtrap screen on 1's man. 1 can really help to set this up, just as he does in a normal front-court pattern, by taking one or two steps to his right and then coming quickly back to his left. Diagram 4-16 shows 1 cutting off 3's screen and 5 hitting him on the move. 1 takes the ball to the middle for a 2-on-1 or 3-on-1 break. If 5 cannot pass to 1, then 1 moves down court and takes the right low-post position; 3 moves over to set a side screen on 2's man, with 2 coming to the middle to receive the pass from 5 (Diagram 4-17). If 5 does not pass to 2, then 2 crosses in front of 5 and 5 brings the ball up court on the dribble. If 5 had passed to 2, then 5 would have crossed in front of 2, as shown in

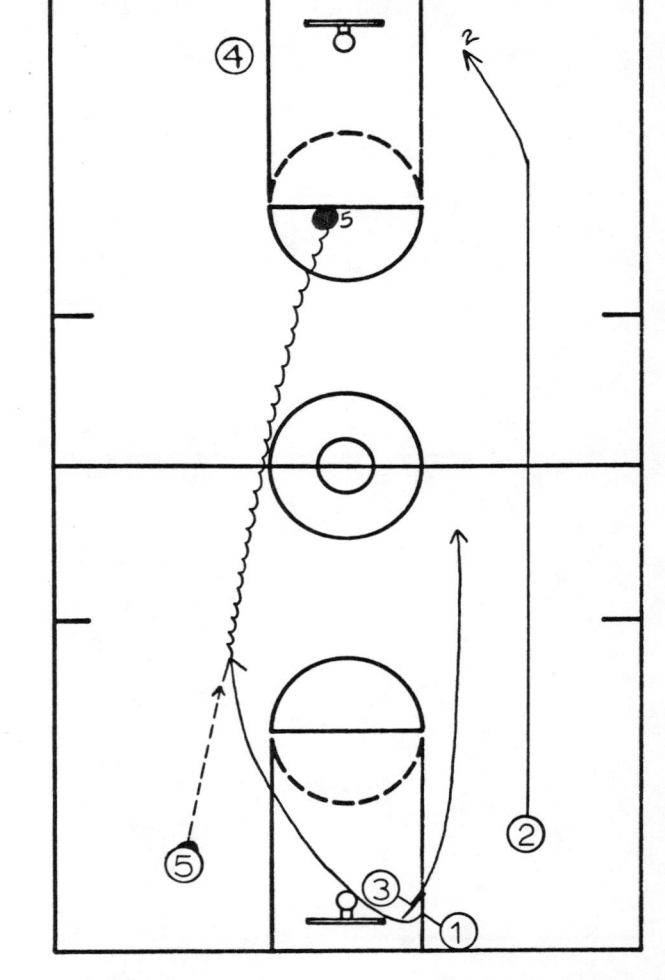

Diagram 4-16

Diagram 4-14. When 5 brings the ball up on the dribble, then he goes to the right wing, 3 takes the point and 2 takes the left wing.

Operating the Stack Full-Court

Another different look that the Five Cutter Attack can give the defense is the stack formation. This is shown in Diagram 4-18. 2 and 4 line up on the same side, 4 behind 2, and 3 and 5 are on the same side, with 5 behind 3. Although we are going into the Identical-Inside-Option 3 play (the way we get into it is by having the 1 man call one of the rear men, 4 or 5, to clear out, and the 2 man in this diagram breaks off 4 as 4 goes around in front of 2), we have found that we

Breaking Man-to-Man Pressure Defenses

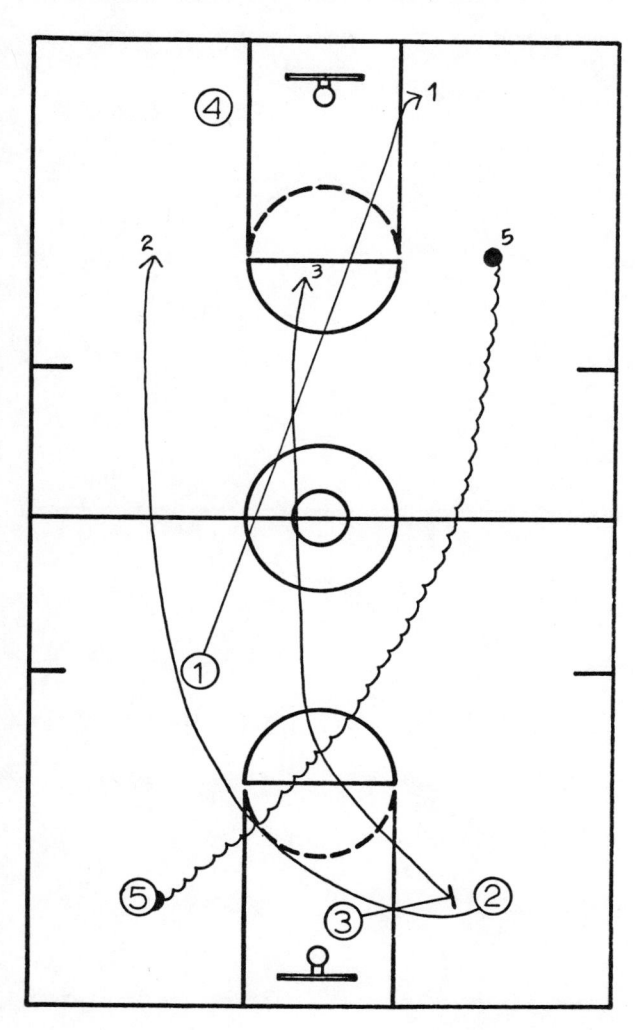

Diagram 4-17

can get the ball closer to the key line than when we run just the straight formation. 3 must remember to break out at the same time 2 does so that 5 will have a good angle to backtrap on. Another point in favor of the stack over the straight 1-2-2 formation is that the big men are not going to have to handle the ball on the first pass, because one has cleared deep and the other is backtrapping. After the 4 man clears out and 2 moves to get the ball, the pattern is run exactly as it is shown in Diagram 4-12. *Coaching Hint:* It is important to have the 2 man break off the 4 man so that there is no daylight between them. 2 should actually make some contact with 4 as he moves off him. We go to the stack only when we find that we are having difficulty in getting the ball in-bounds from the regular 1-2-2 Five Cutter Formation.

Diagram 4-18

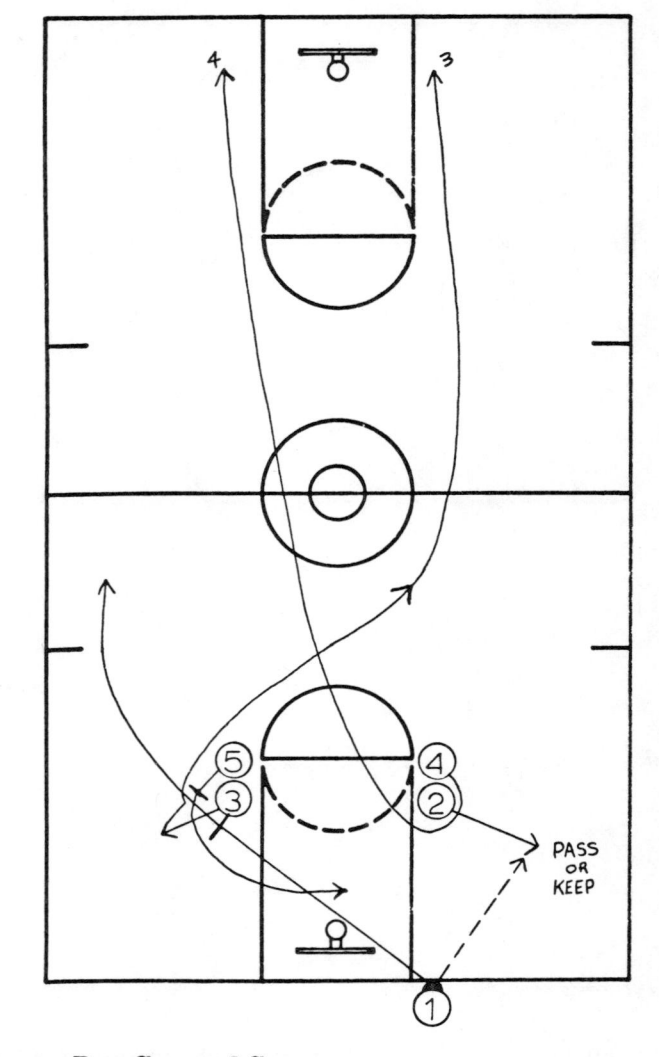

Box Special Setups

The 1-2-2 Five Cutter Formation is shaped like a box when we are using it full-court and the 1 man is out-of-bounds. For this reason, we call the following special plays Box Specials. Any time either the 4 or 5 man feels that he can beat his man, he just takes off. This cannot be done too often, but in a tight situation it can result in an easy basket. Also, a set playoff, having the front man going up and setting a screen on the rear man, and then having the man who set the screen take off deep for the long bomb, is another Box Special that can provide the easy shot in a difficult situation. This should be set up

Breaking Man-to-Man Pressure Defenses 149

Diagram 4-19

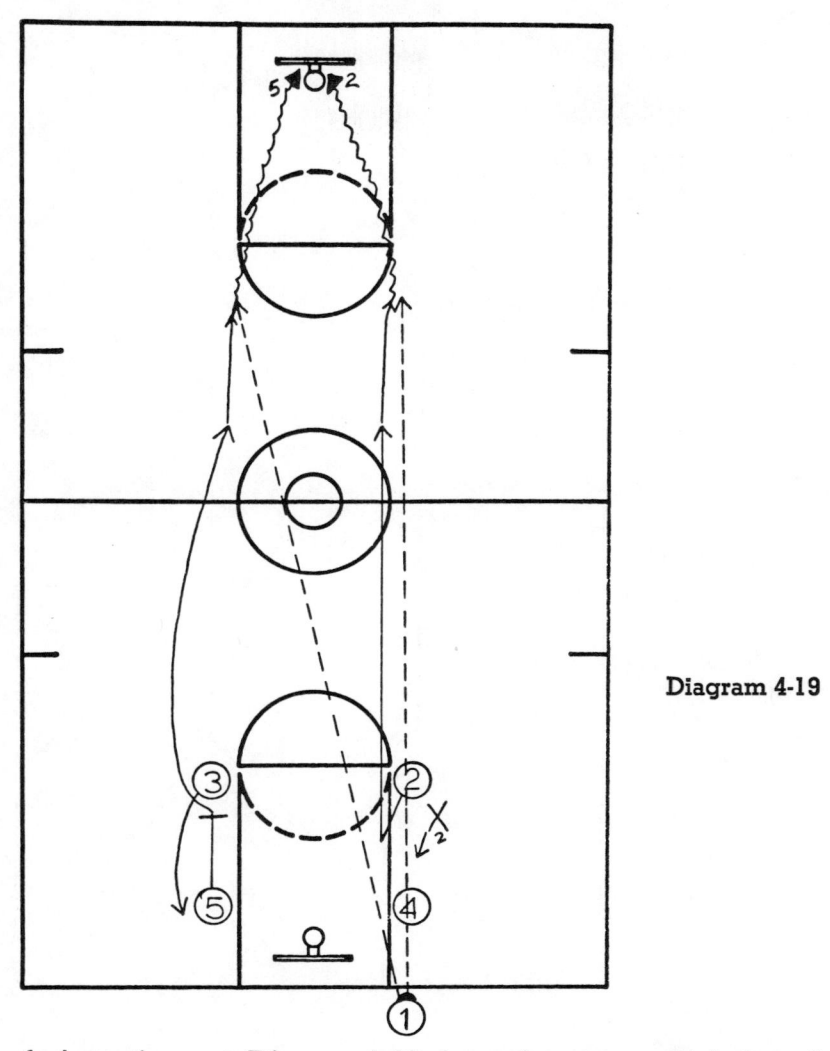

during a time-out. Diagram 4-19 shows these two special plays. 2 and 4 execute the straight takeoff, while 3 and 5 use the screen-and-go play.

Special X Play

The 1 man taking the ball out can yell "X it." Then he yells "Go" and the low-post man on the side of the ball boes first, heading into the bucket area at an angle. The opposite-side low-post man goes next, then the opposite-side wing from the ball goes and the wing on the side of the ball goes last. The players try to time their cuts so that they all cross about the same time in the middle of the opponent's

Diagram 4-20

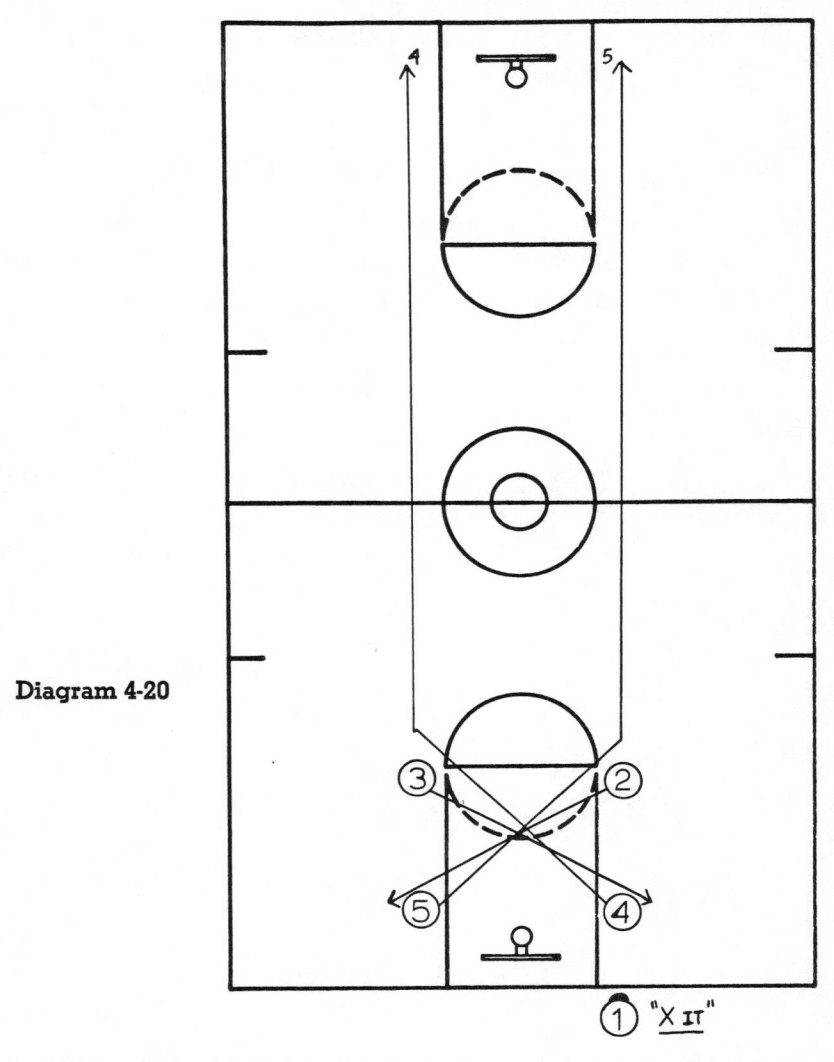

bucket area in front of the basket. 4 and 5 take off deep, as shown in Diagram 4-20, and usually the man at the low-post position on the side of the ball will be a little ahead of the other post man on their move down court. 1 will throw the long bomb if one of the men going deep is open. If 1 cannot do this, then usually he will be able to pass to either wing man, 2 or 3, as they have freed themselves by means of the crossing maneuver. After 1 passes to either 2 or 3, 1 crosses in front of or behind the man he passed to. Diagram 4-21 shows 1 passing to 2. After 1 makes his cut around 2, 3 comes over and crosses in front of 2 as he brings the ball up on the dribble. If you have a left-handed guard, then he should be at the wing spot that sends a man to the

Breaking Man-to-Man Pressure Defenses 151

Diagram 4-21

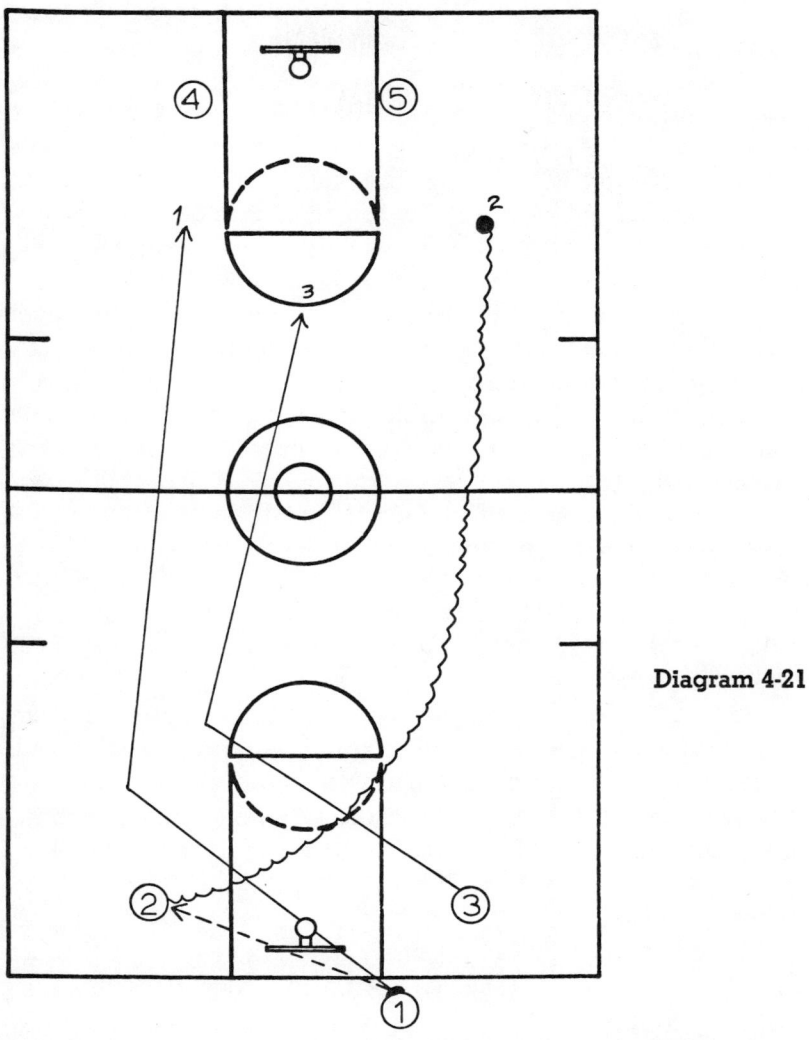

corner so that he can use his left hand to best advantage. If you do not have a left hander, then you should put your guard with the strongest left hand in the wing position to the right of the opponent's basket as the wings are facing the basket, so as to utilize his left hand. Remember that if 1 passes to 3, then the play is run just the opposite, with 1 and 2 screening on the move in front of 3.

Facing Half-Court Man-to-Man Pressure

The section in Chapter 3, Handling the Tight Man-to-Man Front Court Pressure, is exactly what we use for half-court man-to-man pressure. The verbal release call, the dribble release move, the Stack and the Strong-Side Safety Valve from these three maneuvers, along with the Auxiliary Offense to the Five Cutter Attack—all are very effective against half-court pressure. The technique of the guards crossing on the dribble of the Auxiliary Offense is extremely effective in getting the ball to the wing position.

It has been our experience that when running a ball-control type of offense, you do not run into too many man-to-man half-court pressure defenses that meet you at the center line. We feel this is because it is very hard to put denial defense on; there is just too much room for the players to maneuver to get free. Usually, the type of tight man-to-man pressure used against percentage ball-controlled teams in the front court is that which is applied after the ball has gotten into the front court and the man with the ball has stopped dribbling, allowing the defense to overplay.

Regardless of the type of half-court man-to-man pressure, if a team employs the material presented in Chapter 3, it should be able to handle this pressure with a high degree of success. All of these patterns are designed to keep the defense so busy trying to stop the initial action that they do not realize that as soon as the decoy play has been run and nothing develops, the offense is immediately in the Five Cutter Formation, with the ball in the starting position at a wing position. However, the defense must stop the initial decoy technique, because it is designed to apply enough pressure on the defense in the right places so that if the defense falters for a second, an easy basket can be scored. This is especially true of the patterns of the Auxiliary Offense.

When a defense is applying tight man-to-man pressure, regardless of the fact that it is half-court, three-quarters court or full-court, the players must expend a great deal of physical energy in guarding the offensive players, because the defensive players have to move backwards and sidewards, and they do not know which way they are going to have to move in any type of situation. The offensive players know where they are going and they know where they can expect to receive help if they get into trouble. The defensive players do not know where they are going to get their help if it is needed because they have to cover too great an area. This in itself should be enough to give the offense the confidence it needs to beat the pressure, regardless of the plays the offense runs against the defense.

CHAPTER 5

Using Percentage-Controlled Movement Against Zone Defenses

Without a doubt, the biggest headache that keeps basketball coaches awake at night drawing x's and o's, regardless of the type of offensive system used, is the zone defenses. The percentage-controlled team is in for even more problems in facing zones than any other type of offensive system, as zone defenses are designed to force the offense to shoot from outside of the high-percentage shot areas. Percentage or ball-control teams do not like to shoot from beyond the 15- to 17-foot distances; thus, they do not like to face zones, because they cannot get the type of percentage shot they are constantly seeking against the zone style of defense.

Zone defenses have become more complex and difficult to handle over the past 10 to 15 years because of one major development that has taken place. This development has been prompted by the offensive team, not the defensive team. The disappearance of the one-hand set shot and the development of the jump shot has allowed zones to become more effective. The jump shot is more difficult to execute, slower to get off and less accurate from 17 to 25 feet than is the one-hand set shot, which has been replaced by the jump shot.

Over the years, when the one-hand set shot was

being used, zones were not the problem they are today. Teams used to employ the basic old 1-3-1 formation and merely moved the ball from player to player, until somebody got free for a one-hand set shot or a short-range semi-jump shot. Diagram 5-1 illustrates the old 1-3-1 setup, which had a point man or "quarterback" at the top of the foul

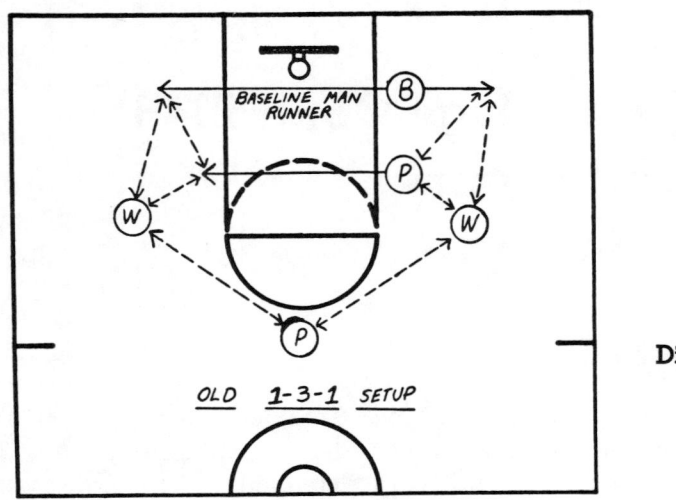

Diagram 5-1

circle, two wing men, a middle-post man and a base-line low-post man who ran the base line. The middle-post man and the low-post man simply positioned themselves on the same side of the court the ball was on, and moved from side to side as the ball was moved from one wing man to the point man to the other wing man. Many teams used this one basic attack against all types of zones with a great deal of success. Zones were not a problem as teams could shoot over them successfully with the one-hand set shot.

All of a sudden, with the disappearance of the one-hand set shot from the individual player's repertoire, the old 1-3-1 technique of moving the ball with a base-line runner was no longer effective. The main reason behind this was that the players found it difficult to be as accurate with the jump shot from just 17 to 20 feet as the one-hand set shooters were at 23 to 25 feet. A good one-hand set shooter can be as accurate at 25 feet as a good jump shooter can be at just 20 feet. Another problem with the jump shot, when using it against zones, is that the release of the jump shot in getting it off is slower than the one-hand set shot release, because the jump shooter has to bend his legs in order to gain the needed momentum to shoot the ball into the basket. On the other hand, the set shooter just takes a step with the leg on the

Using Percentage-Controlled Movement Against Zone Defenses 155

same side of the shooting hand, in a slightly bent position, and releases the ball just before the leg touches the floor. The jump shooter, in taking the extra second or so to bend his legs to gain the needed momentum, allows the defense to cover him quicker as the zone shifts to his side of the floor. Also, the jump shooter, once he is in the air, has committed himself and he must get rid of the ball; whereas, the set shooter can make another move if he is not open for the shot. I feel that the jump shot has been the main reason why zone defenses are more effective today than ever before, because the jump shot has replaced a very strong weapon—the one-hand set shot.

I feel so strongly about this that I insist players learn to use the one-hand set shot, and I also require them to use it when facing zones. We do not like to take jump shots from beyond the 15-foot distance at any time, regardless of the defense employed against us. We have spent a great deal of time teaching the fundamentals of the one-hand set shot, especially in our lower-grades system. Teaching the one-hand set shot is not an easy thing to do. It is very difficult to sell players today on the value of being able to use the one-hand set shot, because they just do not see this shot being used today to any great degree in either the college or professional ranks. However, we ask them to tell us what type of shot they use when taking a foul shot. The answer, of course, will be the one-hand set shot, except that they do not step forward to shoot the ball, but instead bend their legs just enough to get the needed momentum to shoot the ball into the basket (in taking the foul shot). I went back to teaching the one-hand set shot and forced the players to use it against zones two seasons ago. The past two seasons, we have used the old 1-3-1 just-move-the-ball attack as a supplement to the Five Cutter Formation, and we have experienced less difficulty with zones than ever before. I definitely believe that the one-hand set shot is the best weapon a zone offense can have in its arsenal of attack.

Employing the All-Purpose Formations

We use the Five Cutter Formation and the Auxiliary Formation against zone defenses. The Five Cutter Formation is the 1-2-2 setup and is used against both even-front and odd-front zones. The Auxiliary Offense is a 2-3 setup that can be used against odd-front and even-front zones, too.

The Five Cutter Formation Against Zone Defenses

When employing the Five Cutter 1-2-2 Formation against zone

defenses, we make a few minor adjustments in the formation from our man-to-man 1-2-2 Five Cutter setup. First we must know if we are facing an odd-front zone or an even-front zone. Diagram 5-2 shows the Five Cutter Formation against an even-front zone. The low-post

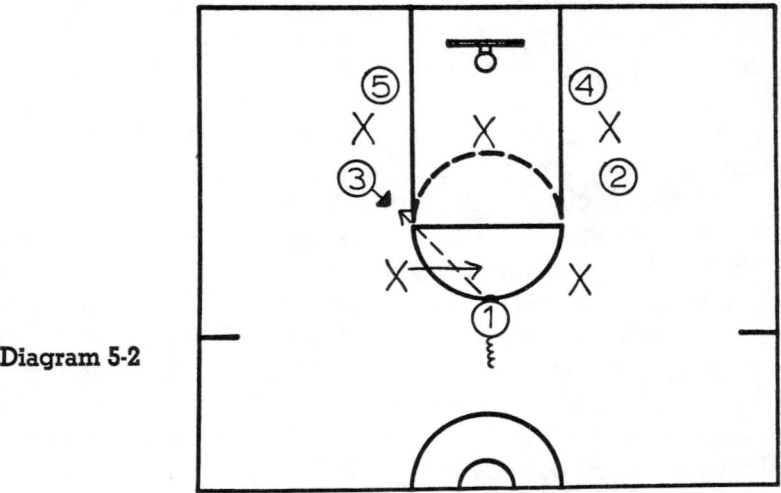

Diagram 5-2

men, 5 and 4, station themselves in the low-post areas near the key line, even with the basket and behind the back defensive men of the zone. This forces the defensive players in the back of the zone to turn around slightly in order to see the 5 and 4 men. The wing men, 2 and 3, move down the key line toward the basket two or three steps from the foul line instead of staying even with the line. The 1 man at the point tries to split the front two men of the zone; thus, he moves into the circle, if possible, instead of stopping at the top of the circle as when facing man-to-man defenses. As 1 splits the defense, one of the front men must pick him up. 1 should pass to the wing on the side that the defender came from to pick 1 up. This is shown in Diagram 5-2.

When facing an odd-front zone, the Five Cutter Formation must make the following adjustments: The post men, 5 and 4, still stay low and try to stay behind the rear defenders in the zone. Meanwhile, the wing men move up the key line and back (even with the foul line extended), trying to stay even with the defenders in their area and to the outside of them, as shown in Diagram 5-3. The point man does not try to penetrate the top of the foul circle when facing the odd-front zone.

The Auxiliary Formation Against Zone Defenses

The 2-3 Auxiliary Formation that is used against zones is almost exactly the same when used against either the odd-front or even-front

Using Percentage-Controlled Movement Against Zone Defenses 157

Diagram 5-3

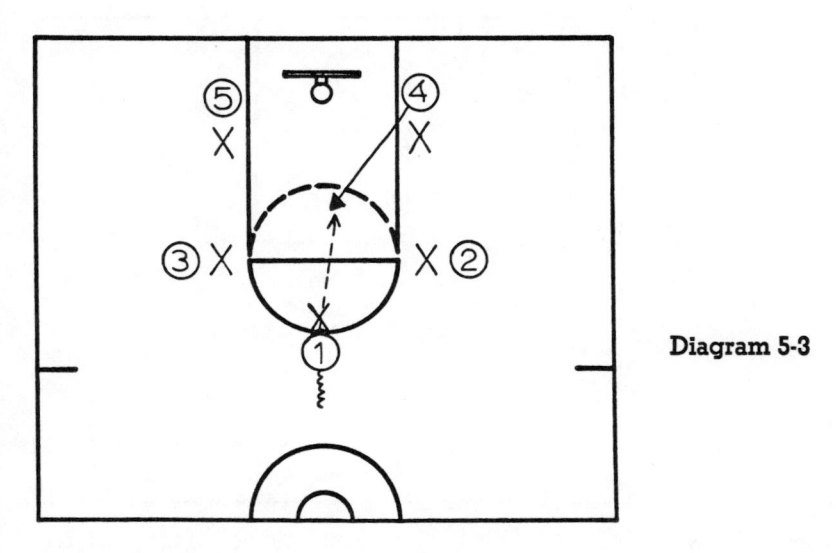

zone. The only change is that the post man is in front of the forward on the side of the ball instead of behind him, as in the man-to-man Auxiliary Formation. Diagrams 5-4 and 5-5 show the Auxiliary Formation that is used against any type of zone defense.

Player Movement Offenses

We use two types of movement offenses against zones. The first is the player movement attack. This just means that we move players to the ball by cutting them in either a preplanned pattern or by allowing the players to cut to the ball on their own when they feel they will be

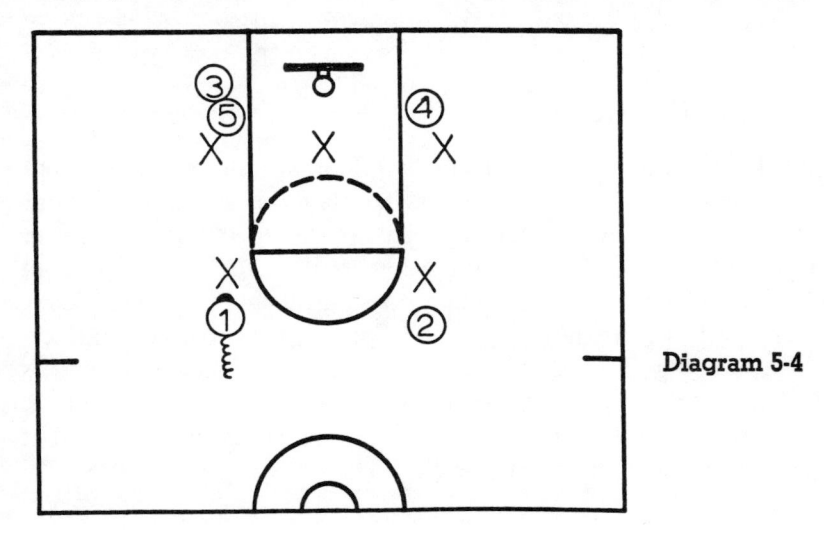

Diagram 5-4

158 Using Percentage-Controlled Movement Against Zone Defenses

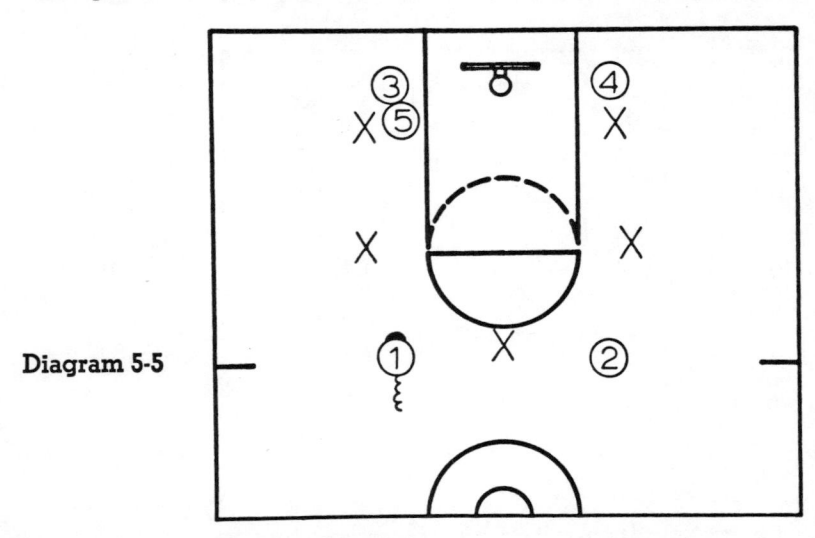

Diagram 5-5

open. Usually, when we are using the preplanned disciplined patterns, the ball stays still after the initial pass gets it to a wing position, and then we move three to four men to the ball.

Ball Movement Offenses

The ball movement attacks simply consist of moving the ball from player to player and having just the low-post man and the middle-post man move to the side of the court that the ball is on. The player movement offenses move three and four players, whereas the ball movement offenses move only two men. The ball is moved from player to player in no predetermined pattern, and the open man gets the shot. It is simply the old 1-3-1 movement of the ball with a baseline runner.

Mixing the Movement Attacks

We like to mix player movement offenses with ball movement offenses because after the zone starts to play the situation without moving too much, then this usually opens areas in the zone that the movement offense (which was not being used) will be able to take advantage of. Zones have a tendency to stand around against player movement patterns, as they can usually pick up the patterns, anticipate what is going to happen and guess just about where the play is going to take place. By quickly switching to the ball movement attack the zone can be beaten, because it does not move as quickly until it can adjust to the movement of the ball.

Using Percentage-Controlled Movement Against Zone Defenses 159

This is just as true when a team is using the ball movement attack and the zone becomes accustomed to moving quickly. Usually zones can cover the offense fairly successfully because the ball movement offense does not put too much pressure in the corners against any type of zone. By quickly going to a player movement attack, the offense can get many shots in the corners before the zone can adjust, and when the zone does adjust to the player movement patterns, then it is right back to just the ball movement attack again. By mixing the two movement offenses, the offense keeps the zone off guard, and it is constantly changing the pace at which the zone is moving.

The Five Cutter Formation and the Auxiliary Formation both have player movement offenses and ball movement offenses, which can be changed from one to the other in either of the formations by a simple hand signal. By constantly changing the movement offenses, the zone defense cannot establish the defensive rhythm it needs to be truly effective. The changing of the movement offenses will keep the defense guessing, and this should cause some confusion, allowing the offense to determine the tempo at which the ball is going to be moved against the zone. This forces the zone to adjust to the offense, not the other way around.

The Five Cutter Offense with Player Movement

When employing the Five Cutter Offense with Player Movement, the first thing that must be determined is the position of the wing men. This, of course, as has been previously mentioned, is dependent upon the type of zone, either odd front or even front, that is being used by the opponents. The wing men play even with the foul line extended and outside the defensive wing men against an odd-front zone; when facing an even-front zone, the wing men drop down the key line two or three steps and try to split the defensive men on their side of the court. The post men always try to station themselves behind the rear defenders in the zone, provided they do not have to go behind the backboard in order to get behind the rear of the zone.

Regardless of the type of zone the offense is facing, once the attack is started, the patterns are run exactly the same for both the odd-front or even-front zone. The diagrams will show the Five Cutter Offense with Player Movement against the odd-front zone, which would have the offensive wing men even with the foul line extended and outside the defensive wing men on their side of the court.

Diagram 5-6 shows the 1 man bringing the ball up to the top of the circle; it also shows that he can pass to either wing man or either

Diagram 5-6

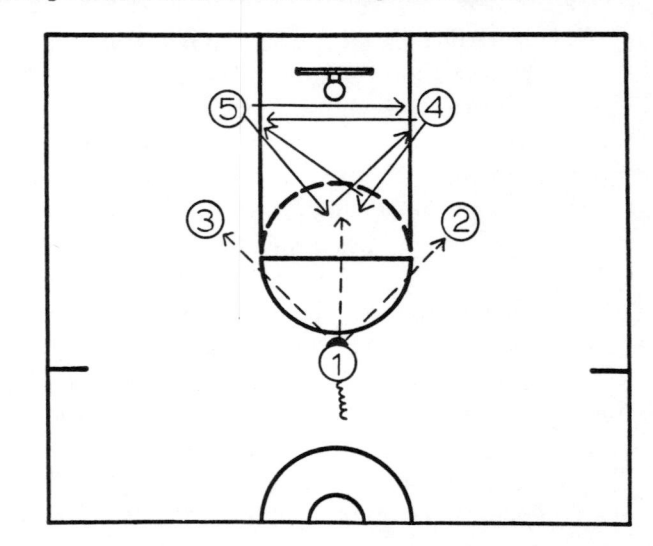

low-post man on the initial move. Regardless of whichever post man breaks into the middle, if he does not receive the pass, then he rolls to the opposite-side low-post position, with the other low-post man moving over across the base line to take the low-post spot that was vacated by the man breaking up into the middle.

Changing the Five Cutter Offensive Identical Inside Option's 3 play Against Zones

The only actual change in the Five Cutter Offensive Identical Inside Option's 3 play, when using it against zone defenses rather than man-to-man defenses, is that the wing man who stays is not back-trapped by the low-post man on the wingman's side who stayed, and the backtrapper does not get a side screen from the point man. The wing man who stays just cuts immediately to the middle of the lower half of the foul circle on a straight line, as shown in Diagram 5-7, instead of moving to the outside of a backtrap screen and then into the power lane. Diagram 5-7 shows 3 breaking into the middle of the lower half of the foul circle. His signal to go into the middle is exactly the same as the man-to-man signal. Either the 1 man uses the verbal release call to signal the wing to go or he passes to a wing (the 2 man in Diagram 5-7), and then the wing starts the play by passing the ball back to the point and either going or staying. We only use the 3 play of the Five Cutter Attack when facing zone defenses. We do not use the 1 or 2 play because it puts the ball in the corner and keeps it there too long, allowing the zone to shift and cover the play fairly easily; whereas, the 3 play always keeps the ball at the wing position, where it

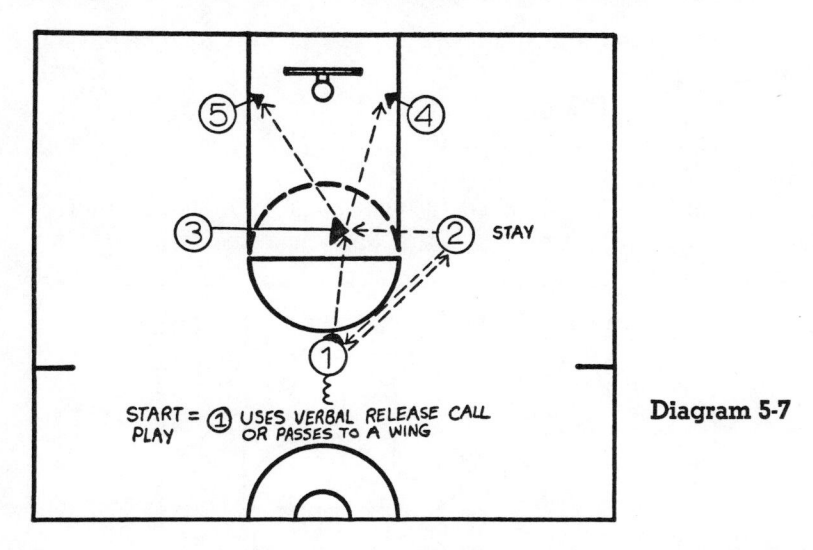

Using Percentage-Controlled Movement Against Zone Defenses   161

Diagram 5-7

START = ① USES VERBAL RELEASE CALL
PLAY   OR PASSES TO A WING

can easily be moved to the other side of the court. Diagram 5-7 shows 2 passing the ball back to 1 and staying, so the 3 man goes. He breaks on a straight line directly into the lower half of the foul circle and stops for one count. If he is open, then he should receive a pass. He may receive the pass from either the 1 man at the point or the 2 man at the opposite wing spot. If 3 is open, then he should take the shot. If he gets the ball but is not open, then he should look for either low-post man on the base-line low-post spots and feed either one of them. Diagram 5-8 shows what happens when 3 is not open in the middle. 1 has passed to 2. 3 now breaks down towards the 4 man and moves to the outside of him into the corner to establish an overload. 2 looks to

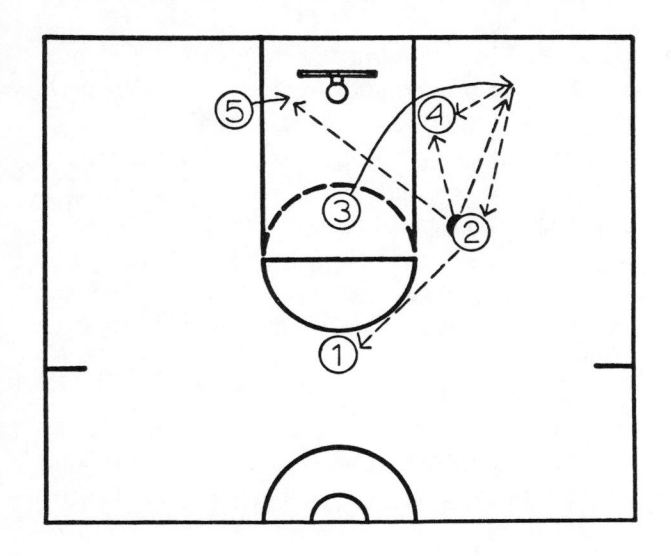

Diagram 5-8

hit 3 in the corner, feed 4 at the low-post spot or pass to 5 at the left power lane spot. If 2 cannot hit 3, 4 or 5, then he can return the ball back to 1 at the point. If 2 passes to 3 in the corner, then 3 looks for the shot or he feeds 4 low. If he cannot do either, then he immediately gets the ball back to 2.

In Diagram 5-9, 2 has passed the ball back to 1 at the point. 1 passes to 5, who breaks up to get the ball because 2 stayed after

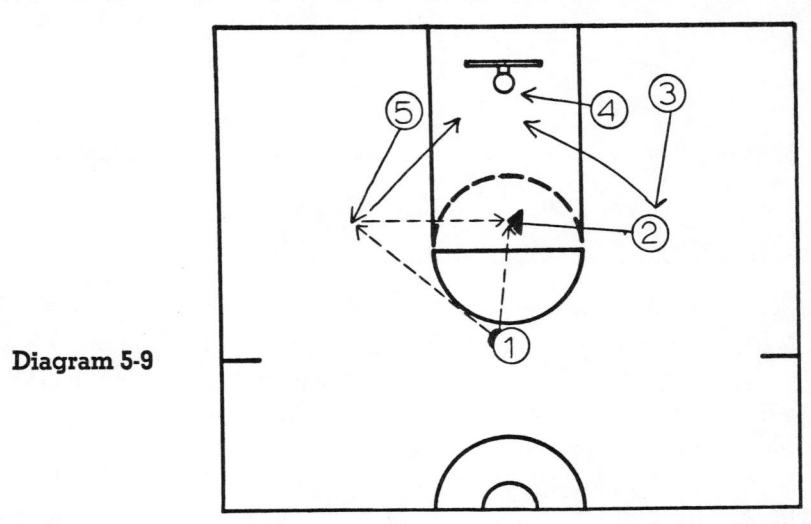

Diagram 5-9

passing to 1. 2 does not wait for a backtrap and breaks quickly to the middle of the lower half of the foul circle as soon as 1 has the ball. 1 may hit 2 if he is open. If 2 is not free, then 1 immediately gets the ball to 5, who has moved up to the left-wing position. 3 starts to move up to take 2's spot when the ball goes to 5. Diagram 5-9 shows 2 taking the shot. Against zones when running the Five Cutter Offense, we send four men to the offensive boards and just keep one man back on defense. We do not employ a half-and-half man against zones. 2 shoots to 5, 4 and 3 go to the offensive boards hard and 1 has defensive responsibility. 2 should follow his shot hard. We have found that by sending four players to the offensive board, we force the defense to concentrate on blocking out or risk giving up the second and third shot; this breaks up the timing of the fast break because it delays the outlet men from getting to their desired positions, as they concentrated on blocking out their area. Thus, by always having a designated man moving into the mid-court area on every shot taken by the opponents as the other four offensive men crash the boards, and by taking only the high-percentage shot which prevents the long rebound if the shot is missed, we have found that this has been enough to stop

Using Percentage-Controlled Movement Against Zone Defenses 163

our opponents from fast breaking us with any degree of success.

If 2 is not open in the middle, then he quickly breaks to the left low-post position. As soon as 2 starts to move from the spot in the middle of the lower half of the foul circle, the 4 man breaks into the middle position vacated by 2. *Coaching Hint:* Remember, any man breaking into the middle should stop for one count before moving out of the 3-second area. 5 looks to feed 4 breaking into the middle; he can also look for 2, who has moved into the left low-post spot and broken out towards the corner a couple of steps. If either 2 or 4 shoot, the men who did not shoot, 5 and 3, go to the boards immediately, as the shooter follows through on his shot and then goes to the board slightly delayed. The 1 man has the defensive responsibility. See Diagram 5-10.

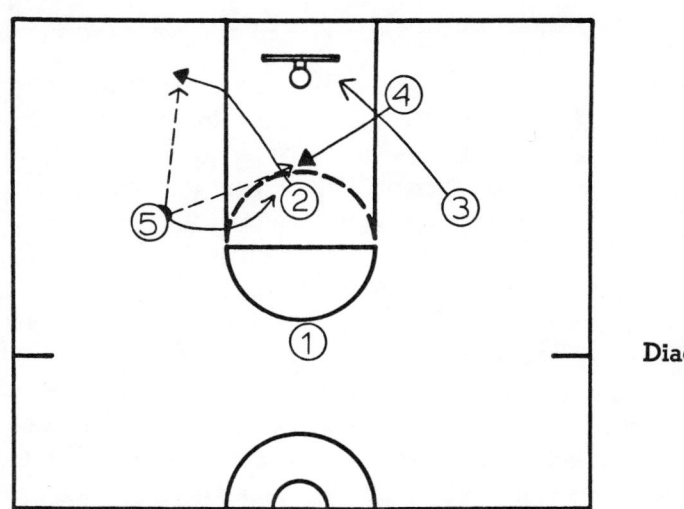

Diagram 5-10

If neither 2 nor 4 are open at this point, the 5 man may have to dribble the ball to take the 5-second count-off, if he is being guarded closer than 6 feet, to prevent the jump ball violation. As soon as 4 realizes that he is not going to get the ball in the middle, he quickly heads to the top of the foul circle to the point position. The 1 man at the point then takes a jab step to his right, moving into the middle of the lower half of the foul circle as 4 is vacating it. 1 should slip into the circle just after 4 has left it, as shown in Diagram 5-11. If 1 is open, 5 should hit him. If 1 shoots, then 2, 5 and 3 go to the boards, and 4, who was moving toward the mid-court area, picks up the defensive responsibility. 5 may hit 2 in the corner, who, in turn, may feed 1 cutting down into the power lane.

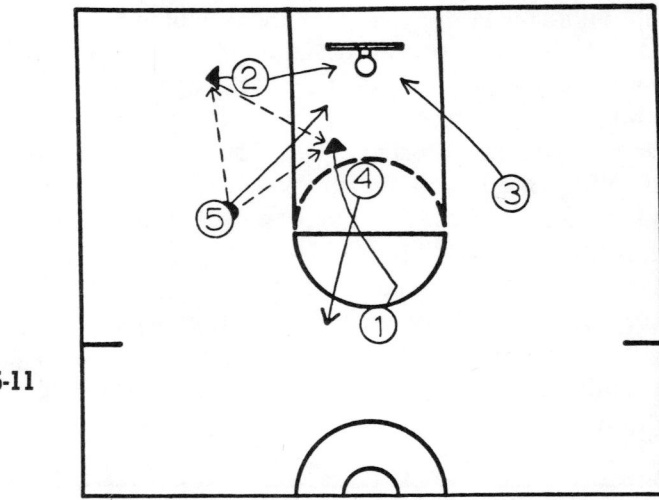

Diagram 5-11

Diagram 5-12 shows that if 1 is not open, then he continues to move on down the lane into the right low-post area. Now the offense is back in the original Five Cutter Offensive Formation, with the ball at the wing spot, ready to run the 3 play. The 5 man will pass to the point and either stay or go, to signal which wing man is to break into the middle. Diagram 5-13 shows what would happen if 5 had passed to 2 in the corner as 1 broke down into the power lane (but did not receive the pass from 5 or 2). 1 moves over to the right low-post spot and 2 just passes out to 5 at the left-wing position.

Diagram 5-14 shows all the cuts that take place when running a 3 play. If a shot does not develop, the players end up in the same positions that they normally would when running the Five Cutter Man-to-Man Attack, with the screening by either the low-post man on the side of the wing man who stayed after the pass to the point, or the screen by the point man on the original low-post backtrap man.

The actual changes in assignments for the Five Cutter Zone Offense compared to the Five Cutter Man-to-Man Attack are the following:

(1) The wing man who breaks to the middle first breaks straight to the middle of the lower half of the foul circle, and instead of going directly to the opposite-side high-post spot, he goes into the right corner. However, when 2 goes through, he then moves up to become the new right-wing man, just as he does after 2 goes through in the man-to-man attack. 3 ends up in the same position, except by a different route.

(2) The second wing man through, the man who stayed, runs the same route as the first wing man, except that he goes in the op-

Diagram 5-12

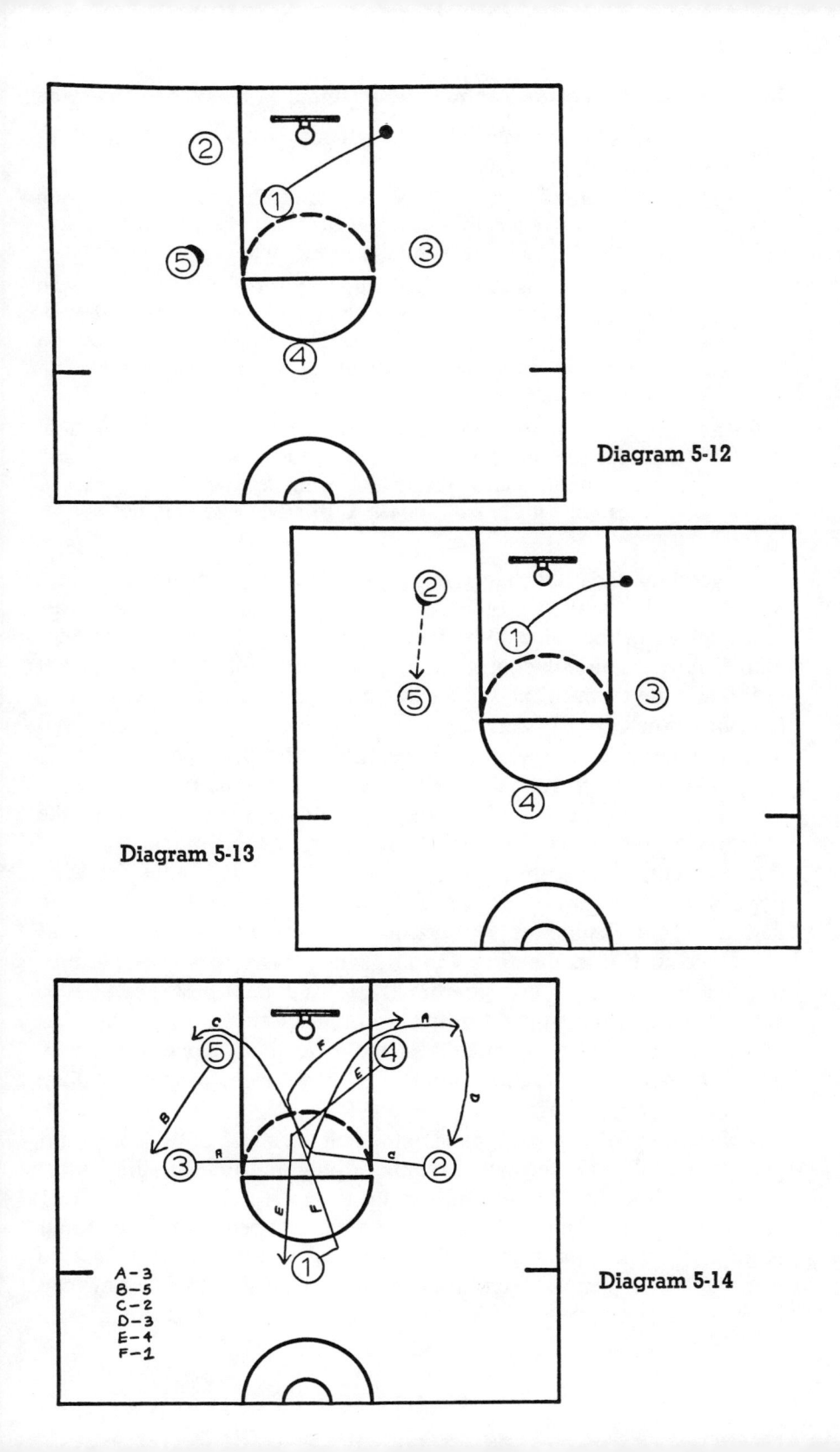

Diagram 5-13

Diagram 5-14

A—3
B—5
C—2
D—3
E—4
F—1

posite direction and takes the left low-post spot if he does not get the ball.

(3) The 5 man (who is on the same side of the court that the wing man, 3, was originally on before he made the first cut) moves up to get the ball just as he did in the man-to-man attack.

(4) The 4 man, instead of backtrapping for the wing man who stayed (the 2 man), moves into the middle of the 3-second area, and if he does not get the ball, then he goes to the point position just as he did in the man-to-man attack, except that his route is a little different.

(5) The 1 man moves into the middle of the lower half of the foul circle instead of setting a side screen for 4, who would be backtrapping on 2 against the man-to-man defense. However, 1, if he does not get the ball, moves to the right low-post position as usual.

Actually, the only change in assignments for the men who do not have the ball is that they break into the middle of the 3-second area and then go to the same spots they would go to against the man-to-man defense. This, of course, forces them into different routes that eventually get them to the same spots if a shot does not develop, and, of course, there is no backtrap screen for the wing man who stayed and no side screen for the man who set the backtrap screen.

Diagram 5-14 shows that 1 received the ball from 2 and 2 stayed, thus causing 3 to have the first cut, as shown by A in the diagram. 5 breaks up to get the ball, so he has the second cut, B. 2 has the third cut, C, and then 3 makes the next cut, D, up to the wing position on the right. 4 has the fifth cut, E, and then 1 has the sixth and last cut, F. There are six cuts in the Five Cutter Zone Attack as compared to five in the Five Cutter Man-to-Man Attack because 3, the first cutter, does not go directly to the high-post position to become the new wing man, but instead breaks to the corner if he does not receive the ball in the middle of the lower half of the foul circle. The 3 man in this situation breaks up to the right-wing spot when wing man 2 goes through.

Diagram 5-15 shows 2 passing the ball back to 1 at the point, and then he goes. This is the signal for the 3 play and that the first cutter through will be the 2 man. 4 moves up to receive the pass from 1. 1 has the choice of first passing to 2 (who has stopped in the lower half of the foul circle), passing to 4 to allow 3 to cut through or passing to 3 at the left-wing spot. Diagram 5-15 shows 1 passing to 3. 3 now can hit 2 in the circle, pass to 5 in the left low-post spot as 2 breaks into

Using Percentage-Controlled Movement Against Zone Defenses 167

the corner around 5, pass to 2 in the left corner or pass the ball back to 1 at the point.

Diagram 5-16 shows that 2 received the pass from 3 in the corner. 2 looks for the shot, and if he cannot get it, he tries to feed 5

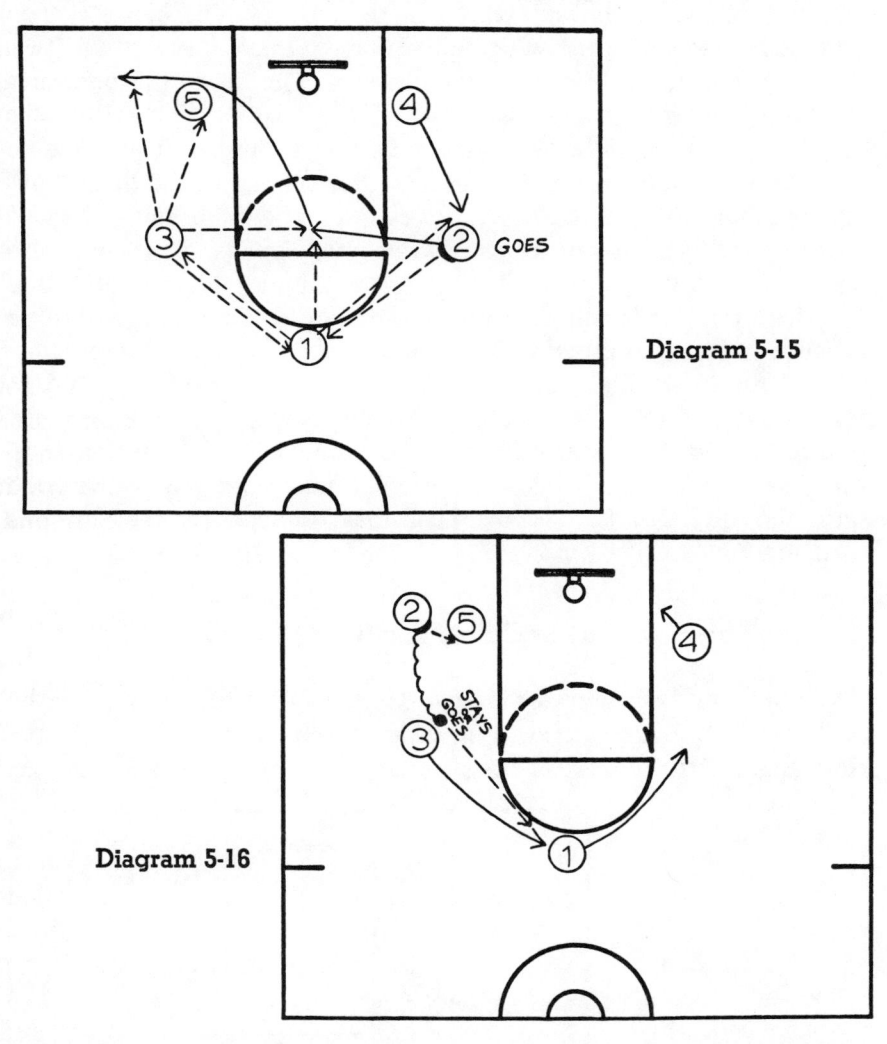

Diagram 5-15

Diagram 5-16

at the post position. If he can neither shoot nor pass to 5, then he can either pass to 3 or dribble to the left-wing position. Diagram 5-16 depicts 2 dribbling to the left-wing spot. 3 moves over to take the point and 1 moves over to take the right-wing position. Now the offense is back into the original Five Cutter Formation, with the ball at the wing position, ready to start a new 3 play.

168   Using Percentage-Controlled Movement Against Zone Defenses

By merely using the 3 play of the Identical Inside Option and running it over and over again, the four cuts to the middle provide more than enough player movement to keep the defense occupied. Usually the zones will tighten up a great deal to shut off the middle to stop the offense, which quickly opens the corners. The ball can then be gotten to either of the wing cutters for the open corner shot if the defense is content to shut off the middle area. The key to this offense is the timing that the players without the ball must develop. There are four cuts to the middle each time a 3 play is run against the zone defense. As soon as one player has made his cut to the middle and has stopped there for one count (and does not receive the ball), then he should quickly move out to his new assigned spot, and the man who has the next cut should start his cut to the middle just as soon as the man before him has begun to vacate the middle. This requires a little practice in order to establish the timing that is so important to make this offense work efficiently. *Coaching Hint:* Each time a man breaks to the middle of the lower half of the foul circle, he should stop for one count and then clear out. Also, he should put his shooting hand up as he cuts into the middle to give the man with the ball a good target to hit. Usually the overhead pass should be used in this situation.

The Five Cutter Offense with Ball Movement

Diagram 5-17 shows the Five Cutter Offense getting into the basic 1-3-1 formation that will have just two men moving most of the time and the other three men stationary, with the ball being moved

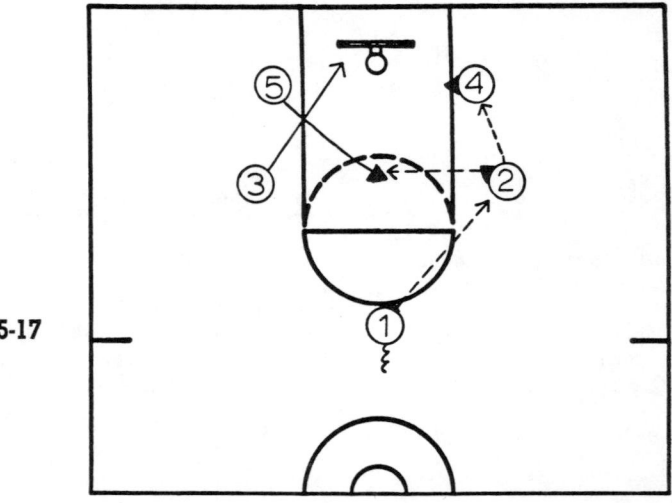

Diagram 5-17

Using Percentage-Controlled Movement Against Zone Defenses 169

from player to player until the open shot is obtained. There will be a greater tendency to take more one-hand set shots with the ball movement offense than with the player movement offense.

1 brings the ball up on the dribble in Diagram 5-17. The Five Cutter Formation is lined up against an even-front zone, as the wing men are stationed two or three steps down from the foul line extended. 1 passes to 2 at the right wing, who immediately looks for the shot. At this point, 5 breaks up into the lower half of the foul circle. 2 looks for either 5 or 4, and if either 5, 4 or 2 shoots, then 3 goes to the board along with the others, while 1 has defensive responsibility. It is important that the low-post men know which player will move up into the middle of the 3-second area and which one will stay at the base line. Usually the slowest and least agile of the low-post men should break up into the middle, because once the offense is moving, he will have to cover a lesser amount of territory than the base-line man.

Diagram 5-18 shows what happens if 5 or 4 is not open and 2 does not get the shot. 5 moves across the 3-second area even with the broken lines of the lower half of the foul circle and then drops down two or three steps to post himself on the same side of the key line extended as the ball is on. The left-wing man, 3, breaks straight into the middle, looking to sneak in behind the defense, and he should receive the pass from 2 at the point he is open as he comes into the circle. If 3 shoots, then 5, 4 and 2 rebound and 1 has defensive responsibility.

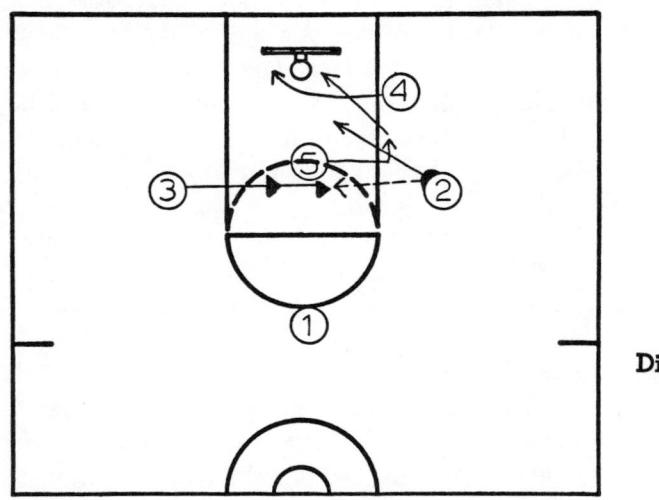

Diagram 5-18

In Diagram 5-19, 2 is unable to hit 3 in the middle, so he returns the ball to 1 at the point. 3, immediately upon seeing this, breaks back to his original left-wing position to receive the ball from 1. As soon as 4 and 5 see the ball go to 3's side of the court, they make their moves. 4 comes across the base line and 5 moves across the middle of the 3-second area. 3 tries to hit either 4 or 5.

Diagram 5-19

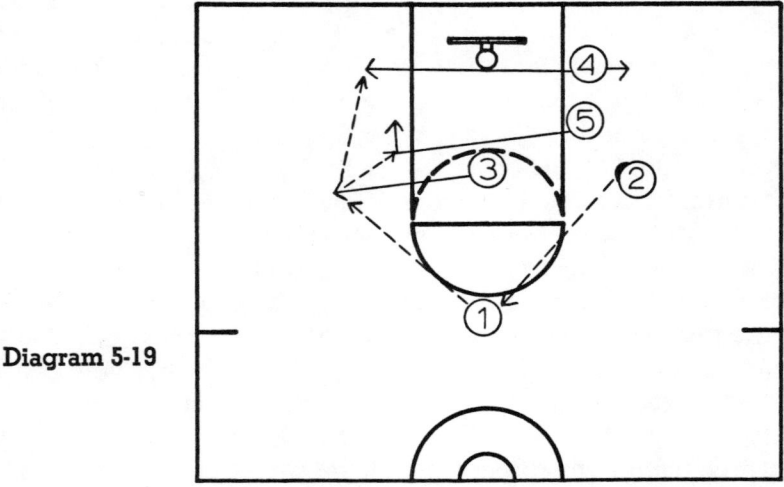

Diagram 5-20 shows what happens if 4 and 5 are not open or 3 cannot get the shot off. 5, after cutting across the middle, drops down 2 or 3 feet, and this is the signal for 2 to now break into the middle, looking to receive the pass from 3. 4, 5 and 3 rebound, 2 follows his shot and 1 has defensive responsibility. *Coaching Hint:* As shown in Diagrams 5-18 and 5-20, when the shot is taken by the wing man who has broken into the middle, this leaves the side of the court that he came from without an offensive rebounder. The base-line rover, 4, should try to get to that side of the court in order to rebound if he has time. 5 will rebound to the power lane on his side of the court, while the wing man who fed the ball to the man in the middle rebounds into the middle of the power lane.

Diagram 5-21 depicts 2 not being open on his cut to the middle. If 3 passes the ball back to 1, then 2 returns to his wing position, as shown by cut A; however, if 3 passes to either 4 or 5, then 2 returns to his side of the court, as shown by cut B + C.

Diagram 5-22 shows another way of getting into the 1-3-1 ball movement attack from the Five Cutter Formation. The ball is passed to 3, and 5, who must break into the middle-post position, moves up the key line extended while 4, who is to become the base-line runner, moves across the low base-line area. Of course, the opposite-side wing man does not have to break into the middle. The rule used here is: If

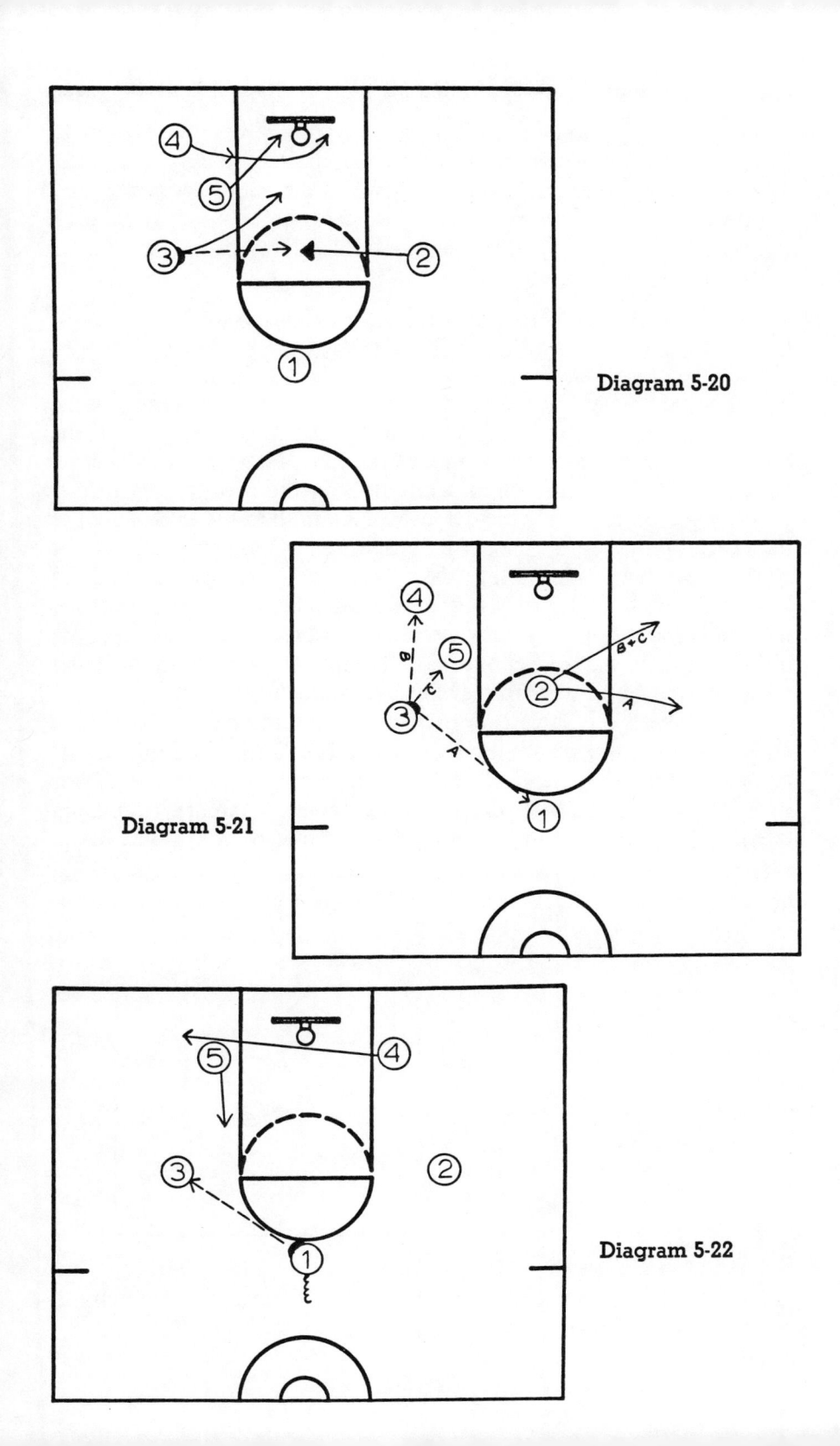

Diagram 5-20

Diagram 5-21

Diagram 5-22

he feels he is going to be open if he goes to the middle, then he should go; if he feels that he will not be open, then he should stay. When the wing man away from the ball stays, then just the middle-post man and the base-line runner move, and we use the old 1-3-1 move-the-ball offense, looking for the percentage shot until it develops.

The Auxiliary Five Cutter Offense with Player Movement

The Auxiliary Formation, used to combat zone defenses, is the same as that employed against man-to-man defenses, except the center, 5, positions himself in front of the low-post man on the side of the ball instead of behind him, as he does in the man-to-man formation. This is done to force the defensive man in the zone in this area to be aware of two men. Also, if 5 must run the base line against the zones, he would be under the basket if he was positioned behind the low-post man. In addition, it puts 5 in a much better position to be fed the ball without having to move, especially when the low-post man on his side breaks out to get the ball. Finally, it allows him a better position from which to go to the offensive board.

5 stays on the same side of the court as the ball, as shown in Diagram 5-23, as 1 passes the ball to 2. 5 breaks across the base line and posts himself on the key line. The cuts that are used by the players without the ball are basically the same as the Auxiliary Formation offensive patterns used to get into the Five Cutter Offense. The major

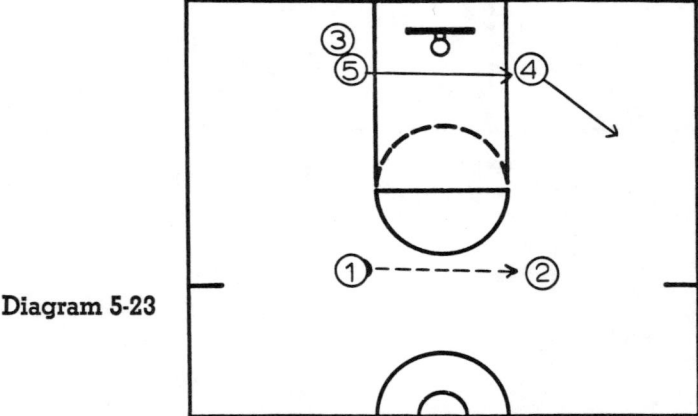

Diagram 5-23

difference is the same as it is with the Five Cutter Offense when employing it against the zone defenses. First there is no screening at

Using Percentage-Controlled Movement Against Zone Defenses 173

all. This means, as shown in Diagram 5-24, that in the man-to-man version of the Auxiliary patterns, 5 does not move around 3 because

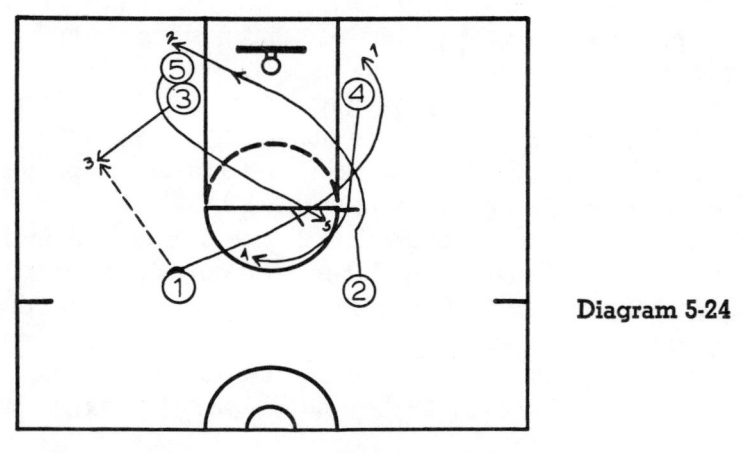

Diagram 5-24

he is in front of him (so that eliminates that screen), 4 does not move up to backtrap for 2 and 1 does not set a side screen for 4. The offense will end up in the same position that it started in (a basic 2–3 formation when facing zone defenses instead of ending up in the Five Cutter Formation when facing man-to-man defenses). However, the basic cuts the players make are essentially the same without the screening, except the 5 man just moves across the base line instead of moving up to the opposite-side high-post position. Diagram 5-25 shows the Auxiliary Five Cutter Offense with Player Movement. 1 brings the ball up

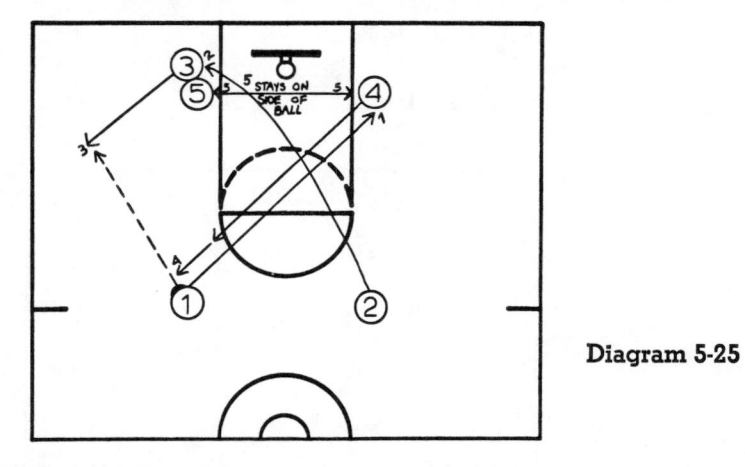

Diagram 5-25

on the dribble. 3 breaks out from behind 5 and receives the pass from 1. 4 breaks into the middle on an angle, heading straight for the place where the foul line meets the key line extended. 4 should break up as soon as 1 stops dribbling. 2 cuts across the 3-second area, stopping behind the 5 man, and 1, after passing to 3, takes 4's position as the right low-post man by cutting directly to that position through the 3-second area.

Diagram 5-26 shows the passing options that 1 has. As soon as 1 stops dribbling, then 3, 4 and 2 must make their moves. 3 breaks out from behind 5 to get the ball, 4 breaks into the middle to get the ball and 2 drops down quickly to a spot even with the foul line where it meets the key line. 1 may pass to either 3, 4 or 2 or he may feed 5 in the low-post area. Diagram 5-27 has 1 passing to 3. When this happens, the 4 man must quickly clear the 3-second area. He does so by going to the point where the key line meets the foul line. 2 immediately breaks to the left low-post area, and he stops behind 5. 1, after passing to 3, moves down to take the right low-post position.

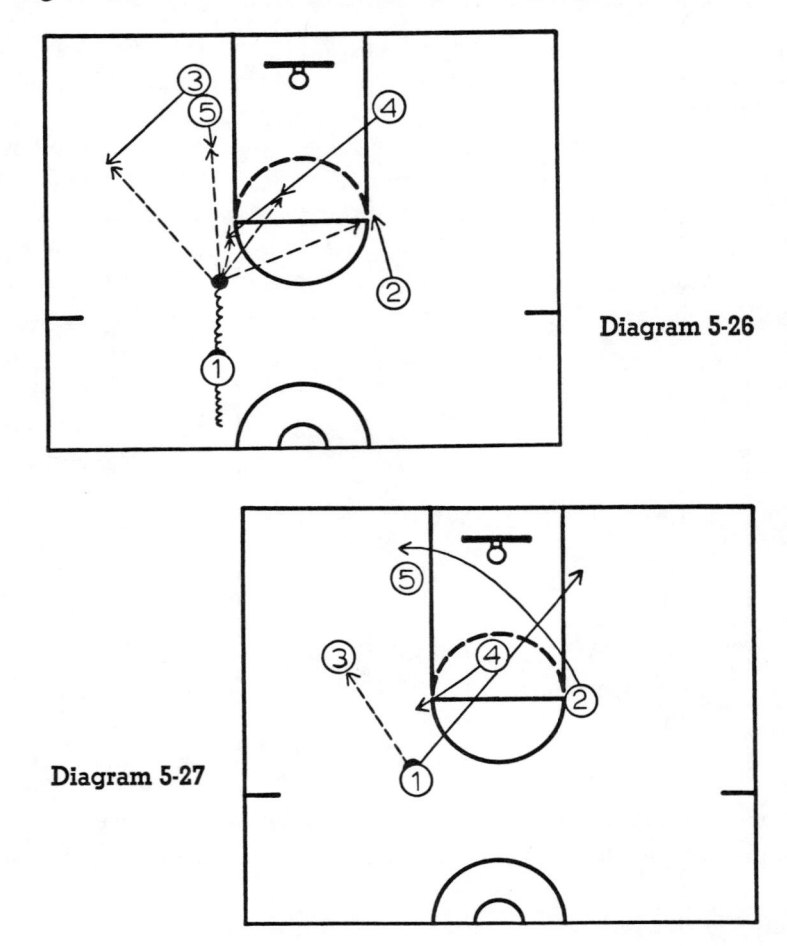

Diagram 5-26

Diagram 5-27

Using Percentage-Controlled Movement Against Zone Defenses 175

Now comes the most important part of the Auxiliary Offense against zone defenses. 3 looks for the shot. If it does not develop, then 3 dribbles once or twice in a stationary position or by taking one or two steps toward the 4 man. As soon as the 3 man puts the ball to the floor on the first dribble, this is the signal for the 2 man to break out from behind the 5 man toward the corner and the 4 man to break out three or four steps from his position at the foul line, as shown in Diagram 5-28. The 1 man breaks up the key line extended to a point even with the broken lines of the lower half of the foul circle.

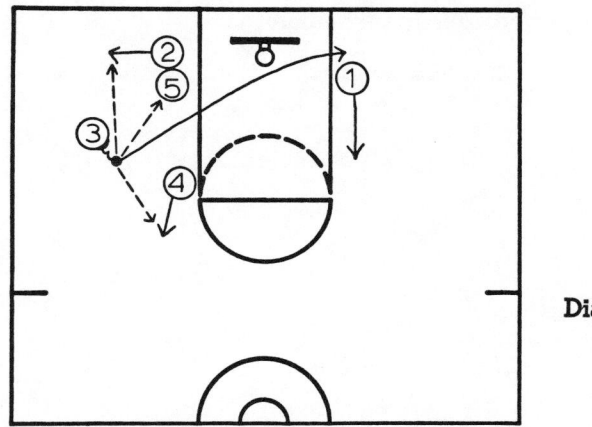

Diagram 5-28

3 now has three choices of who to pass to. He may pass to either 2 in the corner, 5 at the low-post position or out to 4. Regardless of whoever he passes to, immediately after releasing the ball, the 3 man breaks across on a cut toward the middle of the power lane. The 1 man holds to see if the 2 man is going to shoot or if the 5 man is going to take the shot, as shown in Diagram 5-29. If either 2 or 5 shoot, then

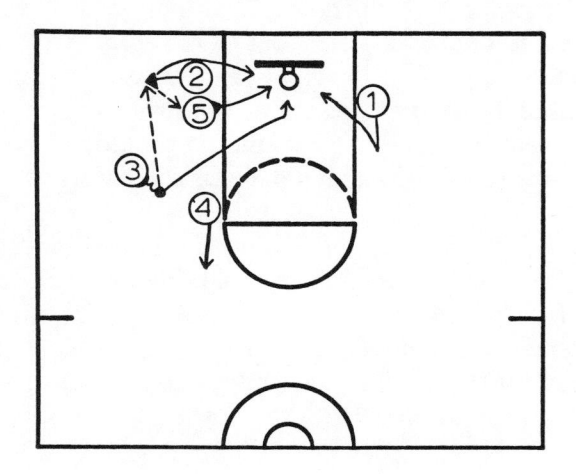

Diagram 5-29

3 probably will not have cleared out of the 3-second area yet. 1 rebounds to the right power lane as 3 rebounds to the middle of the power lane, and either 2 or 5, depending on who did not shoot, rebounds to the left power lane, while the man who shot just follows through and then rebounds. 4 holds for defensive responsibility.

Diagram 5-30 shows 3 passing back out front to 4. 1 quickly moves up the key line extended to receive the pass from 4. 3, of course, moves across to the right low-post spot as 5 moves across the low 3-second area to post himself on the side of the court that the ball is on. The offense is now in the original 2-3 formation, with the ball in position to start the offense again immediately.

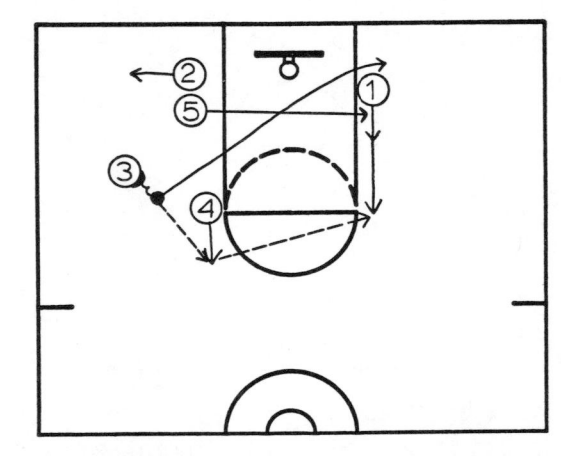

Diagram 5-30

Diagram 5-31 shows 1 taking the shot after receiving the pass from 4. 2, 3 and 5 rebound to the spots shown and 4 has defensive responsibility. 1 follows his shot. 4 should move down to the foul line after passing to 1.

Diagram 5-32 shows what happens if 1 does not get the shot. 2 quickly breaks into the middle as 3 breaks out from behind 5. 1 looks to pass to 2 and 3 cutting, hit 5 in the right low-post area or get the ball back to 4, who should have moved down even with the key line and foul line after he passed to 1. (This puts him in position to get the shot off immediately from the 15-foot area if 1 gets the ball right back to him.)

Diagram 5-33 shows how 1 can use a simple fake to 3 and then get the ball back to 2, who has moved to the foul line to get the easy 15 footer. The fake by 1 usually will move the zone in anticipation of the ball going to 3, and this should leave 2 open at the foul line. This technique is also good for having the zone shift once and starting the offense on the other side of the court. 3, who started to break out to

Using Percentage-Controlled Movement Against Zone Defenses 177

Diagram 5-31

Diagram 5-32

Diagram 5-33

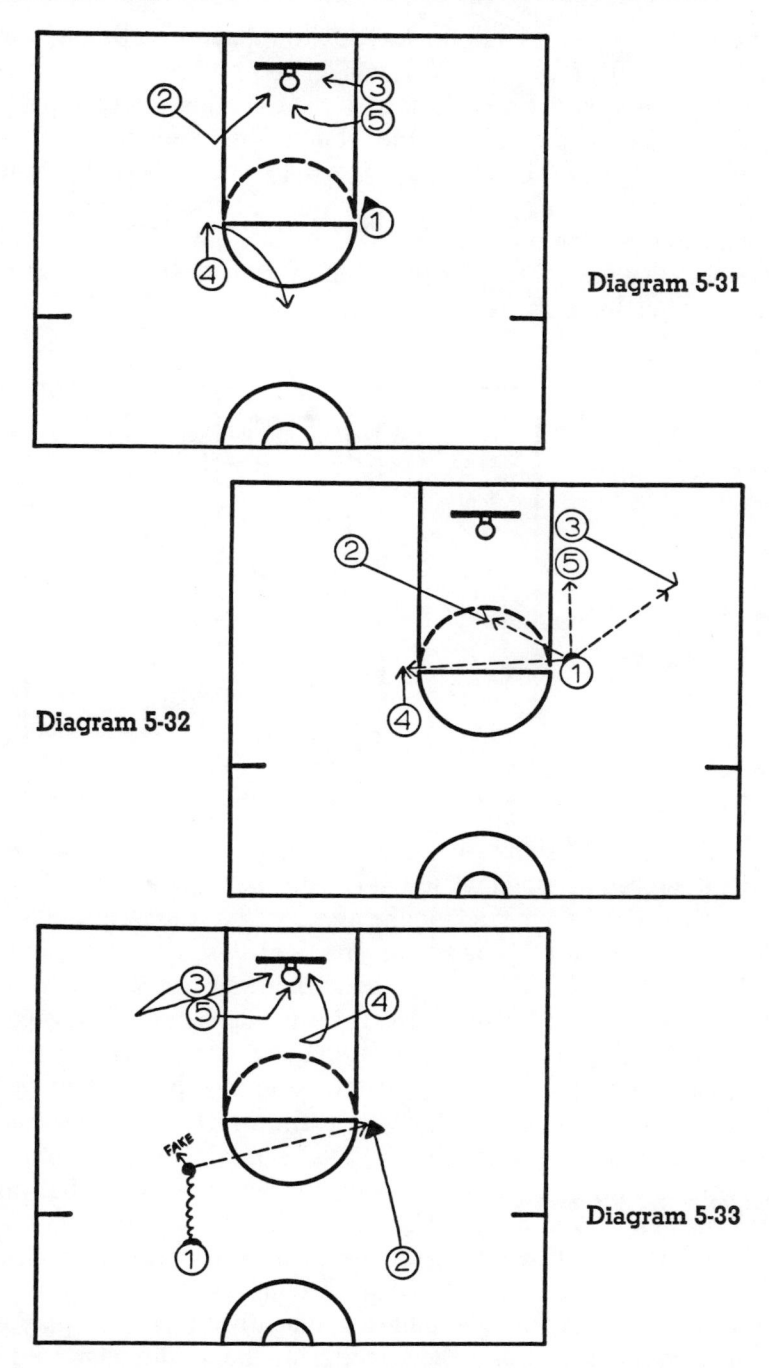

receive the ball from 1, hooks back to rebound to the left of the power lane as 5 covers the middle area. 4, who had started up the middle of

178 Using Percentage-Controlled Movement Against Zone Defenses

the 3-second area, stops and hooks back to rebound on the right of the basket. 1 has defensive responsibility if 2 shoots.

Diagram 5-34 shows 1 faking to 3 and getting the ball over to 2. 3 breaks to the middle if 2 does not shoot. 5 moves across the lane to post himself. 4 moves back toward the right side (where he started to be in position) to receive 2's pass. 2 can hit either 3 in the middle, 5 at the right low-post spot or pass to 4. If he hits any of these men, then he should cut through to start the offense again. 1 should move to the foul line after his pass to 2 in case 2 decides to get the ball back to him.

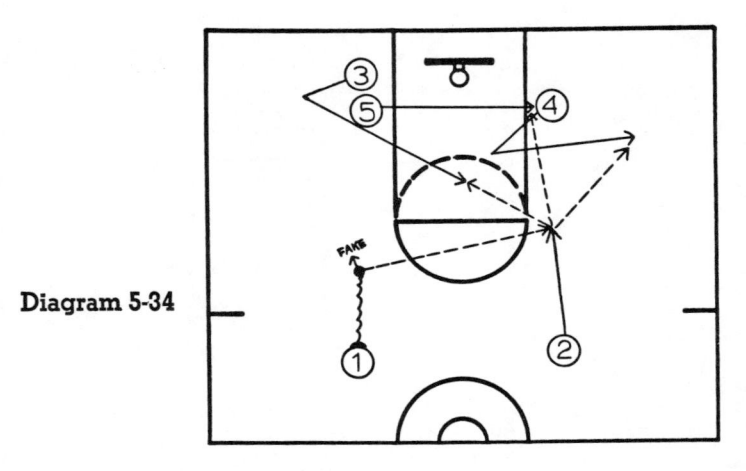

Diagram 5-34

Diagram 5-35 shows the offensive setup if 2 passes to 4 and cuts through. 1 goes to the right low-post spot behind 5; 3 breaks to the foul line where it meets the key line and 2 goes through to the left low-post spot. 4 dribbles the ball once or twice; this is the signal for 1 to break out from behind 5 toward the corner and for 3 to break out to the guard spot. 1 and 3 must break at the same time. The signal, of course, is the dribble by 4. 2 moves up even with the broken circle. 4 now may pass to 1 in the corner, 3 at the guard spot or 5 in the low-post area. *Coaching Hint:* Usually if 1 and 3 break at the same time, this will open up 5 if 1 and 3 are covered. 4 can really help set up 1 by dribbling toward 3, quickly pivoting and then passing the ball to 1 in the corner (Diagram 5-36). The zone will shift in anticipation of the ball going to 3, and by setting the zone up, it will leave 1 open in the corner. The technique 4 employs in this situation is exactly the same as the one the man with the ball uses when running a 31 play in the man-to-man offense. 3 uses the same technique in Diagram 5-28 when the play is run on the opposite side of the court. 4 cuts through toward the left low-post area after passing to 5, 1 or 3, as shown in Diagram 5-36.

Using Percentage-Controlled Movement Against Zone Defenses 179

Diagram 5-35

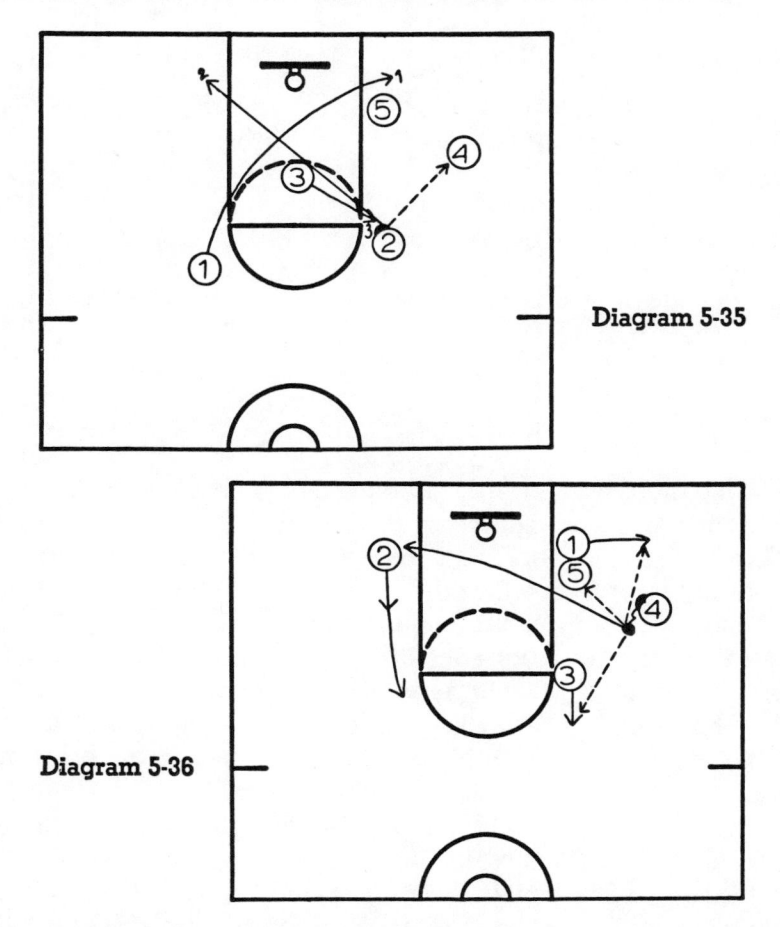

Diagram 5-36

Diagram 5-37 shows that 2 has the ball in the corner after having previously received a pass from 3 (after 2 had moved into the left low-post spot behind 5 and 1 had started the play by passing to 3). 3, of course, passed to 2 and moved through toward the right low-post position. 1, after having passed to 3, moved to the right low-post spot, and after seeing 3 pass to 2 in the corner, moved up the key line to the foul line. (Note: 1 had moved up halfway after he saw 3 dribble.) If 2 passes directly out to 4 (who had broken up the middle to the foul line and then out to the guard spot after 3 dribbled), then the offense is now reset in the 2–3 Auxiliary Formation (4 at the left guard spot, 1 at the right guard position, 2 at the left low post, 3 at the right low post and 5 at the center position on the same side of the ball). The 4 man can start the offense again by either passing over to 1 or by passing to 2, as shown in Diagram 5-37. 3 breaks to the middle as 1 cuts toward the 5 man to post himself behind 5, and 4 heads for the right low-post spot. The offense is now in progress again.

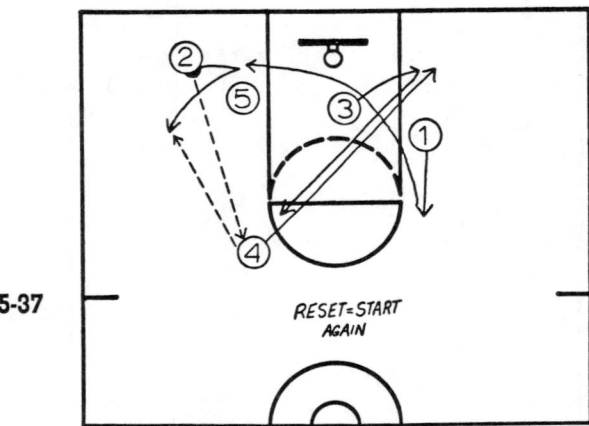

Diagram 5-37

Diagram 5-38 shows the rebounding assignments when the Auxiliary Offense is used against zones as 1 brings the ball up and passes to 3, 5 or 4 for the shot. The 2 man, who is the guard on the opposite side of the court from where the shot is taken, rebounds to the power lane on his side of the court, and the other men rebound as illustrated. If 1 should take the shot after bringing it up, the 2 man would not rebound but instead would have defensive responsibility. The guard only rebounds when the ball is shot on the opposite side of the court that he is on and the shot is not taken by a man in the other guard position.

The Auxiliary Five Cutter Zone Attack can be run continuously from side to side, or repeated on the same side and then run to the other side, as it constantly moves four cutters to the ball each time the pattern is run. It puts pressure on the middle of the zone as there is always a man cutting to the middle, and it forces the zone to widen out to cover the man who is cutting out to the corner from behind a low-post man. The defense also does not know which way the man with the ball in the wing position is going to pass, so that the zone has difficulty in anticipating where it should shift in order to cut off the potential shooter who may receive the ball. This offensive attack gives a team excellent player movement as it puts players in the most vulnerable spots of any zone—the middle and the corners of the zone.

The Auxiliary Formation with Ball Movement

Diagram 5-39 shows the same basic 2-3 formation with the low-post man on the side of the ball behind the 5 man or center. The 5

Using Percentage-Controlled Movement Against Zone Defenses   181

Diagram 5-38

Diagram 5-39

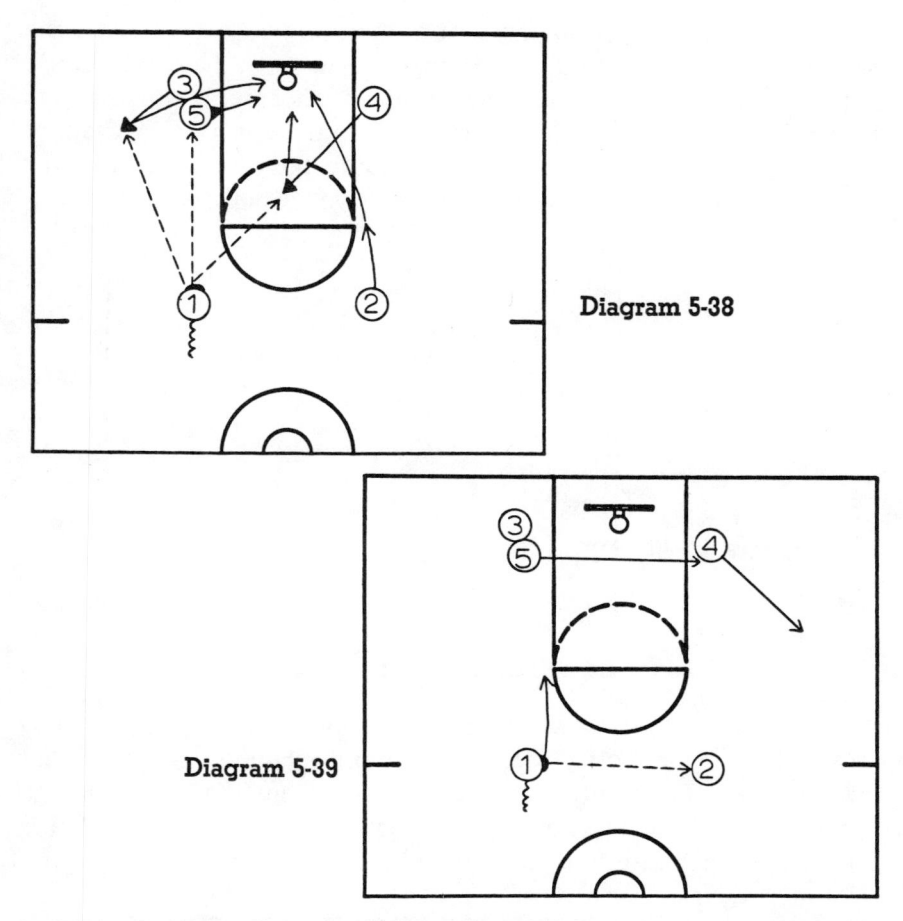

man must stay on the same side of the ball at all times. 1 passes to 2, which forces 5 to move across the bucket area as 4 breaks out to get the ball from 2. 2 passes to 4 in Diagram 5-40, and this is the signal for the 3 man to make his move in the ball movement offense. Again we are only moving two men in the ball movement attack as compared to four men in the player movement attack. 3 has the choice of two cuts when the ball is passed to the opposite-side low-post man. He either goes directly across the base line to the opposite-side corner or he breaks up into the middle as he did in the Auxiliary Five Cutter Zone Offense. If 3 is open there, then 4 will pass to him. If 3 is not open in the middle of the lower half of the foul circle, 4 quickly cuts around behind 5 at the right low-post position and then breaks to the right corner. Diagram 5-40 shows the passing opportunities that 4 has to make on this move. He may feed 3 in the middle, 5 at the low-post spot or 3 in the corner. If the shot is taken by 3, 5 or 4, then the players who did not shoot rebound, and the guard on the opposite side of the court also crashes the boards hard; in this case, it would be the 1 man. Notice that 1 and 2 have moved into the areas where the foul line meets the key line extended, in order to position themselves for the shot in the 15-foot area in case they receive the ball.

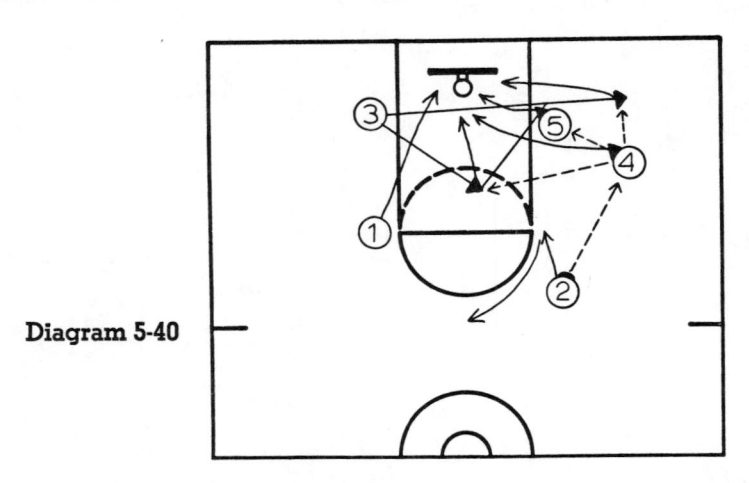

Diagram 5-40

Diagram 5-41 explains the rules the opposite-side guards follow on the shot. The opposite-side guards do not rebound when the other guard shoots. They only rebound when they are the guard on the opposite side of the court from which the shot is taken and the shot is not taken by a man in the other guard position. If the guard does not

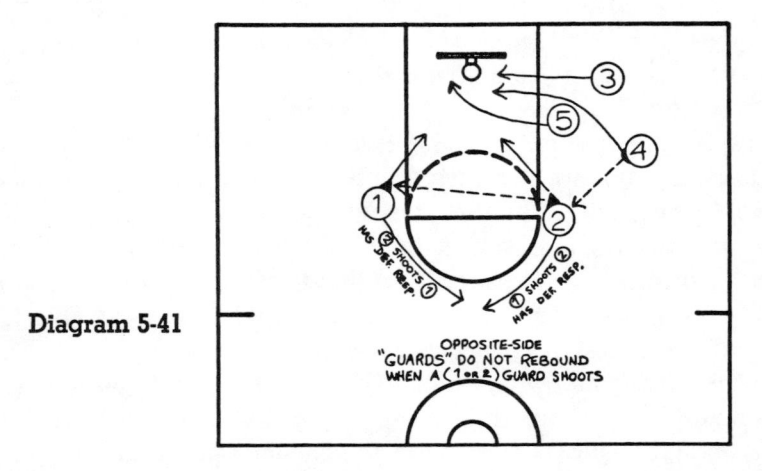

Diagram 5-41

rebound or shoot, then he has defensive responsibility. Diagram 5-41 shows 4 passing back to 2, who either shoots or passes to 1, who is in

Using Percentage-Controlled Movement Against Zone Defenses   183

position to either shoot or pass. If 2 shoots, then 1 has defensive responsibility, and if 1 shoots, then 2 has defensive responsibility. Regardless of who shoots, the shooter follows through on his shot and rebounds. *Coaching Hint:* Notice that when a guard shoots, there is no rebounder on the opposite-side low-post area. The 5 man tries to get to that spot on the shot, if he has time to.

Diagram 5-42 shows 2 passing back over to 1. Note the positions of 1 and 2. They have moved to the foul line to get into better position. The ball started in the right corner from 3 to 4 to 2 and then to 1. 1 does not get the shot, so 3 and 5 move back across the 3-second

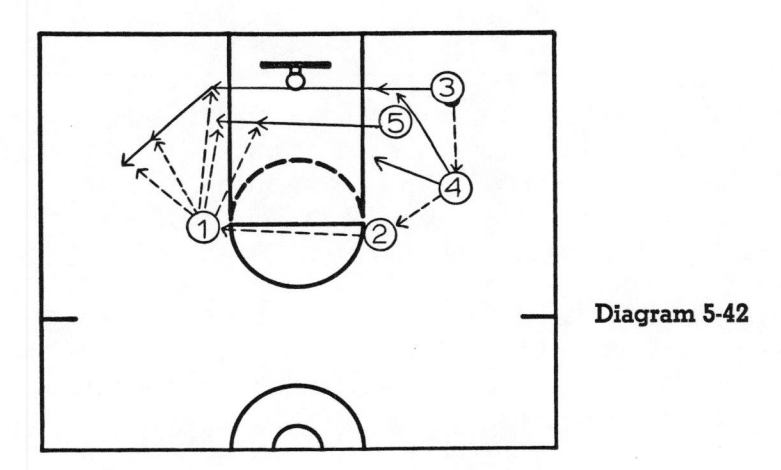

Diagram 5-42

area. *Coaching Hint:* Notice how 3 moved close to the key line after passing to 4. This allows him to be nearer the key line so that he will be able to get back to the other side if 2 passes the ball to 1. 1 looks to feed 3 or 5 as they cut across the lane, and 1 should hit them at any point they are open. Of course, 1 can return the ball to 2 if he wants to. 4 also moves back to his low-post spot as 3 and 5 flash across the power lane. If 3 does not get the ball, then he returns to his low-post spot on the left of the power lane, breaking up to the wing position to get the ball from 1. When 4 sees 3 get the ball, he breaks to the middle and then to the corner if he does not get the ball, or he can go directly to the corner. Diagram 5-43 illustrates 4's moves and the opportunities that 3 has to pass to 5 or 4.

The ball movement attack from the Auxiliary Formation is very simple, as it is similar to the 1-3-1 attack which employs the ball movement theory. The middle man in the post area must stay on the same side of the ball, and then the low-post man on the opposite side of the court from the ball must get to the corner to establish an

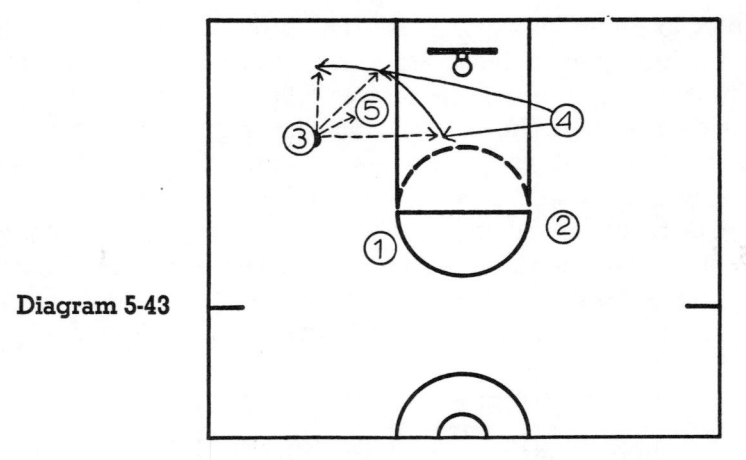

184   Using Percentage-Controlled Movement Against Zone Defenses

Diagram 5-43

overload situation. He gets there by either going directly across the lower portion of the power lane or going into the middle of the 3-second area, and then to the corner by going around the 5 man.

By just moving the ball from side to side and having a base-line runner and a middle-post runner, it makes the zones shift quickly in order to be effective. *Coaching Hint:* Teams should practice and employ the use of faking the pass in one direction and then going in an opposite direction, so as to make the zone commit itself as it anticipates the first pass that is faked. This can be a very effective maneuver against a fast-shifting zone.

Attacking Combination Defenses with the Identical Inside Option

Many teams will employ combination defenses against the percentage-controlled team's offensive patterns in hopes of confusing the offense. When facing combination defenses, we have found that running the Identical-Inside-Option 3 play of the All-Purpose Percentage Five Cutter Offense is all we really need to combat them. The Identical-Inside-Option 3 play has a lot of movement, and it moves the players to a new position each and every time the play is run through, so that eventually the defense will make a mistake. If the offense is patient enough, it should be able to capitalize on the defense's mistake, which should allow the easy percentage shot. Diagram 5-44 shows a combination defense that has X1 and X3 playing man-to-man on 3 and 1, with X5, X4 and X2 playing a three-man zone under the basket in an attempt to cut off the power lane game. We have faced this type of defense many times and it is effective in stopping the

Using Percentage-Controlled Movement Against Zone Defenses 185

power lane game, but it immediately opens up the foul circle shots. 1 should dribble up to the top of the foul circle and force X1 to take him. As soon as X1 picks him up, 1 quickly passes to the open man—in this situation, 2. 2 should take the shot if he is open.

Diagram 5-45 shows 2 not taking the shot because X2 has moved up to take him as X4 covers 4. 2 now has the choice of either staying or going after he has passed back to 1 at the point. In Diagram 5-45, he goes. X3 usually would move over to cover 1 at the point man-to-man, because if he didn't, then 1 would have the shot at the foul line. 2 goes to the opposite-side high-post spot. 4 moves up to get the ball from 1. 5 moves up to set a backtrap for 3, but usually 5 finds no one to screen. 3 moves to the right of 5 into the right power lane. 3 should not stop in the power lane in this situation but instead should continue into the corner, as shown in Diagram 5-46. This forces X2 to cover two men—4 with the ball and 3 in the corner. Usually, the two

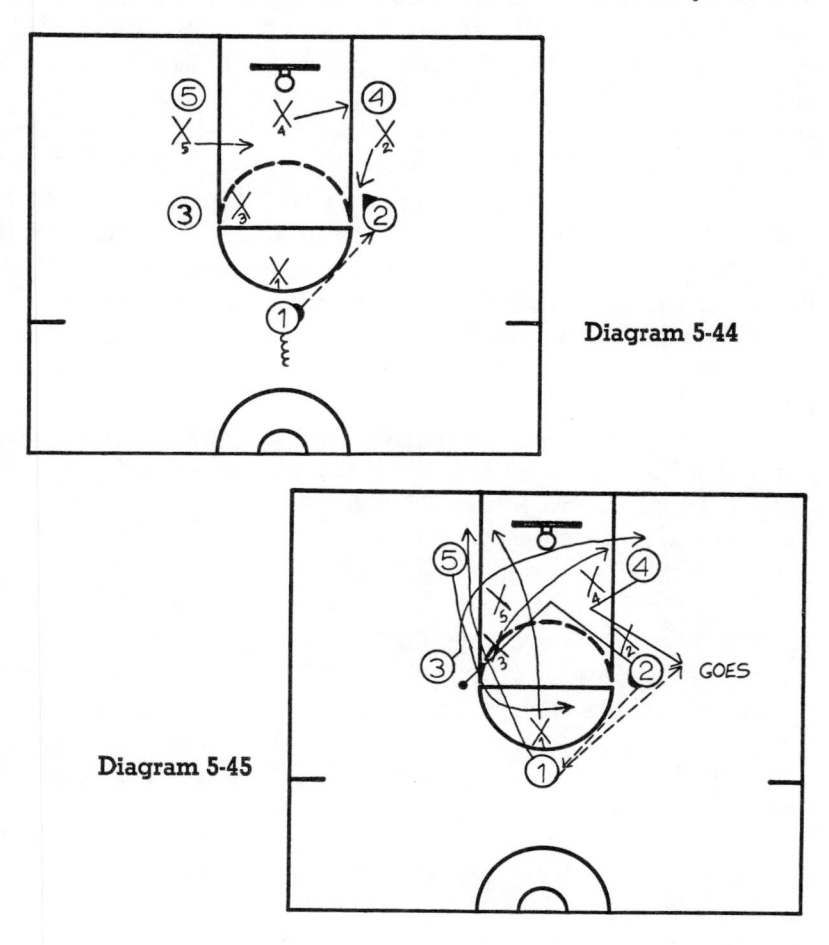

Diagram 5-44

Diagram 5-45

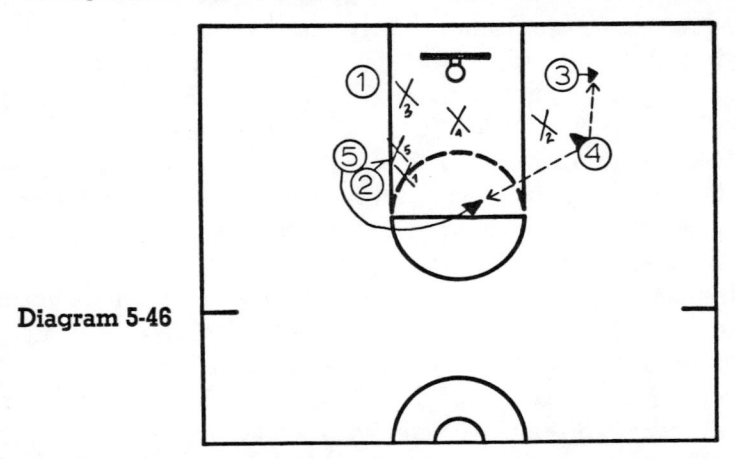

186   Using Percentage-Controlled Movement Against Zone Defenses

Diagram 5-46

men playing man-to-man will cover their men after the initial play. 1, of course, after passing to 4, moves to his left to set a side screen for 5; however, there will not be anybody to screen. X1 has followed 2 and X3 has followed 1 to the left low-post spot. 5 comes off 2's side screen, and again 2 probably will not have anyone to screen. Diagram 5-46 shows how the foul line is open for 5 as he cuts around 2. 4 either hits 5 at the foul line or 3 in the corner. If X4 moves up to cover 5, then 4 should hit 3 in the corner and stay to signal for a 1 play. 31 is a good play to use in this situation if X4 moves up to cover 5. *Coaching Hint:* The reason we run the man-to-man version of the 3 play of the Identical Inside Option instead of the zone version is that we want to keep the middle as open as possible. Also, the man-to-man attack does not take players to the middle of the bucket area as the zone offense does.

Diagram 5-47 shows 2 passing back to 1 and staying. Usually, the reason 2 does not get the shot is that X1 has moved over quickly to take him. The reason that X2 does not pick up 2 is that it would leave 4 open in the corner, and it would be too far for X4 to move to cover 4 in time to prevent the shot. However, if the defense played it this way, then 2 should get the ball to 4 in the corner. He should look to feed 4 low, as he always does in the man-to-man Five Cutter Attack. When X3 sees X1 take 2, then X3 must move up to cover 1 so as not to leave him open at the top of the circle. 2, upon seeing this, forces X3 to take 1 as he passes back to 1. 2 stays and this allows 1 to hit 3, who is open because X3 left him to cover 1. If X5 should move up to cover 3, then this will leave 5 open at the left low-post spot, and if 5 just breaks a step or two to the corner, X4 will not have enough time to cover 5 in the corner. By 2 passing to 1 and staying, it opens

Using Percentage-Controlled Movement Against Zone Defenses 187

Diagram 5-47

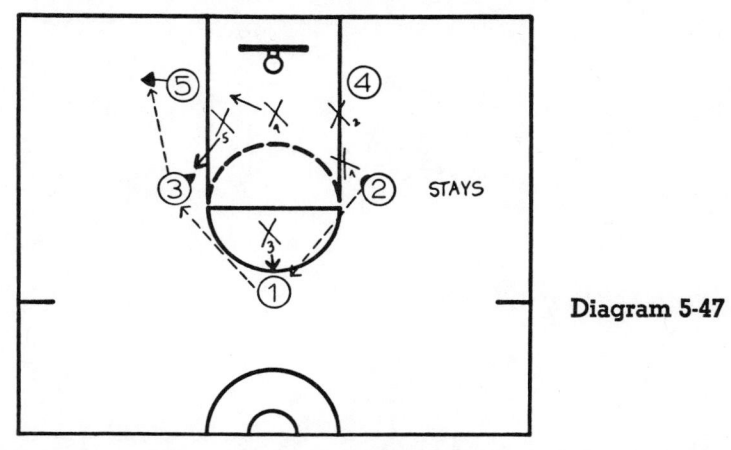

up an opportunity for the free shot. This technique puts a great deal of pressure on the combination defense. Of course 3 can always go through on 2's stay signal after 2's pass to 1, and the 3 play can be run.

Diagram 5-48 shows the back men of the zone, X4 and X5, playing the low-post men man-to-man, while the other three defensive men play a zone out front. We just run a 3 play, with 2 passing to 1 and 2 either staying or going—in Diagram 5-48, 2 goes. 5 sets the backtrap as 2 goes to the high-post spot beside 5, and 4 moves up to get the ball from 1. Diagram 5-49 shows 3 cutting into the power lane unmolested.

The last type of combination defense we have faced is the matchup zone defense. When we face a matchup zone, we immediately go into either the Five Cutter Offense with Player Movement or the Auxiliary Five Cutter Offense with Player Movement. This puts a

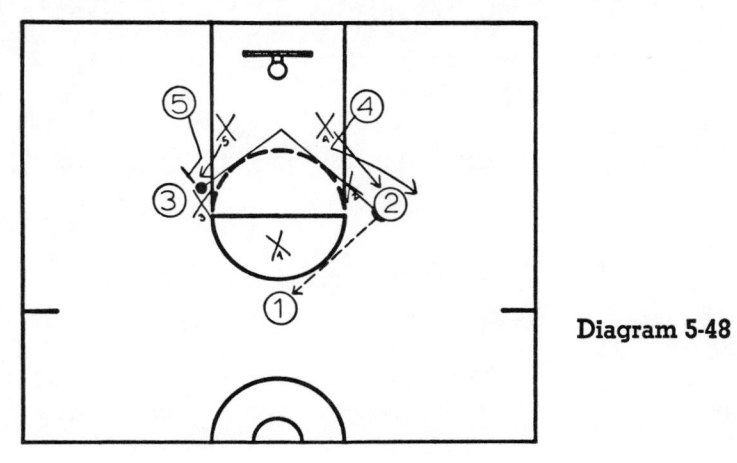

Diagram 5-48

Diagram 5-49

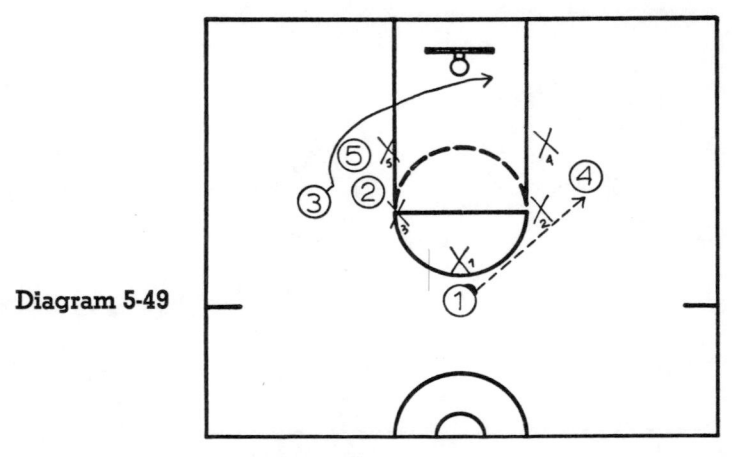

great deal of pressure on the defense, because it makes the defensive players spend a great deal of time releasing players to their teammates as the offensive players cut into their areas and then leave them to go elsewhere. We prefer the Auxiliary Attack to the Five Cutter Attack because the 2-3 setup puts more pressure on the defense by sending cutters continually into the corner away from the dribble by the wing man with the ball. It is very difficult for the defense to cover a man who has cut into a corner when the team is employing a matchup defense. Matchup defenses are very effective against just ball movement zones, but become much less operative when players are continually cut through the middle of a matchup zone and one of the players ends up in the corner. As shown in Diagram 5-50, the 2 man is released by X2 after he goes out of X2's area, is picked up by X4 temporarily and is finally picked up by X3. When matchup zones have to release just one man two or three times, they are creating many problems for themselves. We have found that by sending a cutter into a corner on the same side of the ball and having the wing man with the ball dribble to set up the defense in anticipation of the ball going out front (as the Auxiliary Five Cutter Attack does), the matchup zone is in for a great deal of difficulty in covering the corner successfully.

Solving Fluctuating Defenses with the All-Purpose Percentage Attack

Opponents of the ball-control or percentage-controlled teams have used fluctuating defenses with a high degree of success. By

Using Percentage-Controlled Movement Against Zone Defenses 189

Diagram 5-50

MATCHUP ZONE RELEASES MEN TO THE AREA

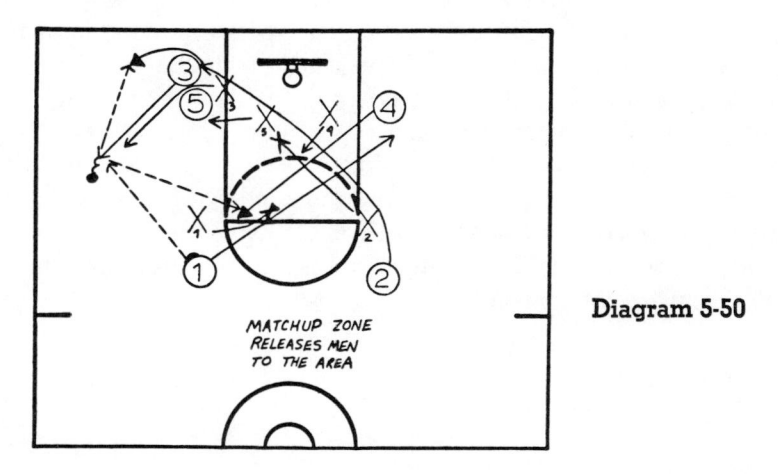

fluctuating defenses, we mean that opposing teams change their defense each time down the floor or on some other type of signal, such as every time they score a field goal or a foul shot. Teams using this defensive strategy will go from a 1-2-2 jug zone, to a 2-3 zone, to a 1-3-1, to a matchup and back again, or they may mix the zones with the man-to-man defense. Regardless of the combinations they used, they can be very frustrating for the ball-control team that is trying to figure out what type of defense it is facing so it can run the special offensive patterns it has prepared for the given defense. This can prove very fatal for the offense, because it wastes so much time trying to figure out what type of defense it is going against that the players stand around too much and make the defense's job that much easier, or the players do not know exactly what they should be doing, as some may think the defense is one type while others may think it is something else. This causes confusion and frustration for the offense.

We usually just run our Auxiliary Offense to the Five Cutter Offense in our man-to-man patterns, regardless of the type of defense we are facing, if the team we are playing is fluctuating its defense. After the 2-3 Auxiliary cuts are run each time down the court, the offense is able to tell whether they are facing a zone or a man-to-man defense. If the offense finds out that the defense is a zone, then we just run the Five Cutter Zone Offense, or if it is a man-to-man, then we run the Five Cutter Man-to-Man Attack with the 31 play, by mixing the 3 play with the 1 play.

If we find that the opposing team is fluctuating its defense, using different zones and not employing any man-to-man defense, then we usually go with the Auxiliary Five Cutter Zone Offense. We do not use ball movement offenses very much against fluctuating defenses because they do not put as much pressure on the defense. They only force it to cover the offense in compact areas; whereas, the player movement attacks make the defense spread out more in order to cover the corners as well as plug up the middle.

We do not worry about whether the zone is an odd-front zone or an even-front zone, as both the Five Cutter Zone Offense and the Auxiliary Five Cutter Zone Offense with Player Movement will work against any type of zone defense.

CHAPTER 6

Centering Zone Presses with the All-Purpose Percentage Offense

All types of offensive systems must expect to face some type of zone press over the course of a season. The deliberate percentage-controlled teams and the ball-control teams must expect to face many more variations of zone presses than the run-and-shoot teams, because these presses speed up the tempo of the game and force the offense away from their set plan of attack. Percentage-controlled teams must be able to handle these presses. Because we have used the percentage- or ball-controlled style as our main offense over the years, we have had to make constant adjustments in our zone press offenses in order to force our opponents out of the zone presses. The only way to do that is to score the easy layup with a penetrating attack.

Objectives of Zone Press Defenses

The full-court zone press defenses are designed not only to harass the offensive team into turnovers, but also to confuse and force them into changing their method of bringing the ball up court. The objectives of the zone presses are just about the same as those of the man-to-man full-court presses, in that the presses are either active or passive ones. Of course, the big difference is that the zone presses use a lot of double-team traps, and they cover areas on the floor instead of individual offensive players.

When facing any zone full-court press defense, we do not care if it is either active or passive because the method of our attack will be the same regardless of the type of press. This differs from our man-to-man full-court press offense as the method against the passive pressure is to go into our half-court All-Purpose Percentage Five Cutter Offense, and against the active man-to-man pressure the objective is to beat the defense down the court and get the 2-on-1 or 3-on-2 situation. The approach to attacking any full-court zone press is that of treating any zone press as an active press.

Many teams are satisfied with just getting the ball up across the 10-second line without losing it against the zone press, and then stopping to reset their offense in front court. This is the case for many ball-control teams, and it had been my philosophy up until five years ago. The problem with trying to reset the offensive attack after successfully getting the ball safely into front court is that the defensive team is allowed to reset its defense, with the defense now determining the tempo at which the game will be played. This should be the job of the offense if a ball-control style of play is employed. In order to combat this problem, I finally decided to use a disciplined, set pattern press offense that would allow us to attempt to score immediately after crossing the 10-second line. When we speak of a disciplined full-court zone press offense, we mean just that . . . every player in a designated position, with a definite assignment based on the position of the ball on the court. We want to be as disciplined on our zone press offense as we are in all our other offensive maneuvers. We call this attack the Middle Lane Blitz and we divide the court into three lanes, as shown in Diagram 6-1.

The Real Secret of Breaking Any Zone Press Defense

The real secret of breaking any zone press is to attack the press at its weakest point. The weakest point of all zone presses is the middle of the court. Most zone presses will allow the first in-bounds pass and then trap the man with the ball when he starts to dribble, using the sidelines as another defensive man. By getting the ball to the middle of the zone, the press loses its effectiveness, because it is virtually impossible to trap a man in the middle of the court (he has too many avenues of escape or help from his teammates). Teams that try to beat the zone presses by trying to bring the ball up the sidelines are

Centering Zone Presses with the All-Purpose Percentage Offense 193

Diagram 6-1

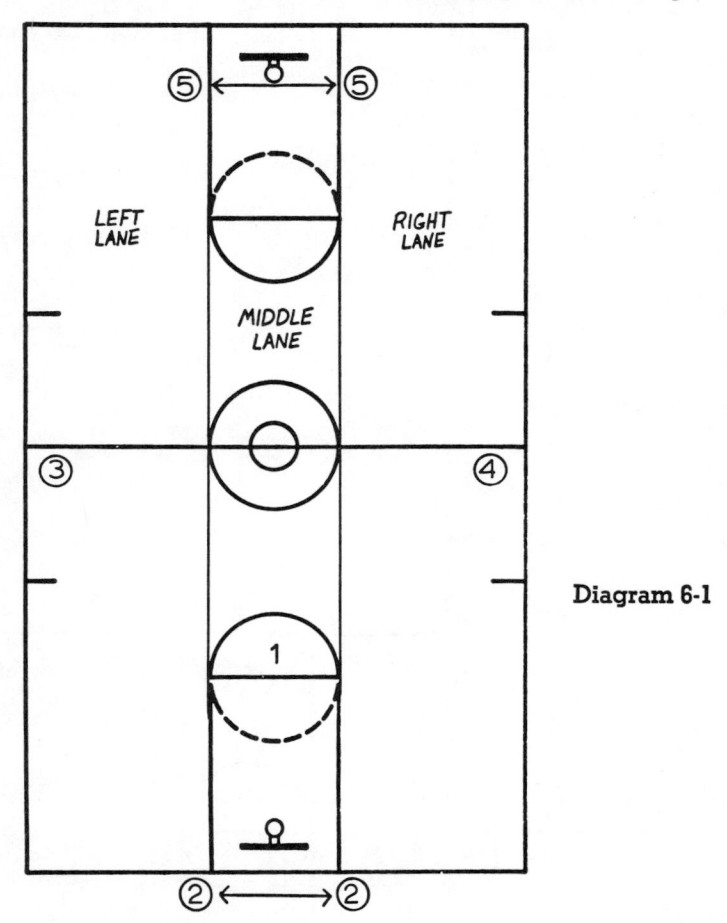

essentially playing into the hands of the pressing team. If the pressing team had a choice of where it wanted the ball to go in order to make a successful trap, it would be in the back court to the sideline, as shown in Diagram 6-2.

Getting the Ball to the Middle

By getting the ball to the middle of the court against any full-court zone press defense, immediately the strongest part of the press is taken away from the pressing team—the double trap at the sideline. When the ball is in the middle lane of the court a great deal of pressure is put on the pressing team, because it is here that the pressing team is so vulnerable to making a mistake that could cost them 2 points. So, by getting the ball to the middle of the court, the offense now gains the advantage by placing the defense in a situation that it

PLAYING INTO THE
HANDS OF ZONE
PRESSES

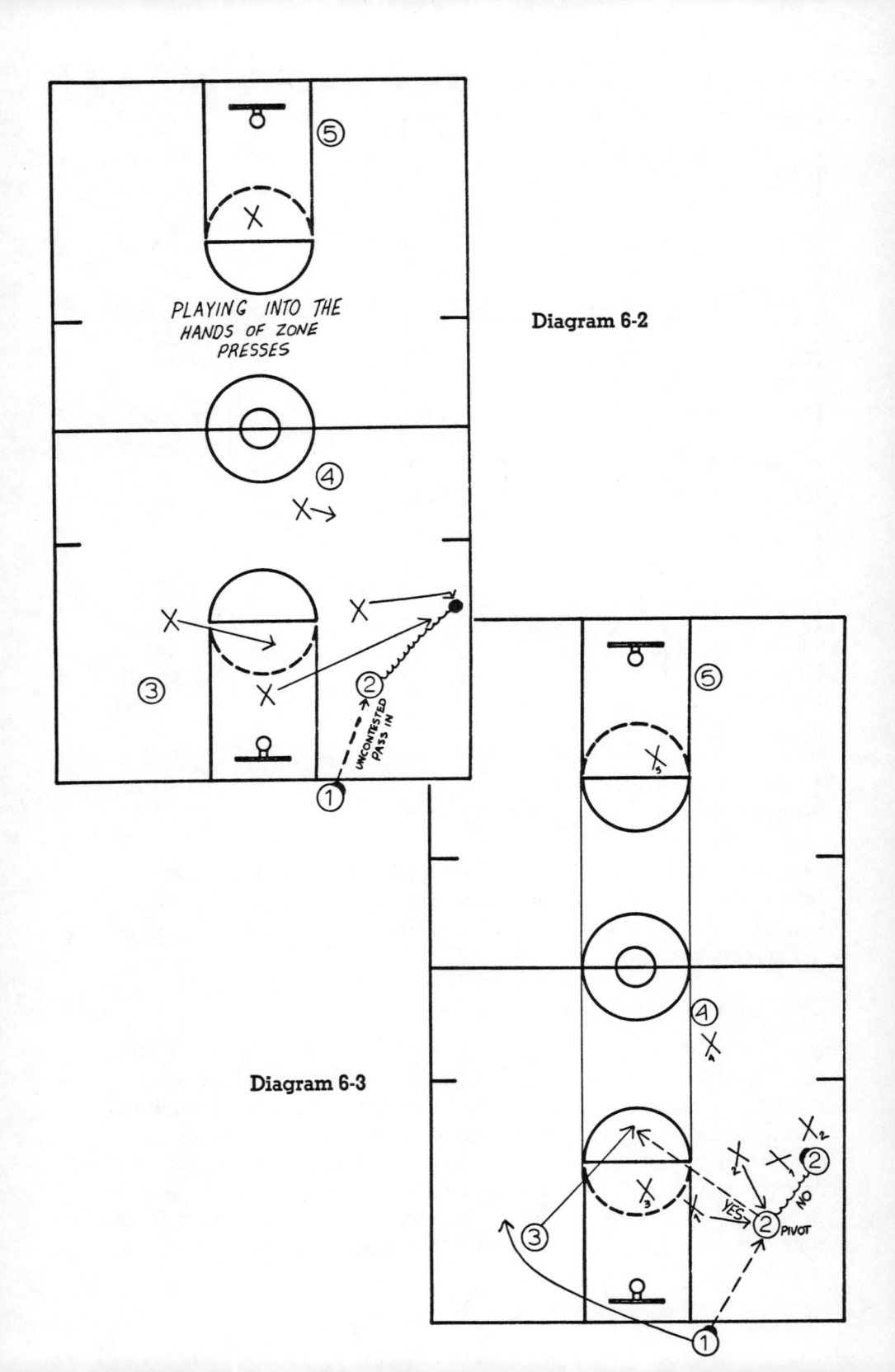

Diagram 6-2

Diagram 6-3

cannot handle. The man with the ball cannot be trapped, and he has enough room to elude the defense because the offense now outnumbers the defense. This takes away the strongest part of the zone press, as shown in Diagram 6-3.

The Two Rule Play

In order to assure a team of getting the ball to the middle of the court, a simple Two Rule Play must be put into effect. Regardless of the offensive formation we use (we only use two formations against full-court zone presses), the Two Rule play is in effect. Diagrams 6-4 and 6-5 show the zone press offensive formations we employ in the All-Purpose Percentage Attack. Both of these formations have men stationed at mid-court and at the sideline, one man on each side of the court.

Rule One

Rule One reads as follows: The man at mid-court on the opposite side from the ball must break to the middle of the court in the direction of the foul line to receive the pass from one of the guards. He should break only as far as he has to, but he must be heading toward the middle in the direction of the foul line to meet the pass, as shown in Diagram 6-6.

After receiving the pass, the man with the ball does not dribble, but instead he pivots and faces mid-court. It is at this point that Rule Two comes into play, as shown in Diagram 6-6.

Rule Two

Rule Two comes into play after the man at mid-court receives the ball in the middle lane and gets ready to start the Middle Lane Blitz up court. It is at this point that the offense has the defense outnumbered, three men to two. The man with the ball in the middle lane now has a Rule Two decision to make. This decision is called Rule Two, and Diagrams 6-7 and 6-8 depict the Rule Two options. 3 must make his decision quickly, for it is at this point that the offense should accelerate in order to beat the defense down court. 3, after receiving the pass, pivots and faces mid-court; at the same time, 4 breaks at an angle to the middle, heading down court. 3 now has the choice (the Rule Two option) of either keeping the ball and dribbling right down the middle or passing to 4 and letting him take it down the middle lane on the dribble.

Diagram 6-4

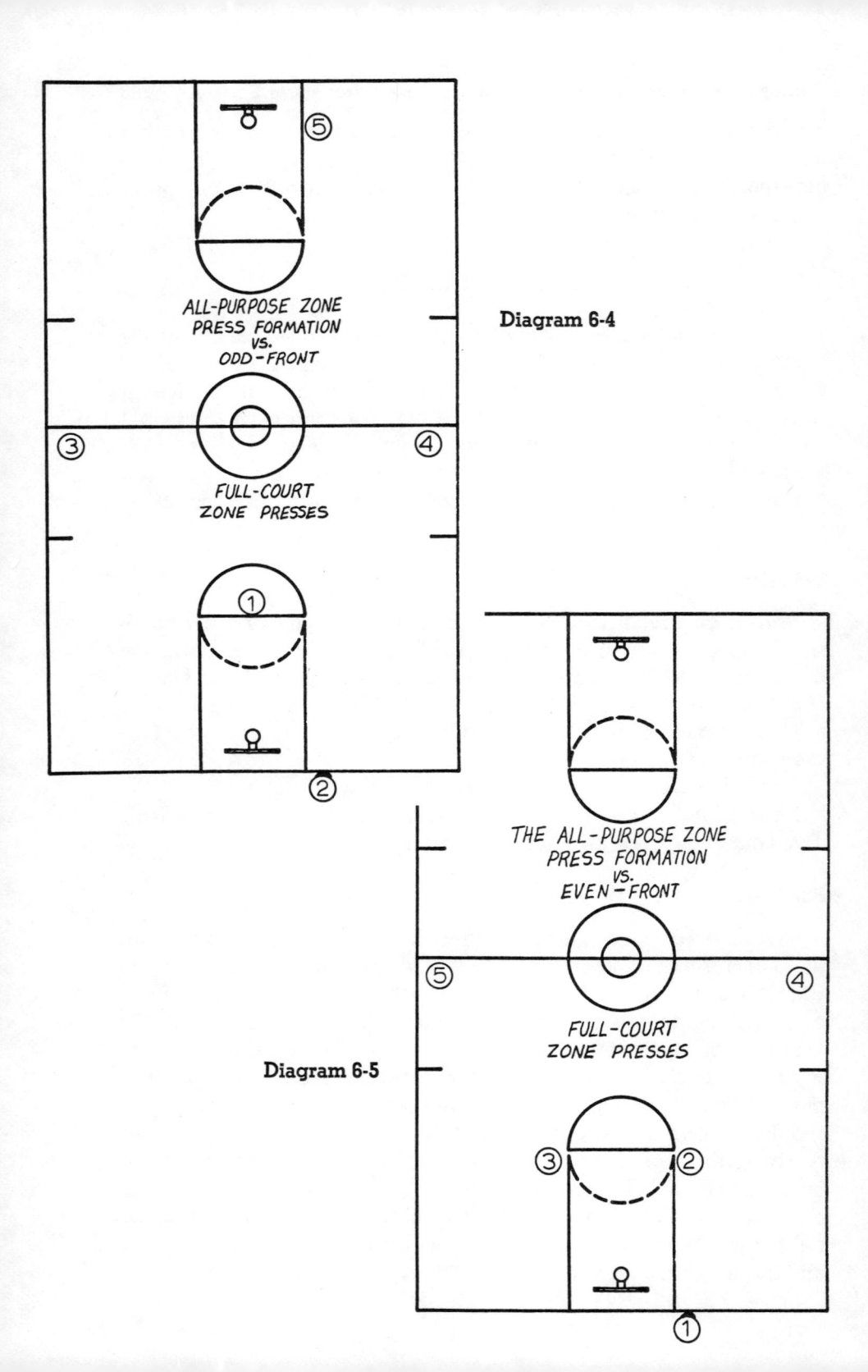

ALL-PURPOSE ZONE
PRESS FORMATION
vs.
ODD-FRONT
FULL-COURT
ZONE PRESSES

Diagram 6-5

THE ALL-PURPOSE ZONE
PRESS FORMATION
vs.
EVEN-FRONT
FULL-COURT
ZONE PRESSES

Diagram 6-6

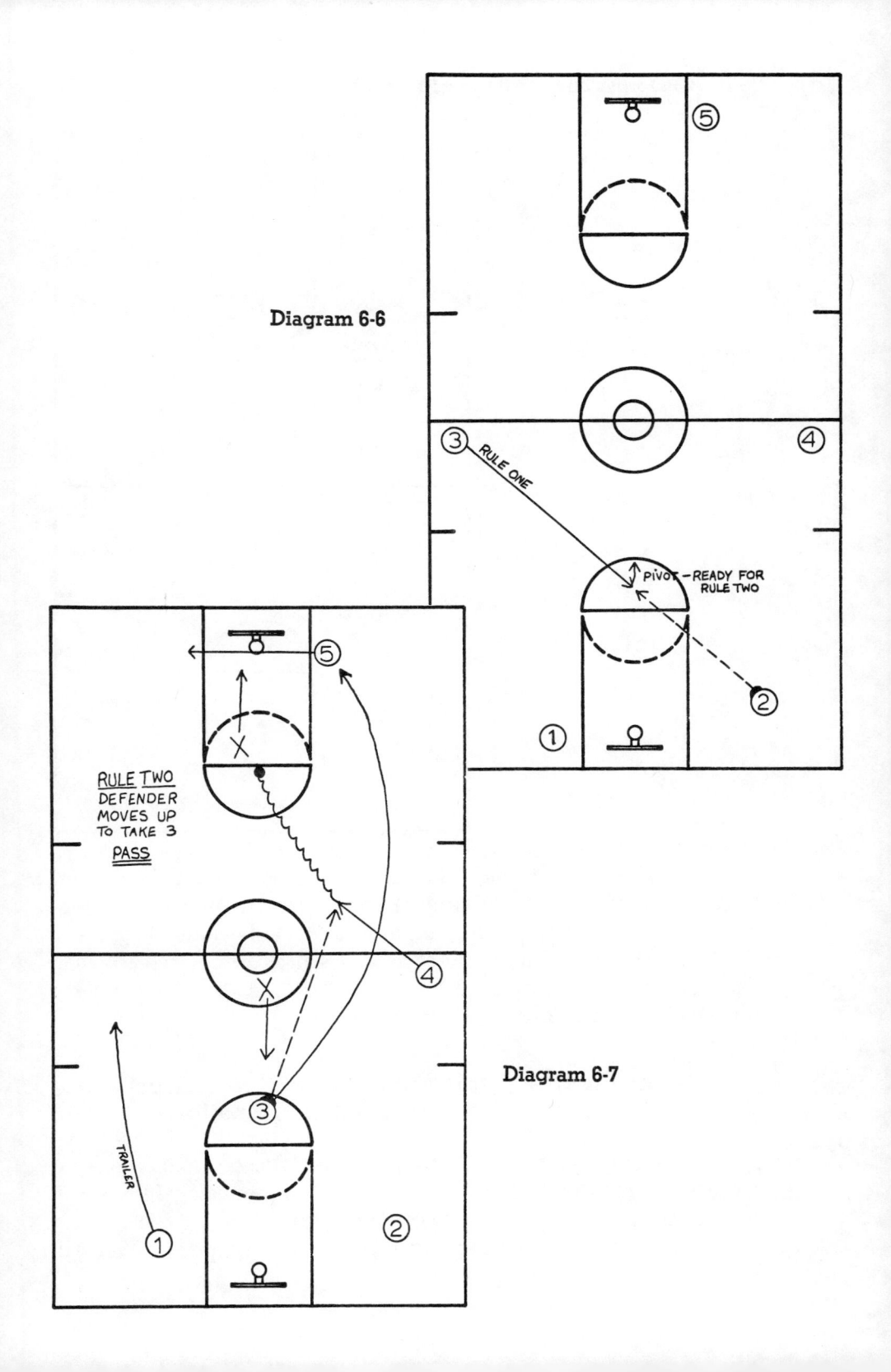

Diagram 6-7

RULE TWO
DEFENDER MOVES UP TO TAKE 3
PASS

TRAILER

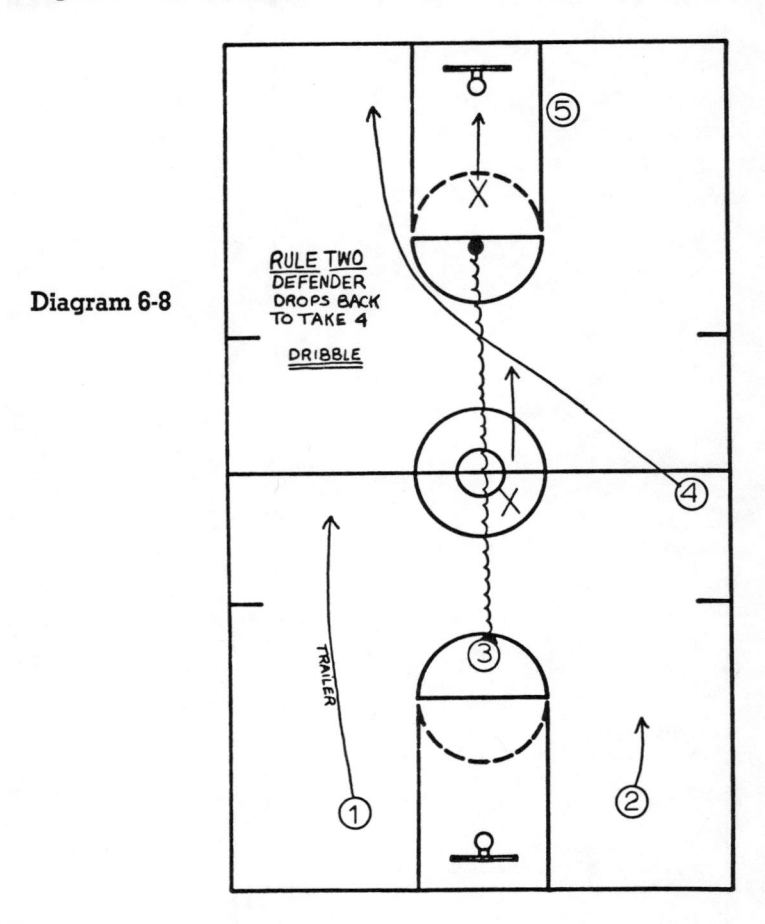

198 Centering Zone Presses with the All-Purpose Percentage Offense

Diagram 6-8

RULE TWO
DEFENDER
DROPS BACK
TO TAKE 4
DRIBBLE

This Rule Two decision is usually based on where the defensive man at mid-court is playing. Rule Two: If the defensive man at mid-court moves up to cover 3, then 3 passes to 4, as shown in Diagram 6-7. If the defensive man at mid-court drops back to cover the 4 man cutting to the middle, then 3 keeps the ball and dribbles it up the middle himself, as shown in Diagram 6-8.

Centering the Even-Front Full-Court and Half-Court Zone Presses with the Five Cutter Formation

When employing the All-Purpose Five Cutter Formation against any even-front full-court zone press, it is set up completely in our own back court, imagining that the basket is at the mid-court center jump circle. The most common even-front full-court zone presses that will

Centering Zone Presses with the All-Purpose Percentage Offense 199

be employed are the 2-2-1 and the 2-1-2; of these two the 2-2-1 is the one the offense will most often face. The only change in the Five Cutter Formation then, when we use it against man-to-man full-court presses, is that the post men are wide. 1 is the point man, who takes the ball out-of-bounds on either side of the backboard. 2 and 3 are the wing men, and they are even and tight to the foul line. 4 and 5 are the low-post men. They position themselves at mid-court near the sidelines, as shown in Diagram 6-5.

By having the low-post men at the mid-court sideline areas, the Two Rule Play can be employed at all times. The wing man on the opposite side of the court (following Rule One) from the ball breaks to receive it. Diagram 6-9 shows the 3 man moving into position. 3 tries to get the ball between the broken lines of the bottom half of the foul circle and the basket, and on one side of the hoop. Wing man 2,

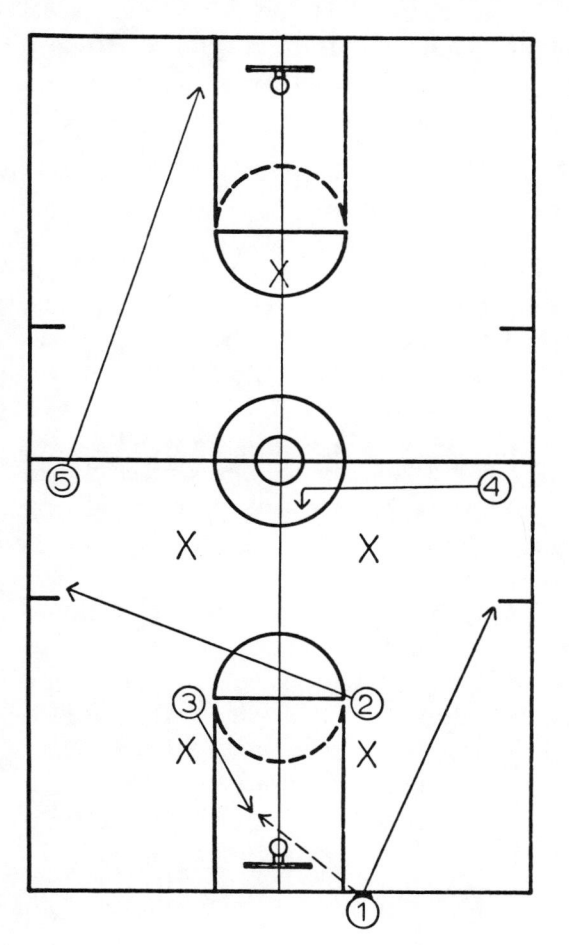

Diagram 6-9

who was on the same side as the ball, breaks quickly across the foul line to the 3-foot mid-court line area to the left. 1, after making his pass to 3, breaks to the the right 3-foot hash marker. 4 and 5 do not move until they see that 3 gets the ball. They must determine which side of the court 3 is on by dividing the court in half right up the middle, using the basket as the center. This is why it is important that 3 gets the ball on either side of the basket. Using Rule One as the guide, the man at mid-court on the opposite side of the ball breaks to the middle of the court, even with the outside center circle in the back court. Diagram 6-9 illustrates the 4 man moving to the middle. *Coaching Hint:* Notice that 4 does not break into the middle lane foul circle area immediately, but instead he waits at the center circle in the back court. 5 then moves down court and positions himself at the base line on the same side he was on at mid-court. We are now in a 1-3-1 formation against the even two-man front of the 2-2-1 zone press. Diagram 6-10 shows the three passing options the 3 man has. If the 3 man had gotten the ball on the other side of the basket, then 5 would have broken to the middle and 4 would have moved down court, again using Rule One.

Getting the Ball to the Middle

Many times the 1 man will never reach his destination before 3 has quickly passed to 4, breaking up the middle. 4 immediately pivots, and now he will use a Rule Two decision. Either he keeps the ball himself and tries to split the middle two defensive men or he passes the ball to either 1 or 2 and lets them bring it up. Diagram 6-11 depicts the 4 man blitzing right down the middle by splitting the defenders as they try to cover 1 and 2. If the 4 man is successful in splitting the defense, then he takes the ball right down the middle on the dribble. 2 fills the left lane and 5 moves over to fill the right lane as 1 trails the play, and 3 has defensive responsibility.

When 4 cannot make the move down the middle, then he looks for 2 cutting diagonally across the court and he passes to him. 4 has made his decision in the Rule Two Play by passing when he cannot make his move. When the defenders hold, the 4 man will have no trouble in splitting, but, as shown in Diagram 6-12, the defender moves over to cover 4 leaving 2 free. 2 gets the ball and dribbles it into the middle to the foul line. 4 follows 2's pass momentum and fills the left lane, with 5 moving over to fill the vacant right lane. 1 trails and 3 remains for defensive responsibility.

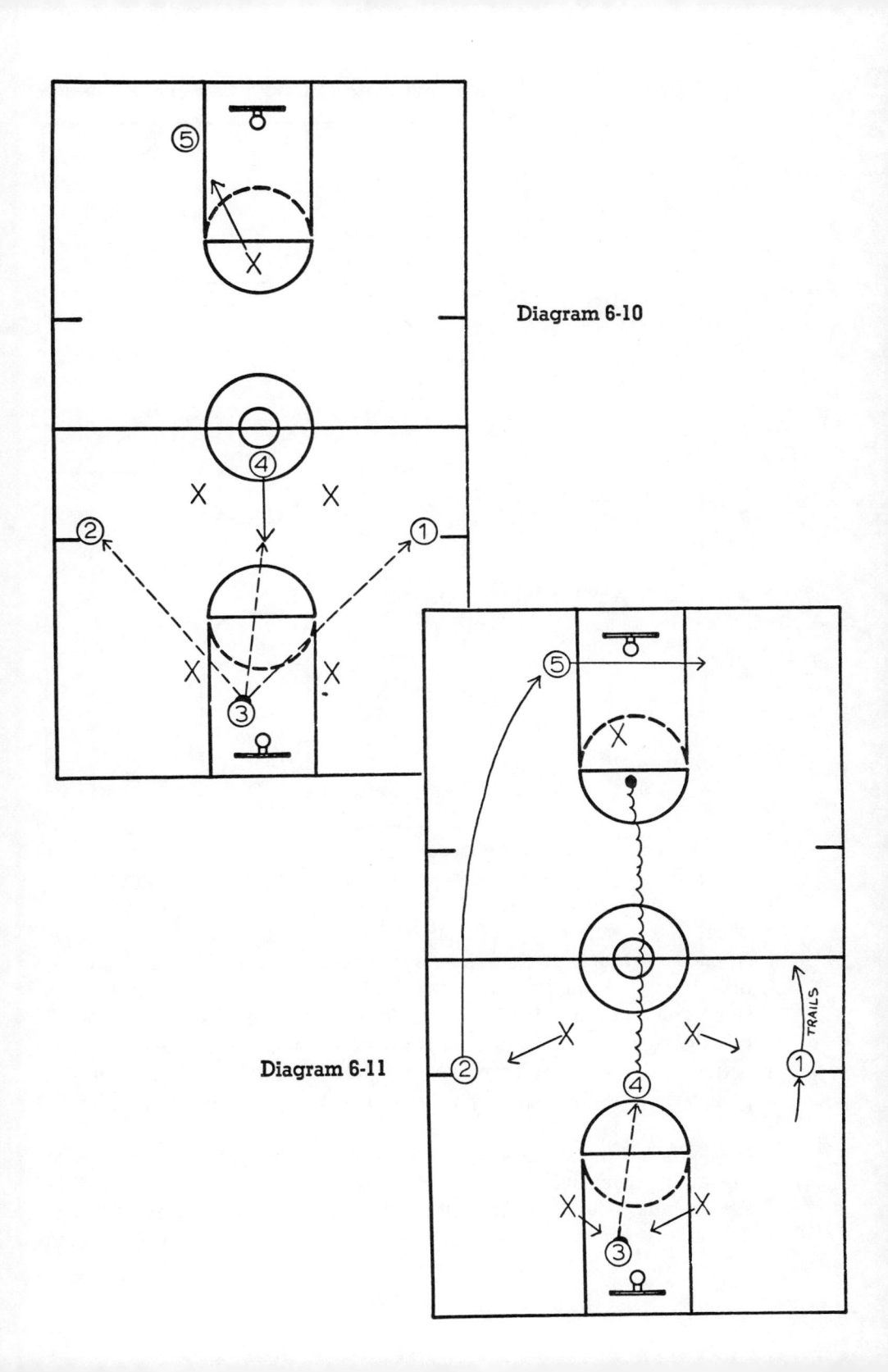

Diagram 6-10

Diagram 6-11

202 Centering Zone Presses with the All-Purpose Percentage Offense

Diagram 6-12

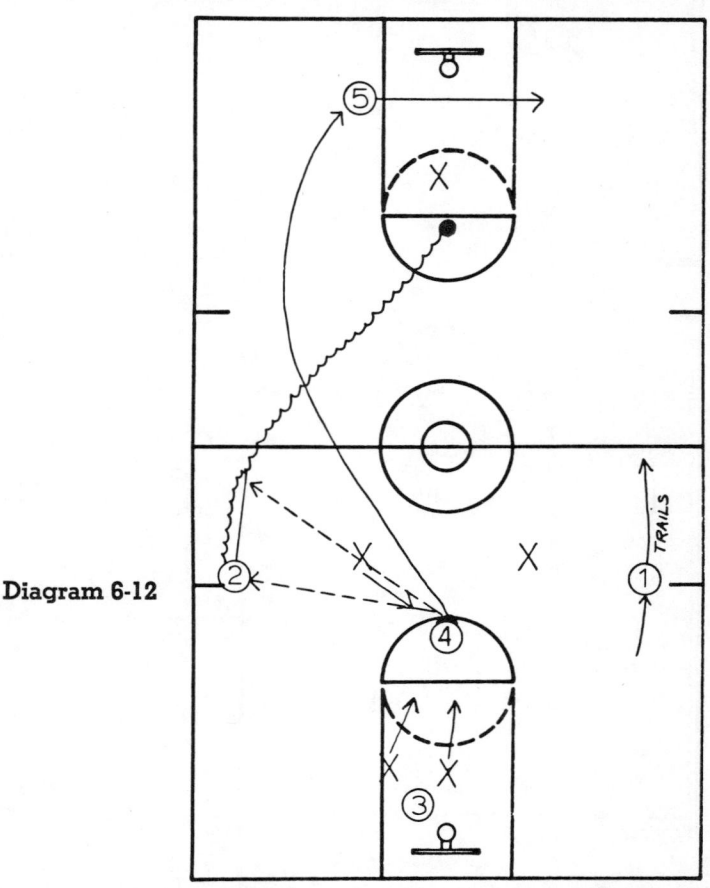

When the 4 man discovers that he cannot split the defense or make the pass to 2, then he must turn and look for the 1 man cutting down the right-side lane. This is an excellent adjustment technique when 2 is covered by the right defender and the middle man, 4, is stopped by the left-side defender. 1, upon getting the pass from 4, dribbles to the middle and down the lane, with the 2 man filling the right lane and 5 holding in the left lane. *Coaching Hint:* The reason 2 fills the right lane instead of 4 is that 2 is ahead of 4, and he is in a better position to get to the lane quicker than 4. 4 then trails the play, with 3 holding for defensive responsibility, as shown in Diagram 6-13.

When 3 finds that 4 is not open because he is covered by one of the middle defensive players, then 3 passes to the side of the court that the defender who is jamming the middle is on. In Diagram 6-14, it is 2 who is open to receive the pass from 3. 2 now has a Rule Two

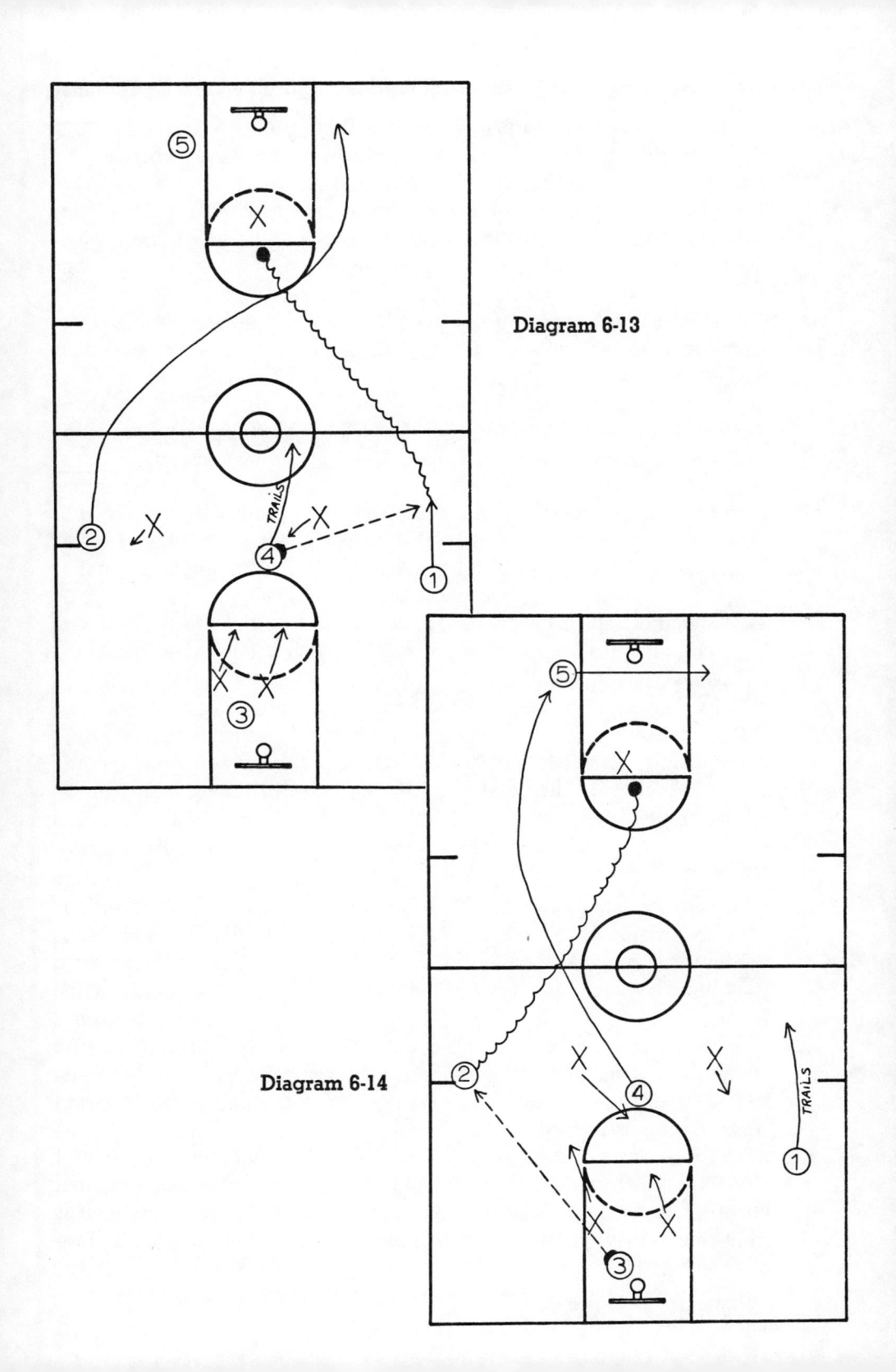

Diagram 6-13

Diagram 6-14

decision to make: Keep the ball and take it himself or pass to 4 cutting down the middle. Diagram 6-14 shows what takes place when 2 decides to keep the ball himself. 2 takes it into the middle lane and to the foul line, as 4 breaks to follow the momentum of his pass and fills the left lane. 5 moves over to the vacant lane as 2 approaches the top of the foul circle. 1 trails and 3 has defensive responsibility. *Coaching Hint:* Many times, especially against the 2-2-1 zone press, the last defender in the zone may move up to stop the dribble. When this happens, the dribbler should stop and feed the open man near the basket, as shown in Diagram 6-15.

When 2 decides to pass to 4 breaking down the middle lane, then 4 takes the ball to the foul line on the dribble as 1 fills the right lane and 5 holds in the left lane. 2 trails and 3 holds for defense (Diagram 6-16). *Coaching Hint:* It is wise to inform 2 that many times when he decides to bring the ball up on the dribble by himself, he may be forced to stop by a defender. In that case, the pass to 4 should be a little deeper than he would normally make it. 2 could actually make the pass to 4 as 4 enters the left lane, as shown in Diagram 6-17.

When 3 finds both 4 and 2 covered, then he must look for 1 on the right side. 3 passes to 1 and 1 has a Rule Two decision to make: Keep the ball himself and dribble it up or pass to 4 going down the middle. This is an excellent move because many times you can catch the zone leaning in the opposite direction. Diagram 6-18 shows 1 passing to 4, with 2 filling the left lane and 5 moving to the vacant lane. Diagram 6-19 has 1 keeping the ball and dribbling it up court, with 4 filling the right lane and 5 holding.

Combating Pressure on the Throw-In

As 3 breaks to receive the in-bounds pass from 1, the defensive man on his side of the court goes with him, trying to keep him from getting the ball. 3 then quickly steps out-of-bounds (remember, only after a score) and 1 passes the ball to 3 out-of-bounds. 4 then breaks to the middle following Rule Two, as he is still the opposite-side man from the ball at mid-court. 5 then breaks down court. 2 moves across to the left mid-court 3-foot mark immediately after seeing 3 step out-of-bounds. 1, who was taking the ball out originally, steps in-bounds immediately after passing to 3. Many times 1 will be open for the quick return pass from 3, as shown in Diagram 6-20.

If the pass goes to 4 in the middle, we run the regular pattern, but if it goes back to 1, then the 3 man who makes the pass cuts to the right-side 3-foot mid-court mark (Diagram 6-21 shows all the passing options that 1 has). *Coaching Hint:* After 1 decides who he is going to pass to, then we just follow the Two Rule Decision Play. The flexibil-

Diagram 6-15

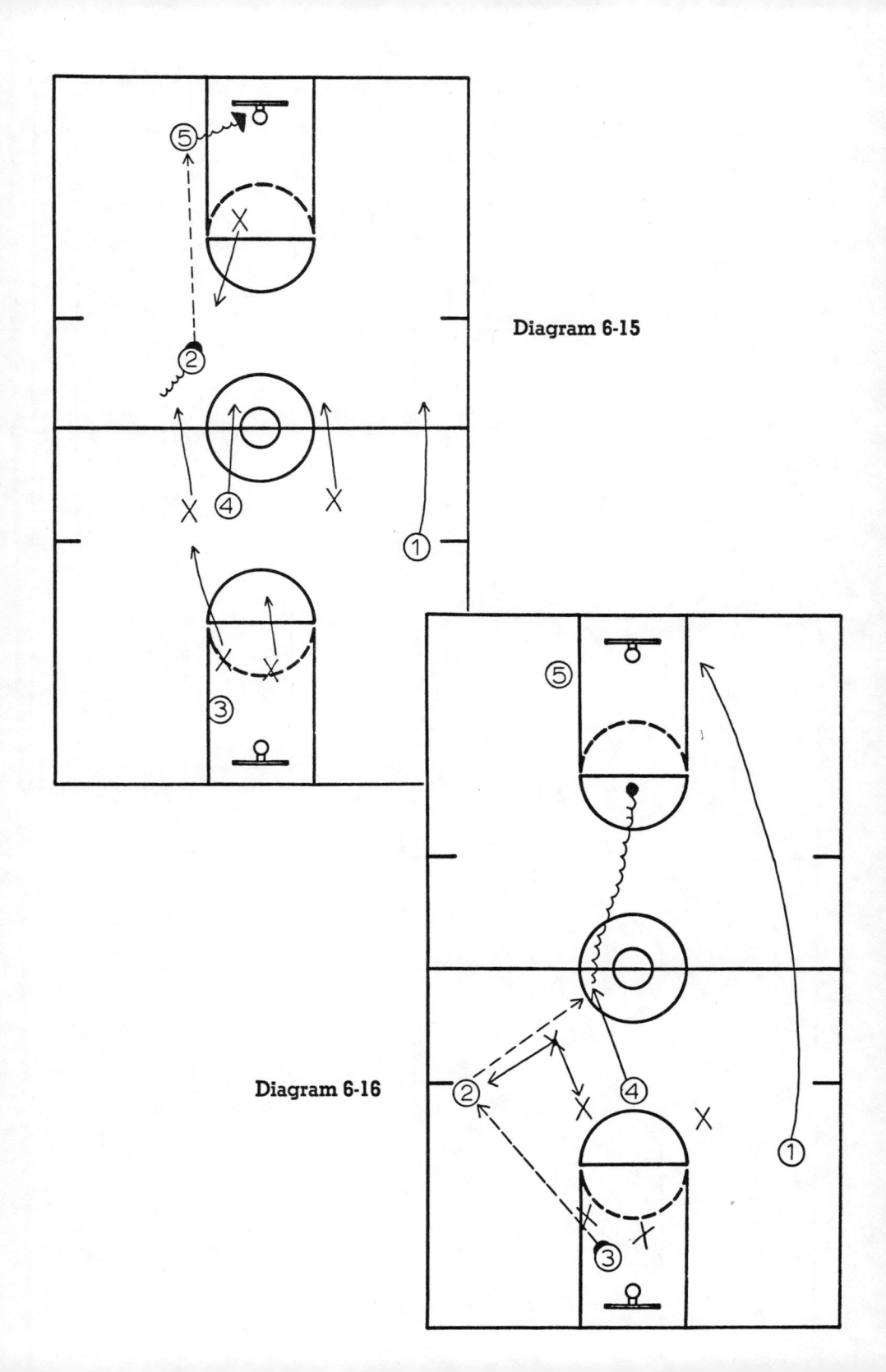

Diagram 6-16

Diagram 6-17

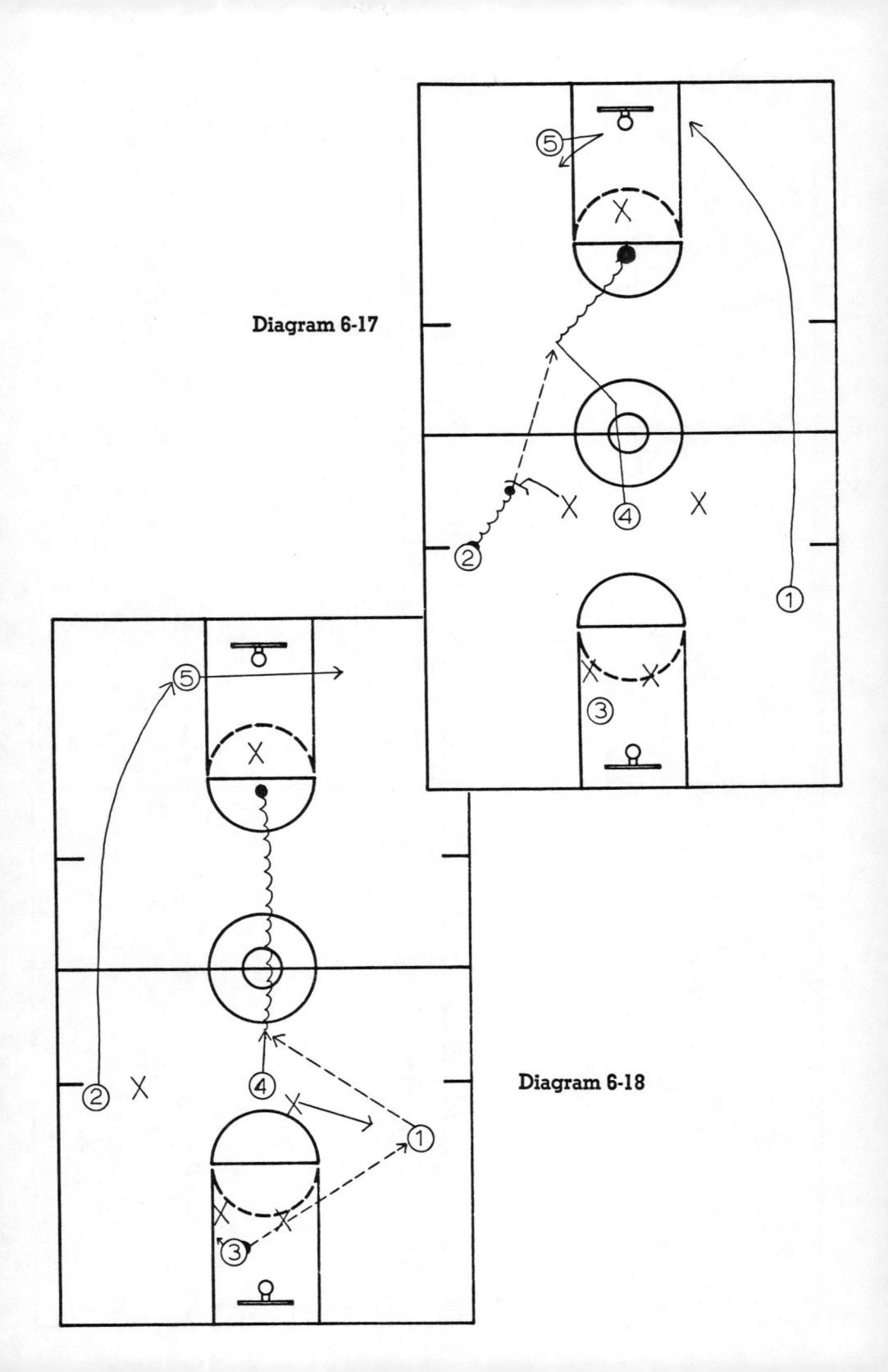

Diagram 6-18

Diagram 6-19

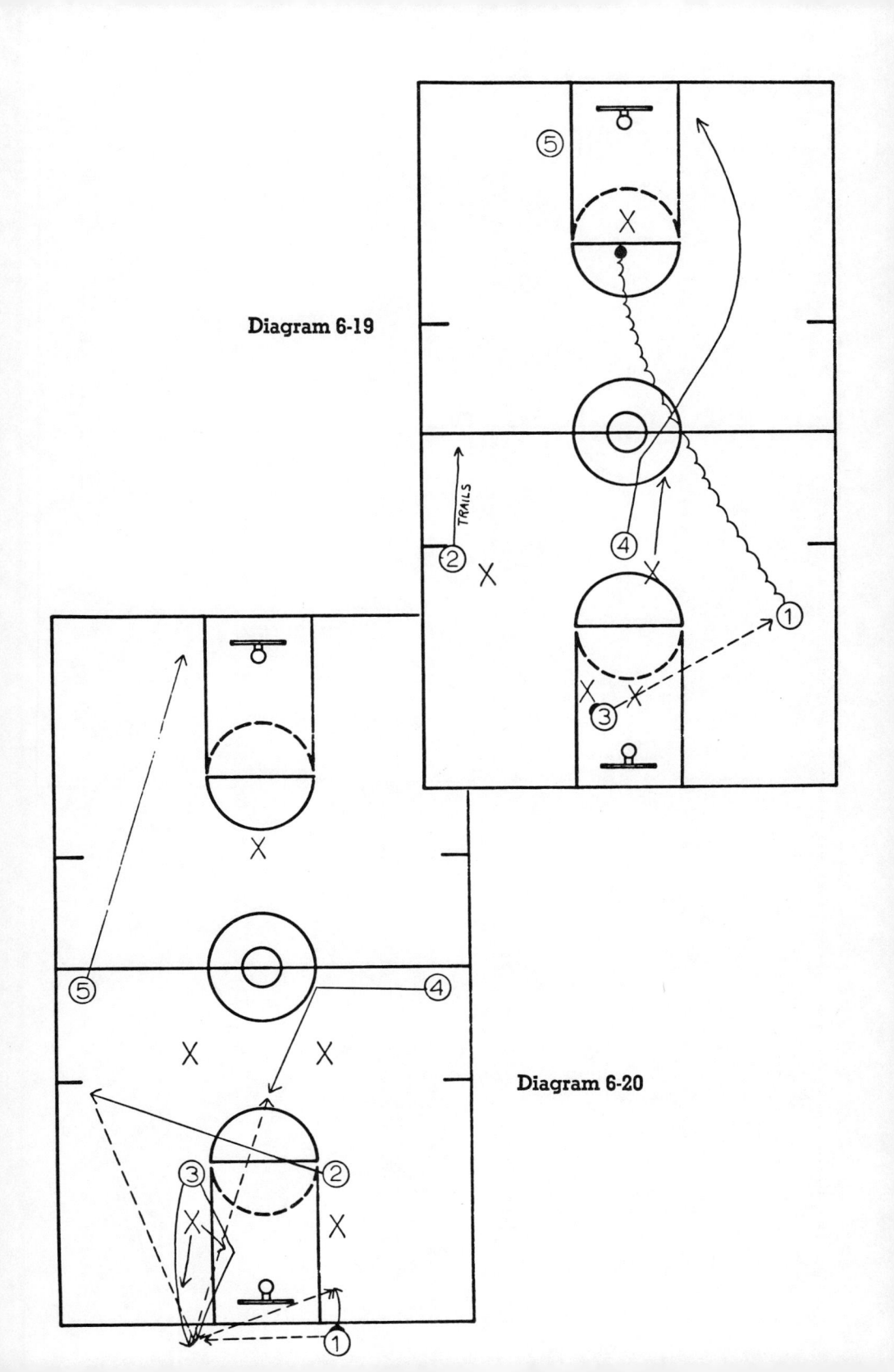

Diagram 6-20

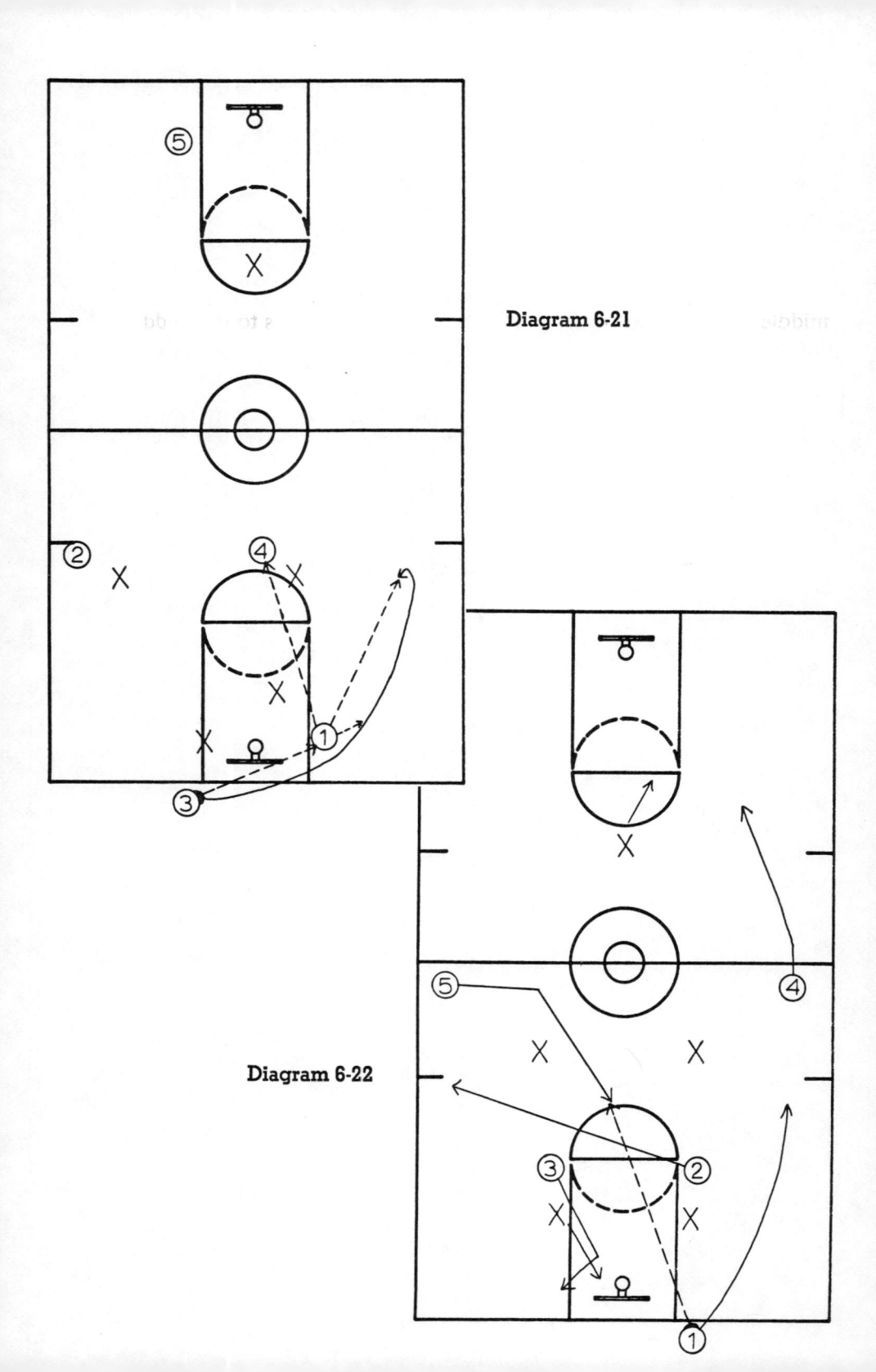

Diagram 6-21

Diagram 6-22

Centering Zone Presses with the All-Purpose Percentage Offense 209

ity this option offers when facing pressure on the throw-in usually discourages teams from trying to continue to apply this type of pressure, because there are too many holes to fill for the defense, and once the pass is gotten in-bounds, then the defense is really vulnerable.

If 3 does not step out-of-bounds and 1 cannot get the ball to him, then the man at mid-court opposite the side of the ball breaks to the middle to receive the pass. In this case, the 5 man breaks to the middle following the One Rule, and the 4 man moves up the floor. Now the offense is set up as 2 moves across to the left mid-court marker area, as shown in Diagram 6-22.

Screening the Zone Press on the Throw-In

Another adjustment maneuver that can be employed when the defensive man is playing so that 3 cannot get the ball is shown in Diagram 6-23. The 2 man moves over and sets a screen on the defensive man, who is denying the 3 man the in-bounds pass. 3 cuts off this screen to receive the pass and 2 continues on to the left-side 3-foot mid-court area mark. 4 breaks into the middle and the offense is ready to go once again. This is a very effective and easy technique to use to get the ball in-bounds. *Coaching Hint:* Remember that if the 1 man takes the ball out-of-bounds on the opposite side of the backboard, it has been shown in this series of plays that the options will be run the same, except that assignments just flip-flop sides of the floor. The men at mid-court must be kept fully aware of this. The man at mid-court on the opposite side of the ball, regardless of where the ball is (provided that it is below the foul line), must break to the middle when needed.

Attacking the Even-Front Half-Court Zone Presses

Whenever we face an even-front half-court zone press, we just use the full-court even-front attack with one slight adjustment. Diagram 6-24 shows the setup. The post man, 5, takes the ball out-of-bounds. He passes in to 1. 2 and 3 station themselves at mid-court in our own back court even with the outside circle of the center jump area. 4 is at the foul line in the front court. After 5 passes to 1, he moves down the floor and tries to sneak in behind the defense at the base-line area on the same side he took the ball out on. 1, after receiving 5's pass, dribbles up court. Once 1 gets even with the mid-court area in the back court between the 3-foot area markers (he must be on one side of the court, not in the middle), we run the same attack as we would when facing the full-court even-front press. The wing man

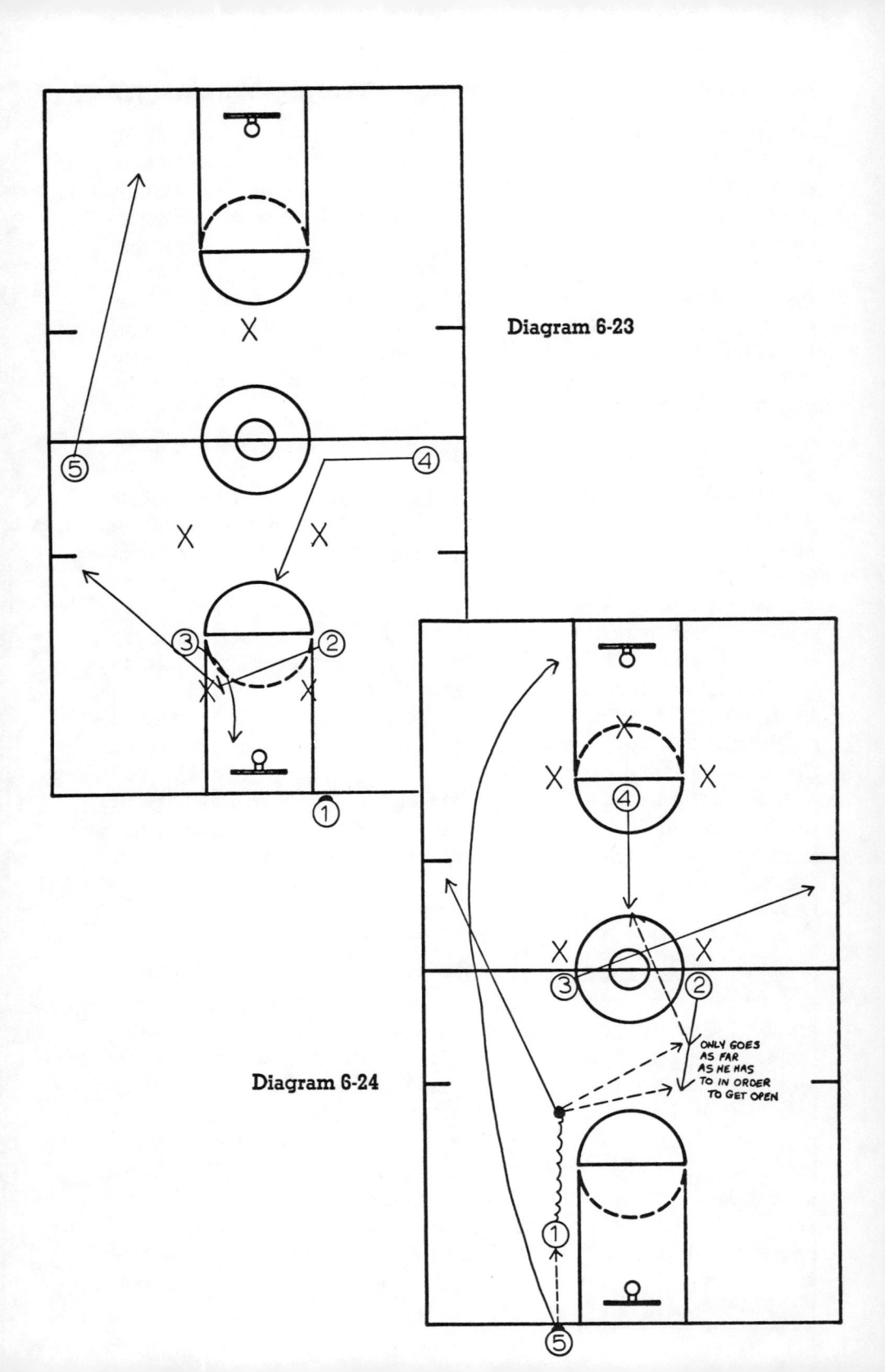

Diagram 6-23

Diagram 6-24

ONLY GOES
AS FAR
AS HE HAS
TO IN ORDER
TO GET OPEN

Centering Zone Presses with the All-Purpose Percentage Offense 211

opposite the side of the ball breaks to get the ball. The remaining wing man, 3 in this situation, moves to the right-side 3-foot mid-court mark in our front court, and 1 goes to the left 3-foot mid-court mark in our front court. 4 breaks up the middle to try to get the pass from 2, who has the ball between the top of our foul circle and the outside circle of the center jump circle. Diagram 6-25 shows 2 feeding 4 in the middle. 1 and 3 fill the outside lanes and 4 takes the ball to the foul line. 4 may shoot or pass to either 1, 3 or 5. 5 may be the man who is open if the defense forgets about him. If 5 can time his move down court (after taking it out), he may be able to get behind the defense without them realizing it. Usually the back two men of the even-front press will be watching the outside lane men, and 5 may be able to slip by them as 4 brings the ball to the foul line.

If 2 cannot feed 4 in the middle, then he may pass to either 1 or 3. Diagram 6-26 shows 2 passing to 3. 3 then has a Two Rule decision to make: Pass the ball to 4 in the middle or dribble it to the middle himself. In Diagram 6-26, 3 passes to 4 and 4 moves to the foul line,

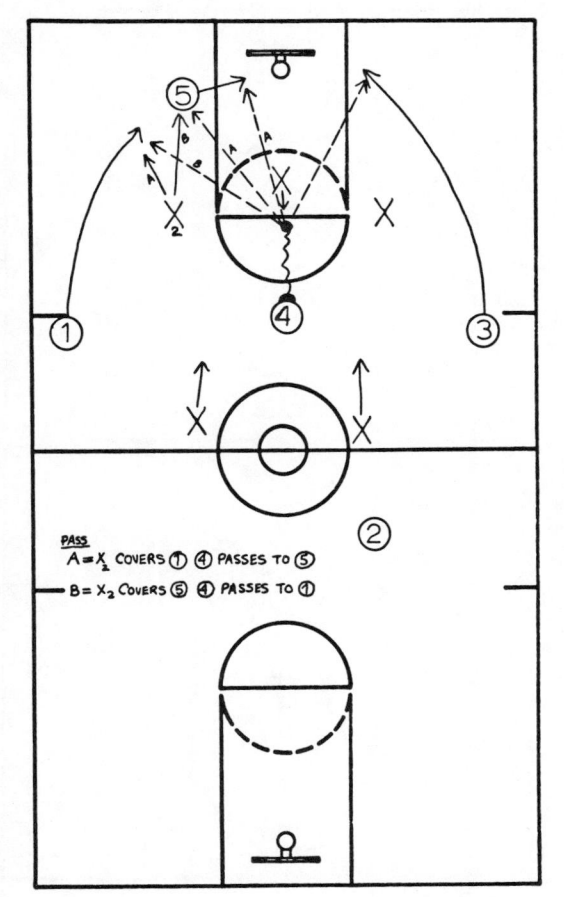

Diagram 6-25

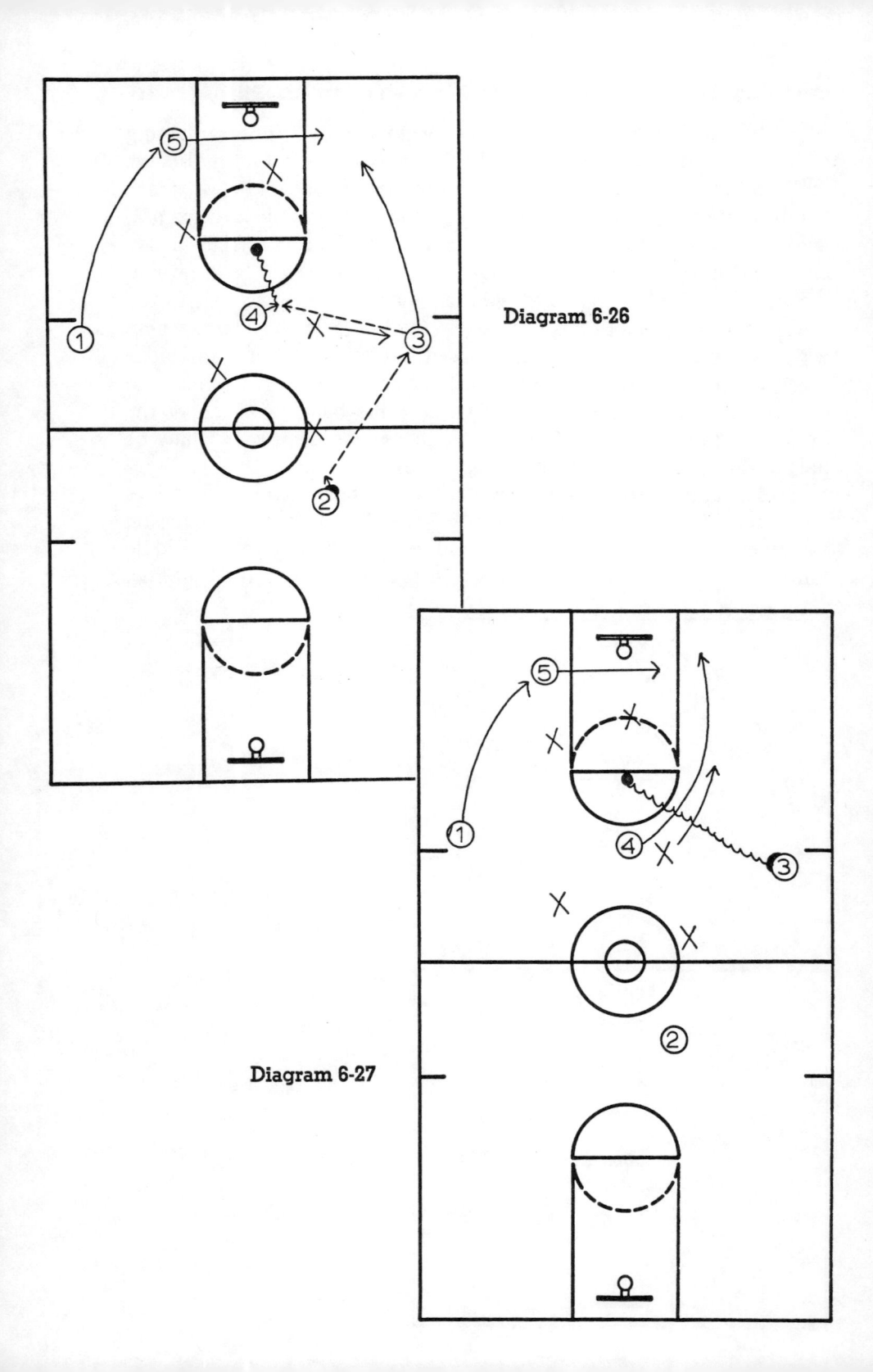

Diagram 6-26

Diagram 6-27

Centering Zone Presses with the All-Purpose Percentage Offense   213

looking to shoot or pass to 1, 3 or 5. Diagram 6-27 shows 3 keeping the ball and taking it to the middle on the dribble, himself. 4 fills the right lane as soon as he sees 3 start to the middle on the dribble. 1 fills the left lane and 5 moves across the base-line area. 2 can shoot or pass as soon as he gets to the foul line.

We have found that this offense works as well against a half-court zone press as it does when it is used full-court.

Centering the Odd-Front Full-Court and Half-Court Zone Presses with the Auxiliary Formation

The method of attacking both the 1-2-2 and 1-3-1 full-court zone presses is the same because both of these presses are odd-front zone defenses. Diagram 6-28 shows the formation that is used when facing these two zone presses. The 1 man takes the ball out on the end line on either side of the backboard, even with the key line extended. The 2 man is on the foul line; the 3 and 4 men are at mid-court near the

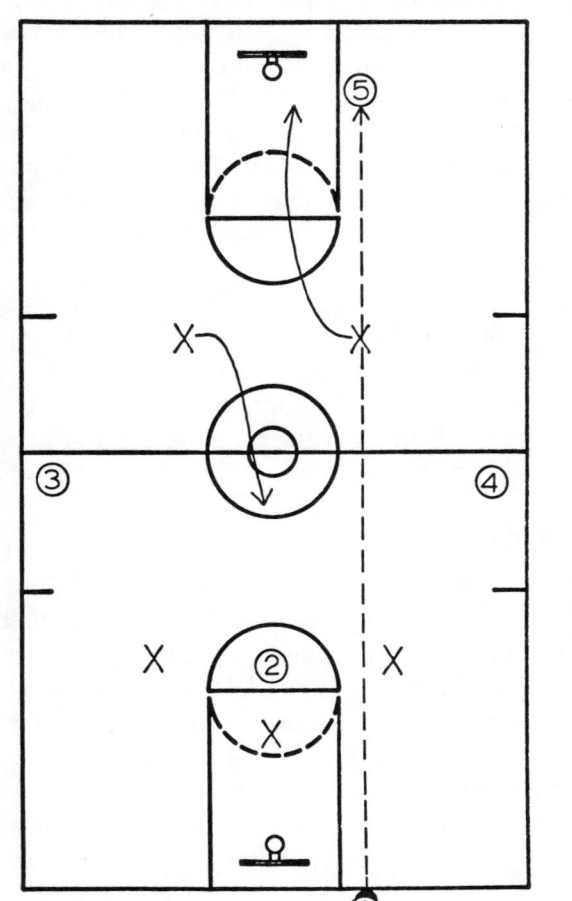

Diagram 6-28

sidelines in the back court. The 5 man positions himself in front of the basket even with the key line, on the same side of the floor as the man (1 man in this situation) taking the ball out-of-bounds in the back court. This formation is sort of a staggered 2-3 setup.

Forcing the 1-2-2 Press into a 1-3-1 Press Formation

By keeping the 5 man deep, it automatically forces the team in a 1-2-2 zone press formation into a 1-3-1 formation. Diagram 6-28 shows how the long pass from 1 to 5 will result in an easy score if the zone did not send a man back to cover the deep man. The offensive 5 man dropping back from the back line of a 1-2-2 zone press automatically forces the press into a 1-3-1 formation, opening up the middle of the court for the offense.

Objective of the Odd-Front Zone Press Offense from the Auxiliary Formation

The main objective of this offense is to get the ball to the middle of the court, keep it there at all times and go to the hoop for a score, just as we do when we are facing the even-front full-court presses. As we have mentioned before, many times teams feel satisfied that they have gotten the ball safely across the center line and slow down, allowing the defense to get back and reorganize. Once the ball has reached the middle of the court and gone across the 10-second line, the offense should try to score the easy percentage shot by achieving the 3-on-1 or 3-on-2 situation.

Since most odd-front full-court zone presses allow the pass from out-of-bounds and then trap the man with the ball when he puts it on the floor (with the dribble, or they pressure the next potential receivers), getting the ball to the center of the court as soon as possible eliminates one of the strongest parts of any zone press—the trap in the back court.

Positioning the Ball to the Middle Lane

First, as we do with all our full-court press offenses, the defense should be allowed to set up its press formation. This assures us that each of the offensive players are in their preassigned spots, as shown in Diagram 6-4. Rule One, Diagram 6-6, must be adhered to at all times by the 3 and 4 men stationed at mid-court on the sidelines. The man at mid-court on the opposite side from the ball must break to the middle of the court in the direction of the foul line to receive the pass from 1 or 2. The man should break only as far as he has to in order to

Centering Zone Presses with the All-Purpose Percentage Offense 215

get the ball, but he must be heading toward the middle to meet the pass.

Diagram 6-29 has 1 taking the ball out and 2 breaking to his own left (he may break either way at his own discretion) to receive the uncontested pass-in from 1. After 2 receives the pass, he does not dribble, but instead pivots and faces mid-court. This is an important technique. The man who receives the ball at any time or any place on the court should always pivot first and then dribble. Now the man at

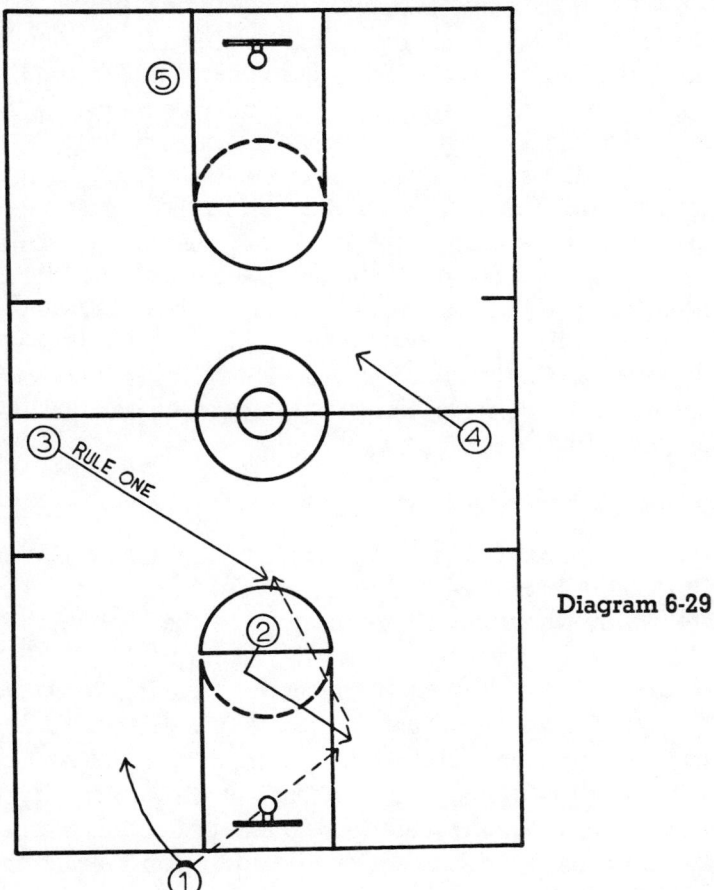

Diagram 6-29

mid-court on the opposite side of the court from the ball, the 3 man, breaks to the middle to receive the pass from 2. The 3 man has completed Rule One.

The 3 Man's Decision

At this point, the 3 man has a decision to make. This decision for the man with the ball in the middle lane is Rule Two, and Diagrams 6-

30, 6-31 and 6-32 show Rule Two. The 3 man must make his decision to keep the ball and bring it up on the dribble or pass to 4 and let 4 bring it up. The 1 man, after making his in-bounds pass to 2, steps in-bounds and goes to the other side of the court, staying even with the 2 man. 1 will become the trailer on the break. *Coaching Hint:* The 3 man's decision, either to keep the ball or pass to the cutting 4 man, will be based on the action of the middle defensive man of the 1-3-1 press. Diagram 6-30 shows the defender dropping back to pick up the 4 man cutting. When 3 sees this, he quickly brings the ball up himself and the 4 man continues his cut, filling the lane to his left; the 5 man holds. The man with the ball will bring it to the foul line on the dribble and then stop at the foul line for the 3-on-1 or 3-on-2 situation. The 1 man trails the play and 2 has defensive responsibility.

Diagram 6-31 shows the middle defender in the zone press moving up to cover the 3 man, who has the ball in the middle lane. This forces 3 to pass to 4, who is cutting to the middle at a sharp angle. 4 then brings the ball down the middle on the dribble and the 3 man fills the lane to his right; the 5 man moves over to fill the vacant left lane. *Coaching Hint:* 3 goes to the lane to his right because his pass to 4 will be to the right side of the court; thus, his body momentum from the pass will carry him in that direction, and he will save valuable time in following his pass.

4 Man's Cutting Angle Keyed on the Middle Defender

Coaching Hint: The 4 man's cutting angle to the middle lane is on an angle directly in line with the left corner. The angle of this cut will be determined by where the middle defender of the zone press is positioned. If the defender moves up to cover 3 who has the ball, 4 will make his cut on the angle straight to the corner, looking to receive the pass as he cuts, as shown in Diagram 6-32. If the defender drops back to cover 4 cutting, then 4 cuts to the middle, but he must make his cut sharper, in order to clear the defender out of the area. This allows the 4 man to come up the middle or be in a position to receive the pass from 3 if the defender jams the middle up to stop 3. Diagram 6-33 illustrates this point.

The 3 man may find that after he has started his dribble up the middle, the middle defender of the zone press may then come up to stop him. If this happens, 3 must stop immediately and make the pass to 4 a delayed one. *Coaching Hint:* Players bringing the ball up court on the dribble in the middle lane must be reminded to look up the court as they dribble. A good rule to follow in a situation where the

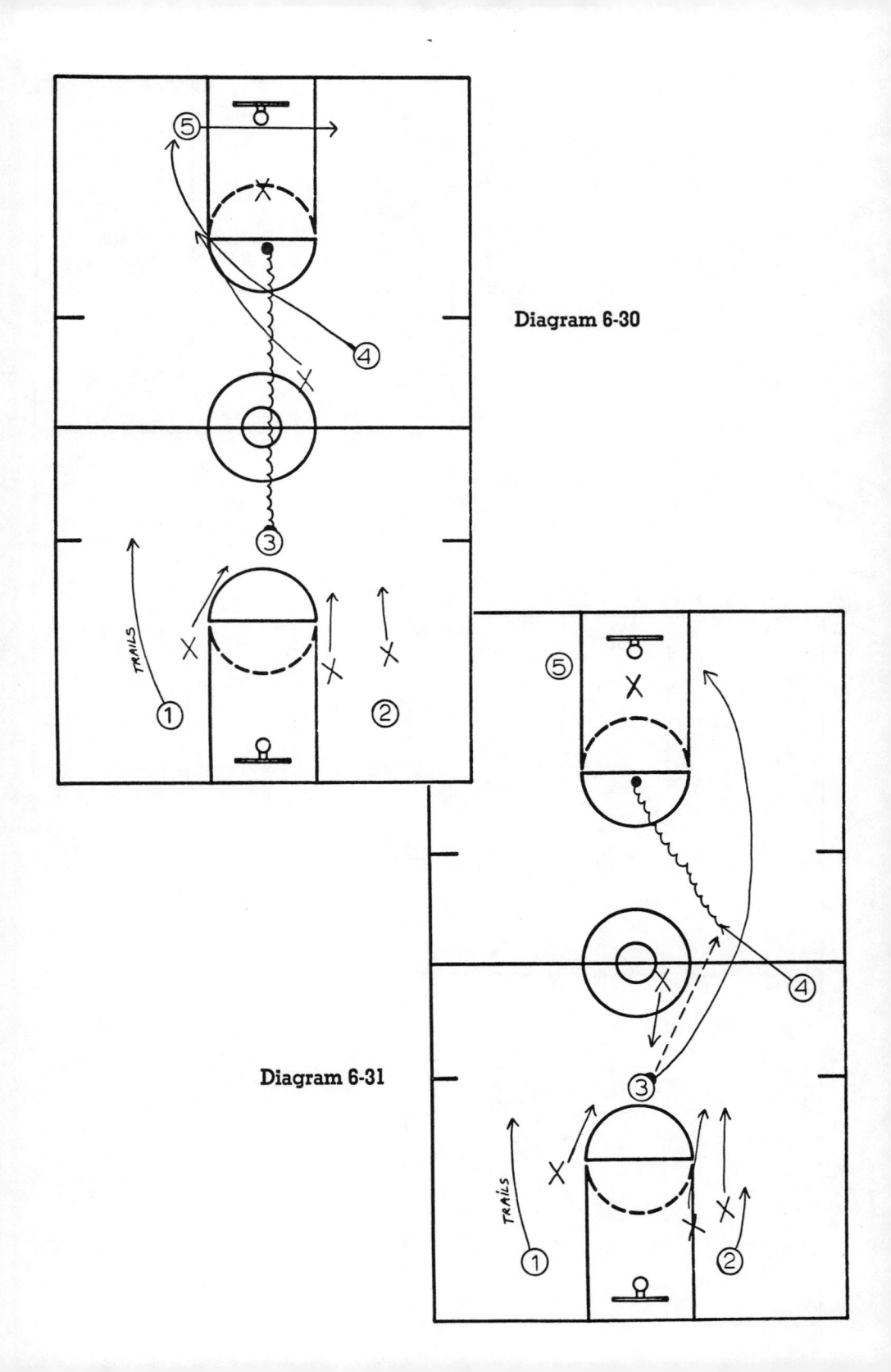

Diagram 6-30

Diagram 6-31

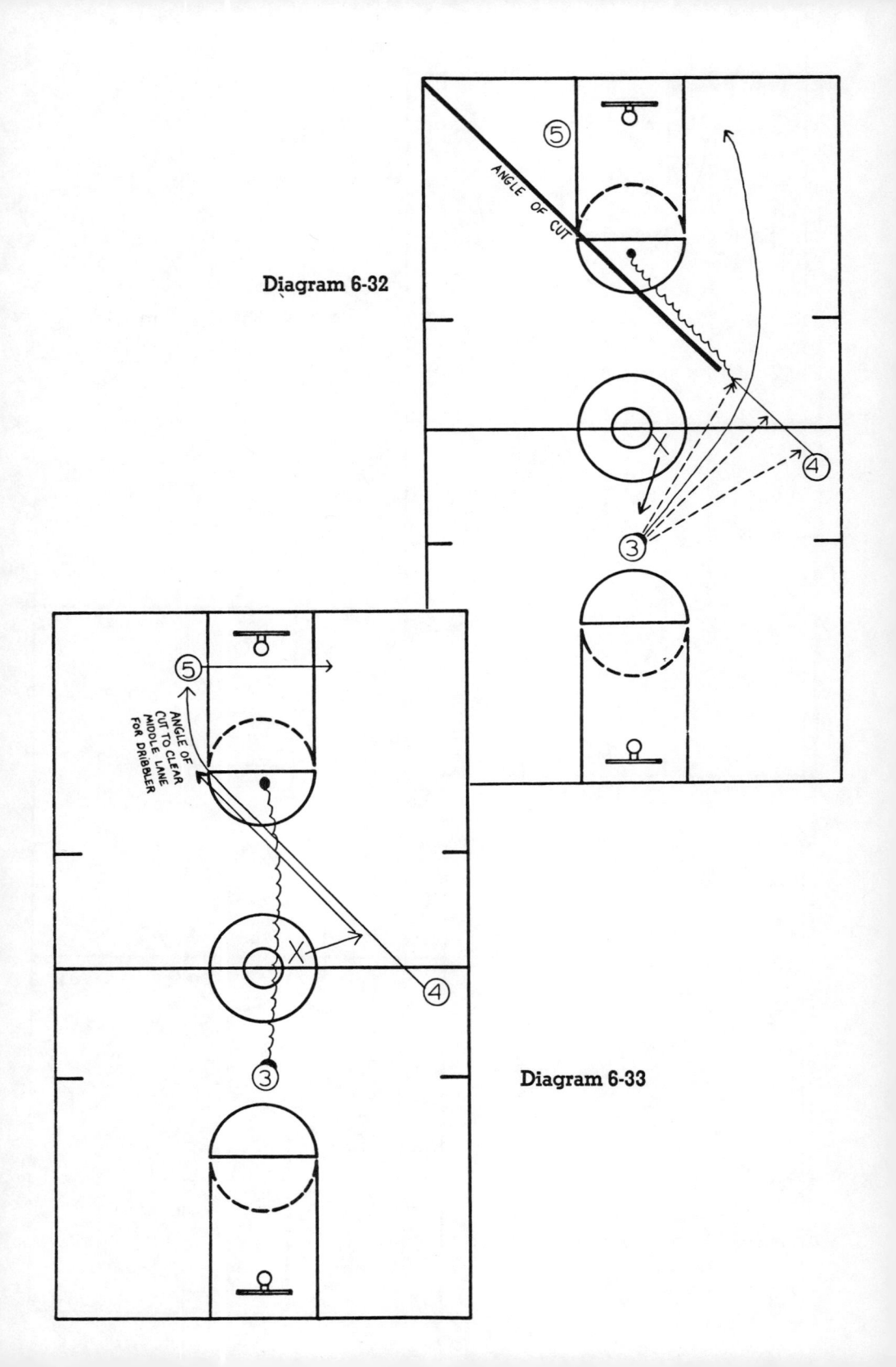

Diagram 6-32

Diagram 6-33

Centering Zone Presses with the All-Purpose Percentage Offense 219

middle man has started his dribble, and then is forced to slow down or stop as the defender comes out to meet him, is that he should not pass to the cutter until the defender is closer to the dribbler than he is to the cutter. Diagram 6-34 illustrates this point. Usually when the middle defender moves up to meet the dribble, the end result will be a 2-on-1 situation instead of a 3-on-2 play, because the 3 man and the middle defender of the zone cannot get back into the front court to be factors in the play. However, it is good to remember that the 3 man may beat the middle defender and come into the pattern as a trailer if the 2-on-1 break is not successful, as shown in Diagram 6-35.

Safety Outlet Pass

If the man with the ball in the middle lane cannot dribble down the middle lane or he cannot hit the 4 man cutting to the middle lane,

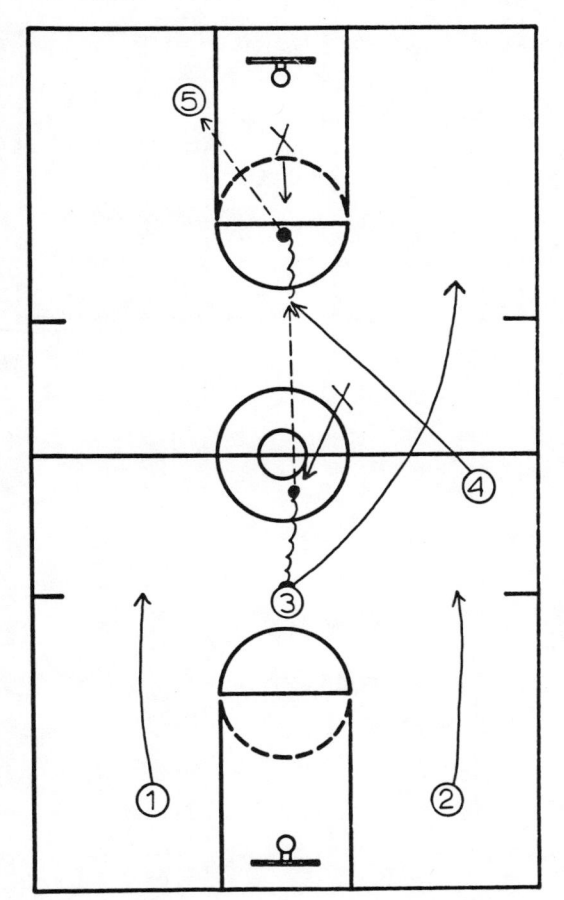

Diagram 6-34

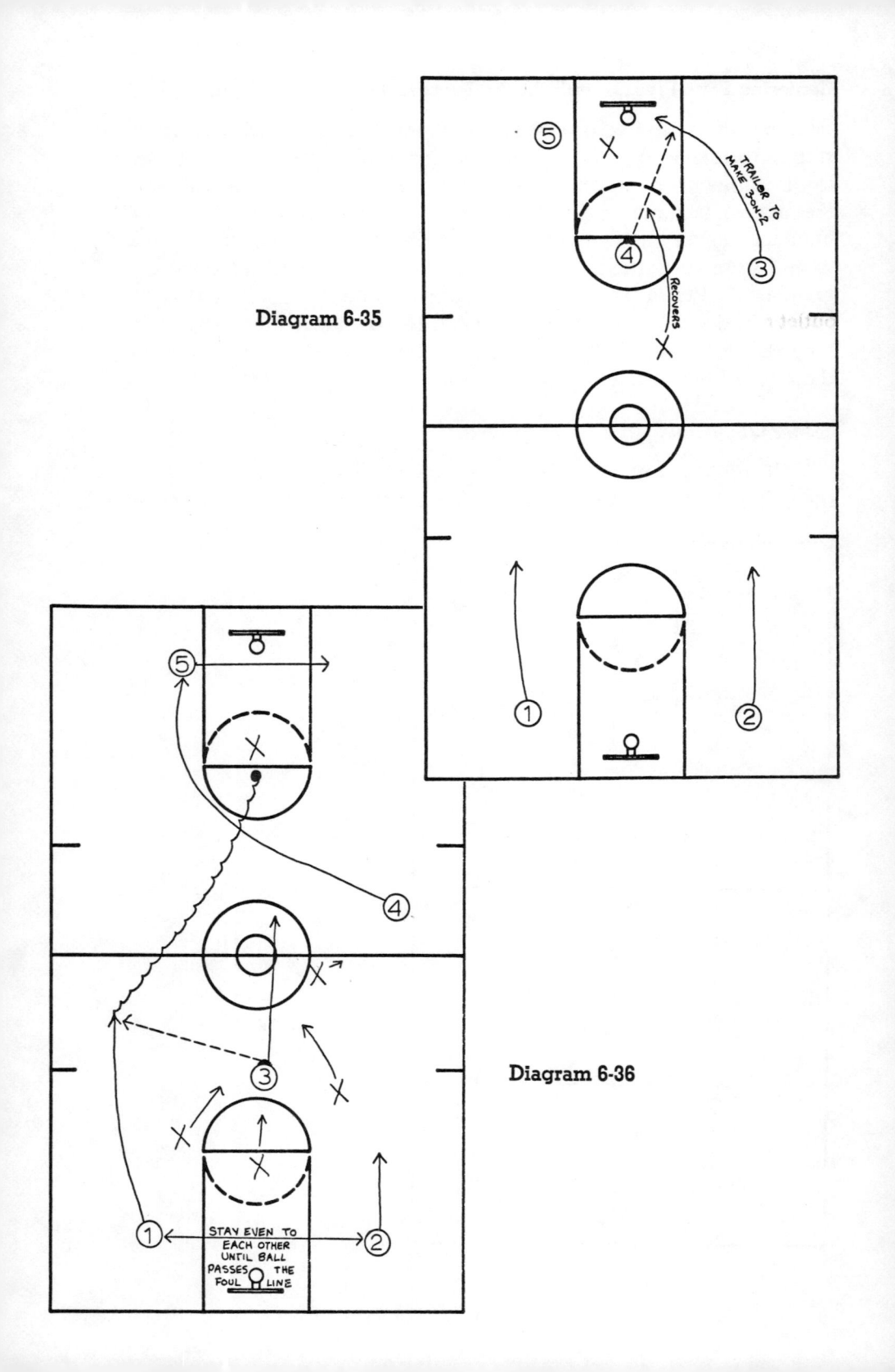

Diagram 6-35

Diagram 6-36

Centering Zone Presses with the All-Purpose Percentage Offense 221

then he does have a safety outlet pass that can be made to the 1 man who is cutting up the left lane. *Coaching Hint:* Remember that 1, after making his pass in-bounds to 2, is required to move to the opposite side of the court from 2 and stay even with 2 until 2 passes the ball to the 3 man in the middle lane. As soon as the pass is on its way from 2 to 3, the 1 man starts up court to be the trailer. However, if 3 cannot get rid of the ball or bring it up himself, then the 1 man is the safety outlet man.

Diagram 6-36 illustrates what happens when 3 passes to 1, who is cutting up the left lane. 1 dribbles the ball into the middle lane, with 4 and 5 filling the outside lanes. 3 becomes the trailer and 2 has defensive responsibility. This maneuver has been very effective when the defenders start to anticipate the play to the middle (after they have seen it run several times) and feel they have the play diagnosed. This is an excellent adjustment technique designed to catch the defense off guard and going in the wrong direction

Sideline-to-Middle Option

This is another adjustment technique that can be used when the offensive team cannot get the ball to the middle from the 1 or 2 men. Defensive teams will start to jam the middle after the offense has scored a few easy points against the press by getting the ball to the middle from the back court to the front court. The 2 man cannot get the ball to the middle lane to 3. At this point, the 2 man has two choices: He may either pass to 1 on the other side of the court or he may pass to 4 at the sideline near the center line, as shown in Diagram 6-37.

Diagram 6-38 shows the pass to the 4 man at the mid-court sideline position. When this occurs, 3, who was in the middle lane near the foul line circle, breaks down the middle lane, and the 4 man now has a Rule Two decision to make. If he cannot pass to the cutting 3 man, he keeps the ball and dribbles into the middle himself, with 3 and 5 filling the outside lanes. If 4 passes to 3 cutting down the middle, then 3 dribbles the ball right down the pike and the 4 man fills the right lane. Again, the 3-on-2 situation is in effect, as shown in Diagram 6-39. *Coaching Hint:* Remember that in using Rule Two, it is going to be the middle defender of the zone press who is going to be the determining factor in 4's passing to 3 cutting, or keeping the ball himself. *Coaching Hint:* The 5 man always fills the vacant lane because he has the least amount of distance to cover and he can see the whole play develop. As shown in Diagram 6-39, when 5 sees the left

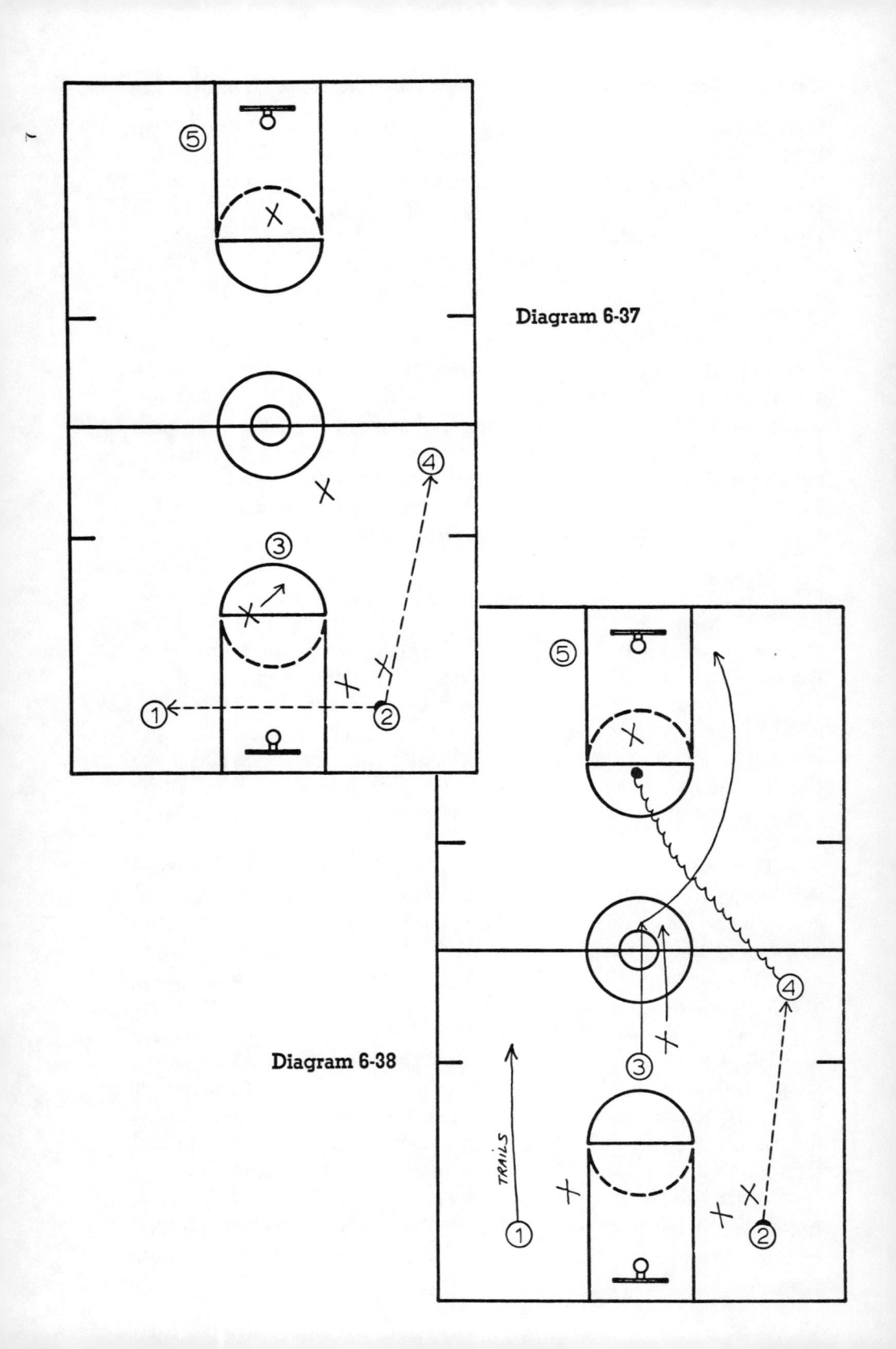

Diagram 6-37

Diagram 6-38

Centering Zone Presses with the All-Purpose Percentage Offense 223

Diagram 6-39

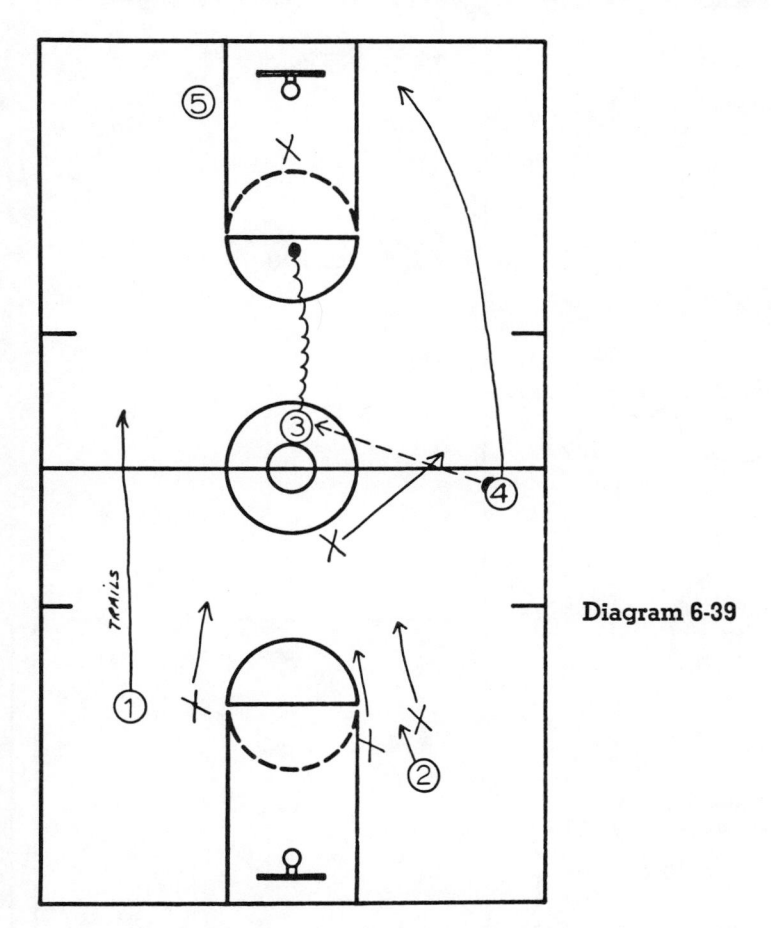

lane is not filled, he moves across the bucket to fill the left lane as 4 comes down the right lane and 3 brings the ball to the foul line.

Cross-Court Pass Option

When the 2 man finds both 3 and 4 are covered, then he can make a return pass cross-court to the 1 man, who is stationed there even with 2. *Coaching Hint:* This is why the 1 man is told to stay even with the 2 man until 2 has released the ball to either 3 or 4. When the 3 man in the middle sees the return pass from 2 to 1, he immediately returns to his original spot at the mid-court sideline position. The 4 man now follows Rule One by breaking to the middle to look for the pass from 1, because he is now the man at mid-court on the opposite side of the court from the ball. In Diagram 6-40, the 1 man passes to the 4 man in the middle lane, and now the 4 man has a Rule Two decision to make as 3 cuts to the middle lane on an angle to the right corner.

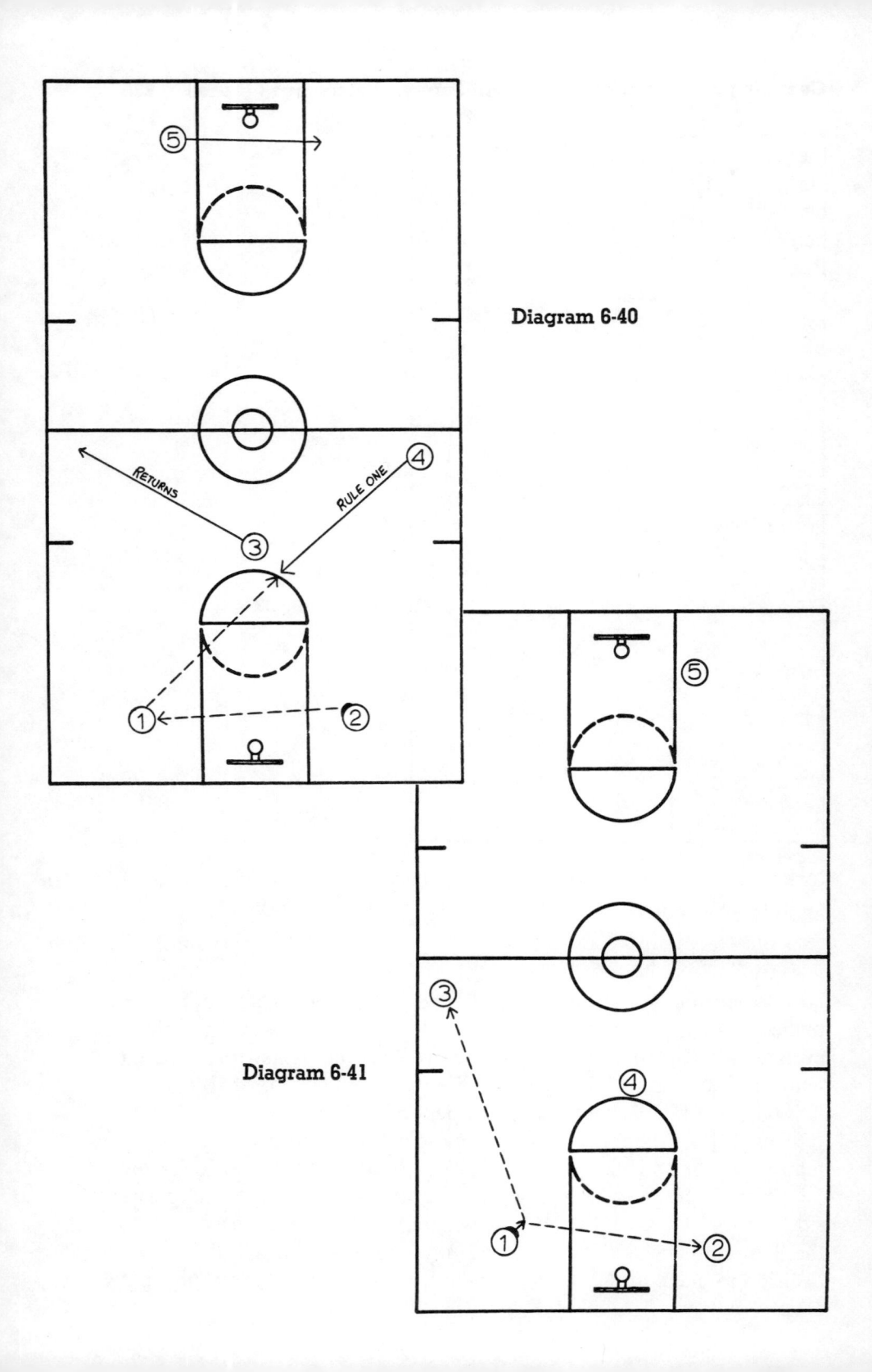

Diagram 6-40

Diagram 6-41

Centering Zone Presses with the All-Purpose Percentage Offense 225

Coaching Hint: Diagram 6-41 shows the safety valve outlets that the 1 man has if he cannot get the ball to the 4 man in the middle lane. He can use the sideline-to-the-middle option by passing to the 3 man near mid-court at the sideline, or he can make a return pass to 2, who has stayed even with 1, thereby using the Cross-Court Return Pass Play. Of course, if 1 passes back to 2, then 4 moves back to his original mid-court sideline spot, and 3 breaks to the middle again following Rule One.

Combating Pressure on the Throw-In

When the full-court zone press defense puts pressure directly on the man who is taking the ball out-of-bounds and tries to discourage the pass-in, then the following adjustment technique should be used: The 1 man, who is taking the ball out, still tries to get the pass to 2, even though both men are being closely guarded. If the pass from 1 to 2 is impossible, then the mid-court man on the opposite side of the ball (following Rule One) breaks into the middle lane toward the foul circle to receive the pass from 1. *Coaching Hint:* 4 only goes as far as necessary to get the ball. Once he has received the pass from 1, he pivots—and now he has a Rule Two decision to make. Diagram 6-42 has the man taking the ball out-of-bounds to the left of his own backboard, to illustrate the play going to the other side, in contrast to previous diagrams in this chapter.

Diagram 6-43 shows the safety valve options the 1 man has if he cannot get the ball to the 4 man (cutting into the middle lane at the foul circle). These safety-valve outlet options are the same as when the 1 man had the ball in-bounds. He may pass to 3 at the mid-court sideline position, or he can look for the 2 man, who has stepped out-of-bounds to avoid his defender. *Coaching Hint:* Of course, 2 may only step out-of-bounds to receive the pass after a score. When the pass goes to the 2 man out-of-bounds, then the 1 man immediately steps in-bounds and the 4 man returns to his original position near mid-court at the sideline. The 3 man, following Rule One, would break to the middle toward the foul circle, as shown in Diagram 6-44.

Attacking the Odd-Front Half-Court Zone Presses

We employ the Auxiliary Offense 2-3 Formation when facing the odd-front half-court zone press, and we run this exactly like we do full-court, except for one slight variation. 1 and 2 bring the ball up and both stay even with each other. The 5 man positions himself at the foul line and makes sure that he moves over to the point where the

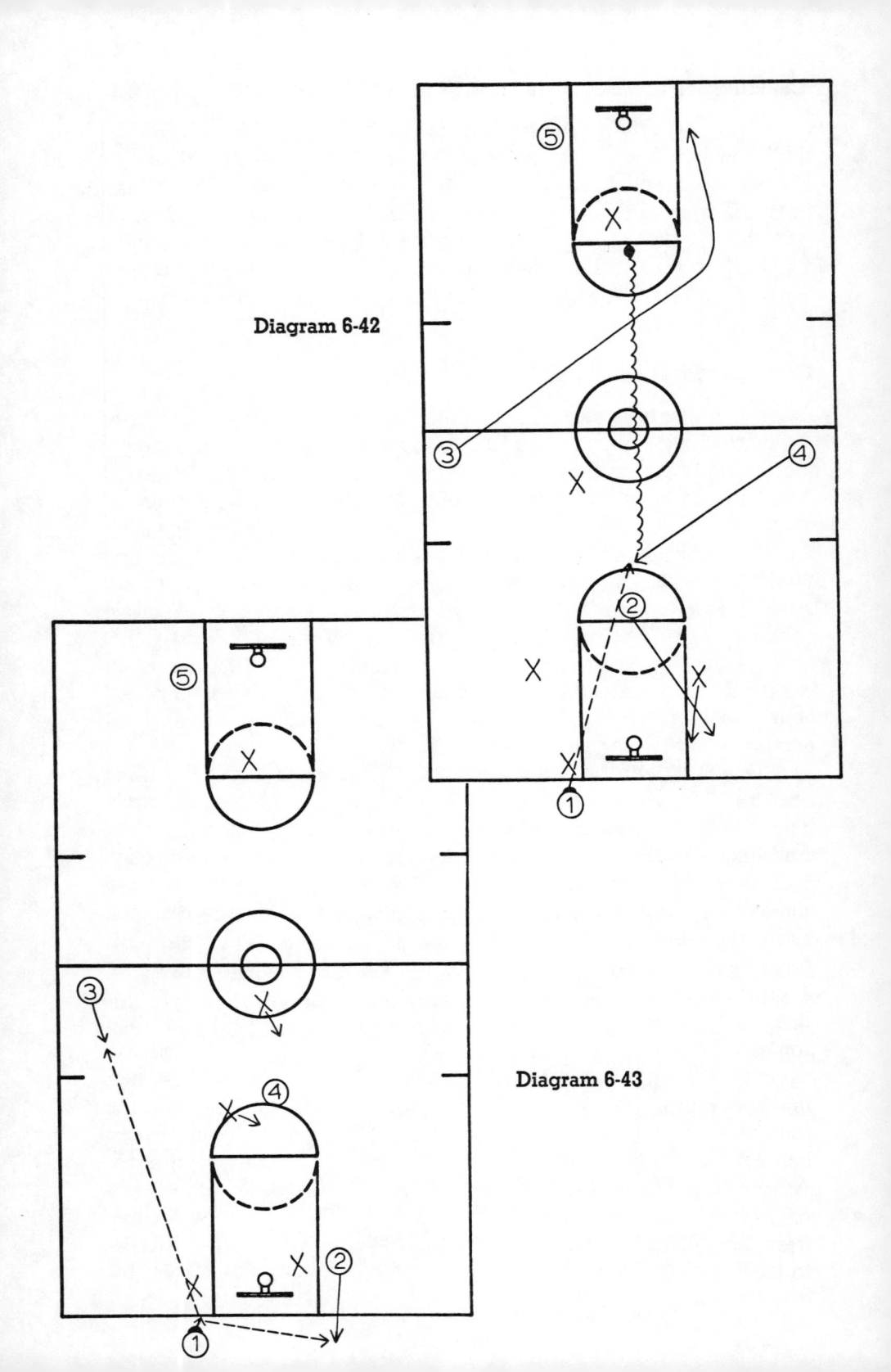

Diagram 6-42

Diagram 6-43

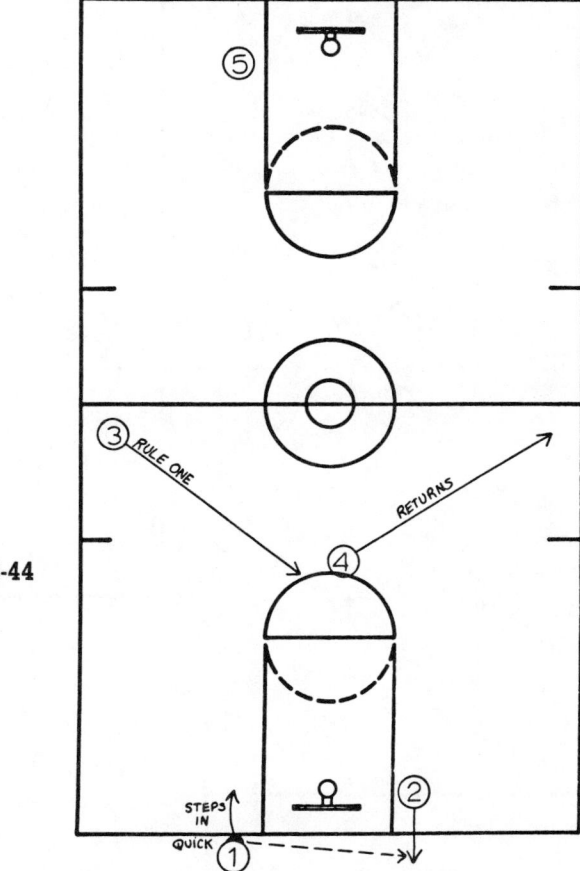

Centering Zone Presses with the All-Purpose Percentage Offense 227

Diagram 6-44

foul line and the key line meet, on the same side of the floor that the ball is on. If the guards exchange the ball, then 5 must move over to the ball side. The 3 and 4 men position themselves even with the foul line and about 3 feet from the sideline on their side of the court. This formation for half-court odd-front defenses is shown in Diagram 6-45. 1 brings the ball up and stops dribbling before he gets to the center line. He holds the ball over his head. The opposite man even with the foul line from the ball (Rule One in the Full-Court Zone Press Offense again) breaks to the middle to receive the pass from 1. It is the 4 man in this situation, as he is the man opposite the ball who is even with the foul line. 1 passes to 4, who is in the middle of the court somewhere between the foul circle and the outside circle of the center jump area. As soon as 4 receives the pass from 1, he pivots and faces the basket. 5 rolls off the high-post position to the same side of the court 4 came from, and 3 breaks to the left-side base-line low-post area. 4 dribbles to the foul line and the 3-on-2 situation develops again. If 4 cannot

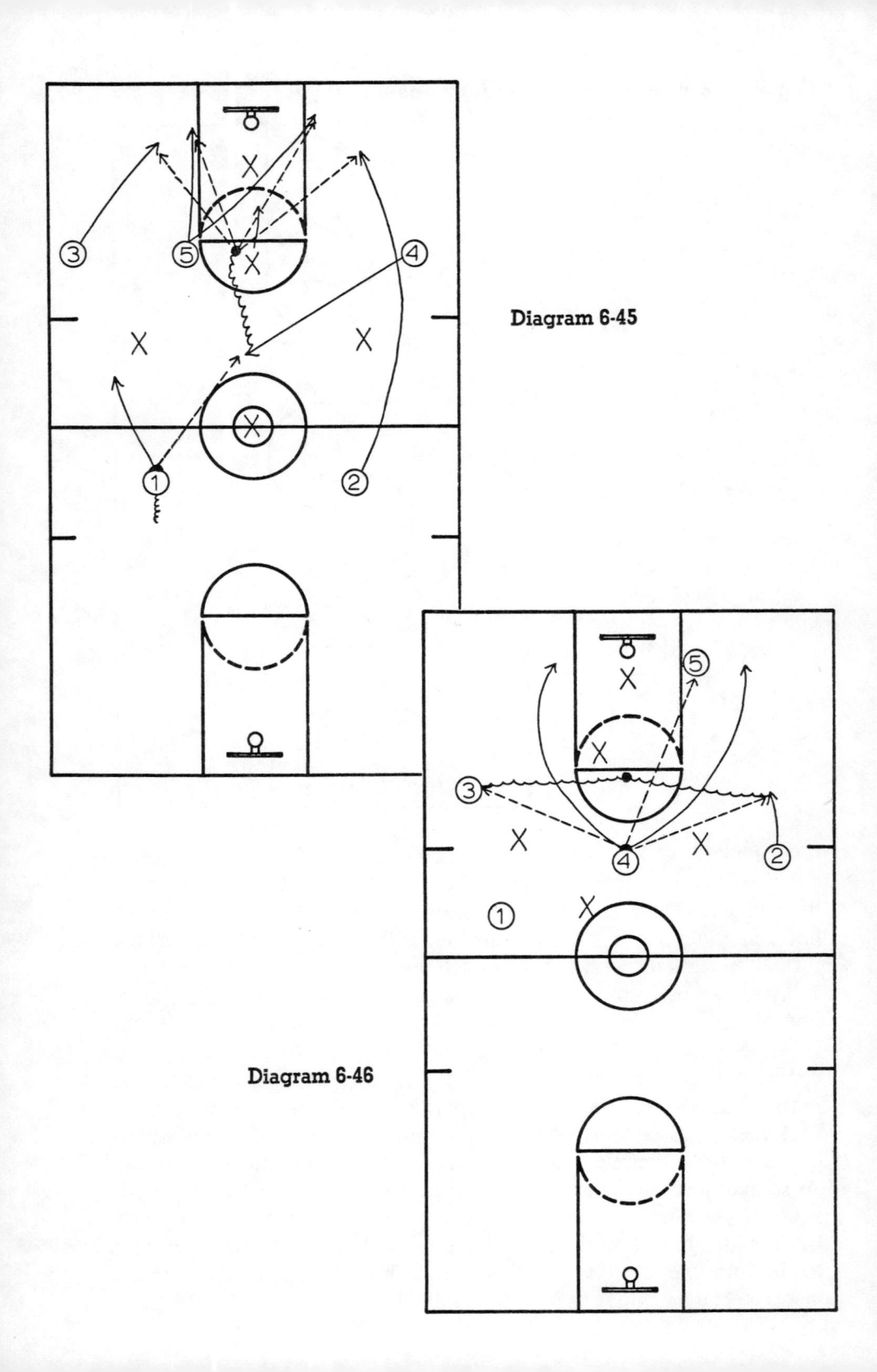

Diagram 6-45

Diagram 6-46

Centering Zone Presses with the All-Purpose Percentage Offense 229

dribble to the foul line, he can pass to either 3 or 2, and the man he passes to goes to the middle on the dribble. 4 then fills the lane of the man that he passed to, as shown in Diagram 6-46. 4 should also look for 5 at the base line if he cannot dribble to the foul line.

If 1 cannot feed the ball to 4 cutting into the middle, then he has two choices: He can pass to 2, who has stayed even with him, or he can pass to 3 on the left sideline. Diagram 6-47 shows 1 passing over to 2. 4 returns to his original sideline position when he sees 1 pass over to 2, and 3 breaks to the middle to receive the pass from 2 (same as Full-Court-Zone Press Offense, Rule One). 5 rolls to the side 3 came from and 1 fills the left lane. 3 pivots and faces the basket and goes for the 3-on-2 situation.

Diagram 6-48 shows 1's pass to 3 on the left sideline. 3 now has a Rule Two decision to make: He can either pass to 4, who is in the middle of the court near the foul circle, or 3 can keep the ball and dribble to the middle himself. Diagram 6-48 shows 3 passing to 4. 4 goes to the foul line. 5 rolls to the side that 4 came from and 2 fills the right lane. Diagram 6-49 has 3 dribbling the ball to the middle. As soon as 4 sees this, he crosses over and takes the left lane. 5 rolls to the right low-post area, and as 3 takes the ball to the foul line, 2 fills the right lane. Of course 3 should pass to 4 in the middle if 4 is open. He should only dribble in this situation if it is a last resort. 1 can move into the middle to act as a safety valve for 3 if 3 gets into trouble. *Coaching Hint:* Many times the 5 man can be hit at the foul line on the side of the ball, if the 1 or 2 men cannot get the ball to the middle to the man breaking there or to the man who is at the sideline. 5 should step out two or three steps and signal for the ball by raising his hand high over his head. If 5 gets the ball, he should pivot and face the basket, looking for 3 and 4 cutting to the hoop. Another move that can be used against any type of half-court zone press (or full-court press for that matter) is that of having the guard with the ball fake a pass to get the defense to move, and then pass in the opposite direction of his fake. This will get the zone to move and then catch it going in the opposite direction of where the guard really wants to pass the ball.

Special Techniques for Coaching Zone Press Offenses

These two simple but effective full-court and half-court zone press offenses, based on the Two Rule Play, can be inserted into any system of play, and with very little practice, can be quickly learned and perfected. Players adjust very quickly to the system by working on the special technique drills to follow the Two Rules of Decision.

Diagram 6-47

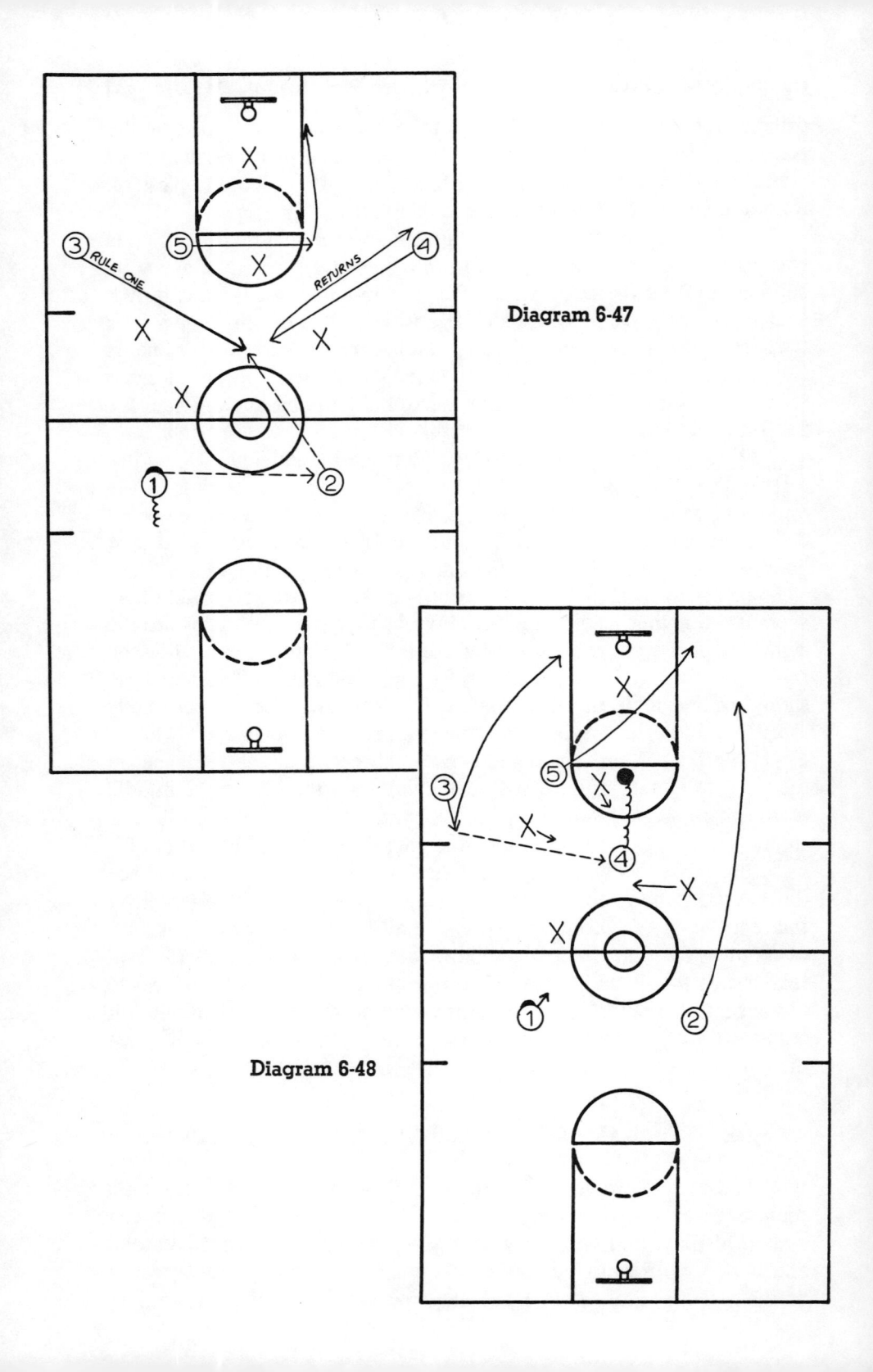

Diagram 6-48

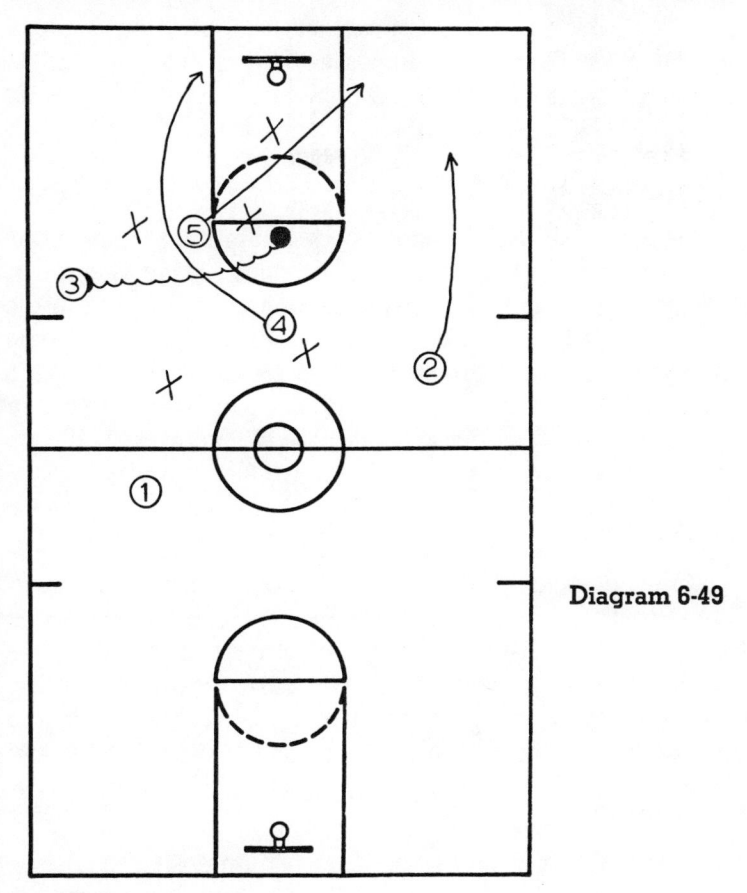

Centering Zone Presses with the All-Purpose Percentage Offense 231

Diagram 6-49

Back-and-Forth Drill

A good drill for teaching Rule One is to have 1 and 2 keep passing the ball back and forth in the back court, and have the mid-court men at the sideline positions keep breaking to the middle toward the foul circle when the ball is not on this side of the court. Also, have the mid-court men return to their original sideline spots when the ball is passed back to their side.

Dribble-or-Pass Drill

An excellent drill for teaching Rule Two is to have a man with the ball in the middle lane, a player at mid-court near the sideline and one defender between them. Have the defender do whatever he pleases, and the man with the ball must follow Rule Two—dribble or pass. This drill also can be executed by having the man with the ball positioned at a mid-court sideline area, another player stationed at mid-court near the back-court center jump circle's outside line and a defender just within the front court, to force the man with the ball to make his decision from this position with regard to following Rule Two. Diagrams 6-50 and 6-51 show these two drills.

Identifying the Press Drill

Break the team into two teams of equal ability, mixing your starters with your reserves to balance the teams. Have one team press—they may use any press they want so long as it is a zone press with an even or odd front. The offensive team tries to pick up the type of defense and goes into the correct offensive formation to meet the press. The defensive team must use some kind of signal that the offense cannot pick up. If the offense scores, they keep the ball, if they do not score, then the defense gets the ball and the teams swap jobs.

3-on-1 and 3-on-2 Drills

Time should be spent on the common 3-on-1 and 3-on-2 fast-break situations that will arise with this offense. Such drills may be incorporated with your fast-break drills as both are directed at the same end result—beating the defense down court, outnumbering the defense and ending up with no worse than a 15-foot shot from the foul line, with excellent rebounding position for the offensive boards.

Timing the Press Offense

By timing actual scrimmages and game situations, it has been established that it takes about 3 seconds to get the ball in from out-of-bounds and about 6 or 7 seconds to get the ball across the 10-second line. By putting a stopwatch on these maneuvers and letting the players know exactly how long it takes them to get the ball in and over the mid-court line each time, they gain a good perspective with regard to this time, without hurrying or panicking. It gives them a great deal of confidence to be able to approximate the time on their own, and it provides that needed assurance when facing any type of full-court pressure defense. *Coaching Technique:* To add zest to this drill, let the players on offense try to guess the length of time it takes them to get the ball in-bounds or across the 10-second line. Assign penalty laps for guesses that are off by 2 seconds, either over or under.

6- and 7-Man Zone Presses

An excellent drill, which gives the offensive team an extra tough time and a hard workout, is that of inserting an extra man or two in

Diagram 6-50

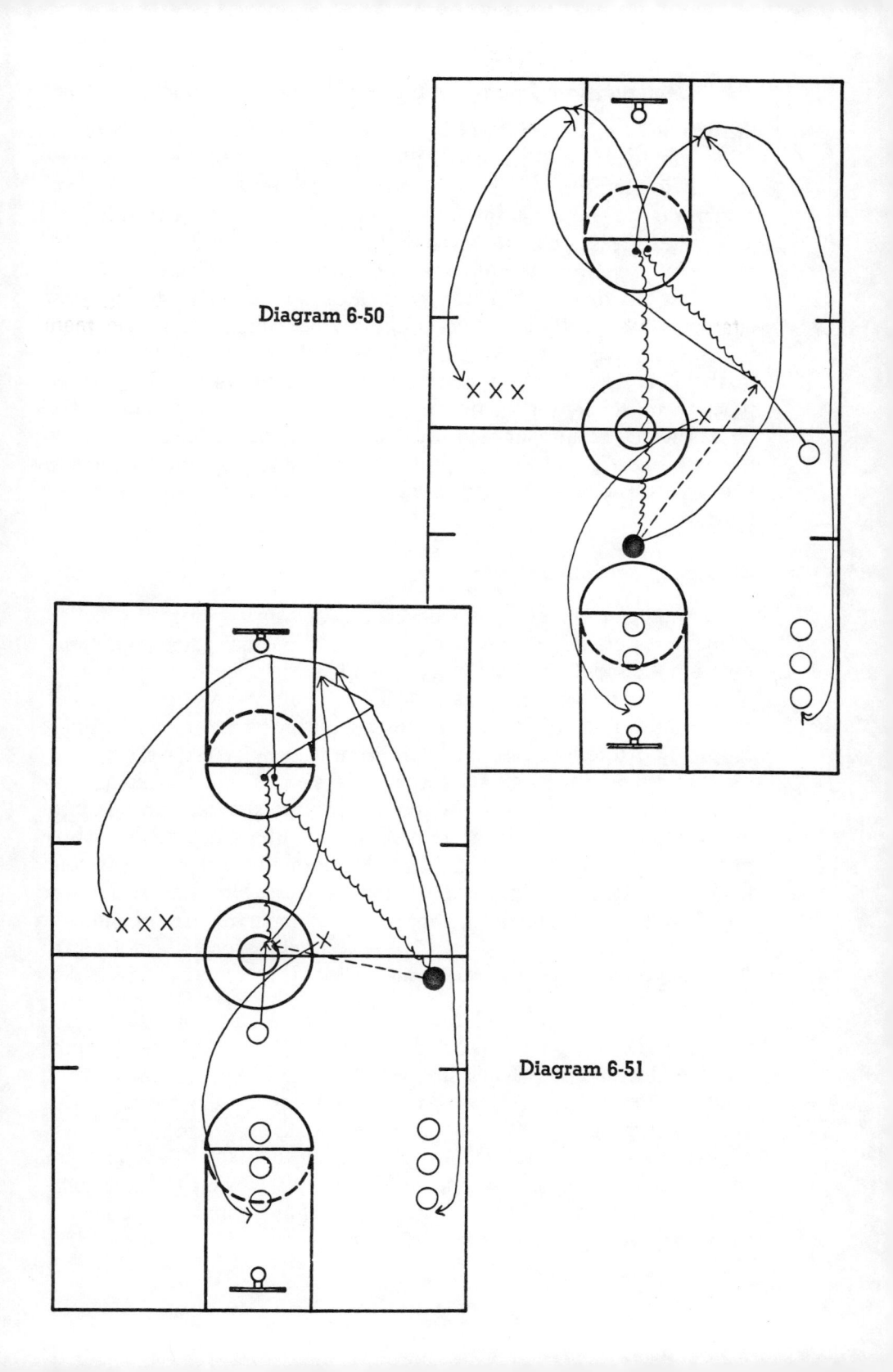

Diagram 6-51

the practice sessions when working against the full-court zone presses. Many times, when these extra players are inserted, the offense is actually in the process of bringing the ball up court, and the offensive players do not know that there are additional men on the court. Sometimes the offense will go through the offensive play several times successfully before the additional men are noticed. *Coaching Technique:* At this time, it should be pointed out to the offense that if they can operate correctly and successfully against six or seven men, then the ordinary five-man press in a ball game should present no problems to them. An extra added maneuver to liven up this hard type of practice, especially for the defense, is to see how long the offense will go before the additional men are noticed. Another added feature of the extra men is that they help plug the weak gaps of the zone press and give the offense needed work against good, hard pressure defenses.

Simulating Game Conditions

Another technique that can be used when working in practice against pressure defenses is to try to simulate actual game conditions by using the scoreboard, pulling out the bleachers all the way to get a crowded feeling and using canned noise. Canned noise is the actual crowd noise that can be tape recorded during some actual game—especially before a large crowd. To make it as noisy as possible, play the tape recorder through a loudspeaker system. These techniques can turn boring, dull and tiring full-court zone practice scrimmages into exciting and near-real game conditions. Set the clock for about 6 minutes to go in the game and then keep score. Make sure the pressing team (usually the second group) have a slight handicap score and then have the losers run five laps after the scrimmage.

Summing Up the Zone Press Offenses

These are the only full-court zone presses I have used during the past five seasons. I find that if these patterns are executed correctly and the One and Two Rules are followed to the hilt, a team will get opportunities for layup after layup, which breaks the backs of the zone press people and forces them into doing something else. Even though the tempo of the game may pick up, it is the offensive team that is causing this increase in speed, and this is what the true ball-control team must do in order to be successful—control the tempo of the game, even against pressure defenses.

Index

A

Active presses, 128–129
Adjustment techniques:
   against sagging, switching and anticipating defenses, 99–113
   circling defense, 98, 106–108
   double screening defense, 98, 102–103
   going over top or topping defense, 98–99, 101–102
   man-to-man, 98–113,
     (*see also* Man-to-man)
   screen rolling defense, 98, 103–106
   special offensive, 42–43
   team special offensive, 108–113
Advantages:
   All-Purpose Percentage Offense, 18–19
   percentage-controlled attack, 29–31
All-Purpose Percentage Attack, 188–190
All-Purpose Percentage Offense:
   advantages, 18–19
   attack, 29
   ball-control theory, 26–27
   biggest problem encountered, 18
   building, 35–47
   coach, 27–28
   continual ball movement, 38
   continual player movement, 37–38
   control amount of time with ball, 17
   control tempo of game, 17
   criteria for selecting percentage shot, 21–24
   diagrams, 20, 22, 24, 25, 26, 36, 39, 41, 46, 47
   disciplined options, 36–37
   foundation, 17–34
   functional cure-all, 19
   getting percentage shot, 25–26
   half of practice on defense, 18
   high-percentage shot close to basket, 17
   maintaining disciplined defensive floor balance, 41–42
   man-to-man offense to zone offense, 43–44
   moving layup shot, 19
   necessary yearly adjustments, 17
   not too many patterns to learn, 18
   1-2-2 formation, 46–47

All-Purpose Percentage Offense (*cont'd*)
   only two offensive formations, 18
   over the years, 17
   patterns enjoyable to execute, 45
   patterns fun to run, 45
   penetrating patterns to get the percentage shot, 39–40
   percentage-controlled offense, 29–32
     advantages, 29–31
     disadvantages, 31–32
   percentage-controlled team, 17
   percentage factors to strive for, 17
   percentage shot areas, 24–25
   percentage shots, 19–24
     (*see also* Percentage shots)
   player positioning, 35–36
   players, 28
   player's reactions, 32–34
   positioning offensive rebounders for second and third shots, 40–41
   simple to comprehend and execute, 18
   6 to 15 footers, 21
   special offensive adjustment techniques, 42–43
   stationary power shot, 20–21
   substitute for player, 19
   10-point game strategy, 32
   two basic options per formation, 18
   2-3 offensive setup, 47
   type players in lineup, 19
   used against any defense, 18
   utilizing time clock, 44–45
   varying calibres of team talent, 18, 19
Anticipating defenses, 99
Attack, 29
Attributes of coach, players, and offense, 27–29
Auxiliary Five Cutter Offense with Player Movement, 172–180
Auxiliary Formation, 156–157
Auxiliary Formation, odd-front zone press offense from, 214
Auxiliary Formation with Ball Movement, 180–184
Auxiliary Offense:
   breaking man-to-man pressure defenses, 136–140
   setting up percentage man-to-man attack, 121–126

Index

B

Back-and-forth, 26
Back-and-forth drill, 231
Backtrap, 49
Backtrap rear screen, 76
Backtrap screen, 51, 75, 101, 108–109
Balance, floor, 41–42
Ball, movement, 38, 168–172, 180–184
Ball-handling skills, 28
Ball movement offenses, 158–159
Box Specials, 148–151

C

Circling defense, 98, 106–108
Clock, time, 44–45
Coach, 27–28
Combination defenses, 184–188
Confidence, 28
Continual movement:
 ball, 38
 player, 37–38
Continuity attacks, 18
Corrections, 28
Criticism, 28
Cross-court pass option, 223, 225

D

Diagrams:
 All-Purpose Percentage Offense, 20, 22, 24–26, 36, 39, 41, 46–47
 man-to-man attack, 49–67, 70–83, 85–92, 94–96, 100–111, 113, 115–126
 man-to-man pressure defenses, 130–141, 143–151
 zone defenses, 154, 156–158, 160–165, 167–183, 185–189
 zone press defenses, 193–194, 196–199, 201–203, 205–208, 210–213, 215, 217–220, 222–224, 226–228, 230–231, 233
Disadvantages, percentage-controlled attack, 31–32
Discipline, 28
Discipline continuity pattern, 29
Disciplined options, 36–37
Disciplined players, 23
Double screening defense, 98, 102–103
Dribble-or-pass drill, 231–232
Dribble release move, 114–116
Drills:
 back-and-forth, 231
 dribble-or-pass, 231–232

Drills (cont'd)
 identifying the press, 232
 simulating game conditions, 234
 6- and 7-man zone presses, 232, 234
 3-on-1 and 3-on-2, 232
 timing the press offense, 232

E

Even-front half-court zone presses, 209, 211, 213

F

Fast break, 26
"Fast broke," 69
Five Cutter Attack, 121–126, 136–140
Five Cutter Formation:
 against zone defenses, 155–156
  adjustments, 156
  against even-front zone, 156
  facing odd-front zone, 156
  1-2-2 setup, 155
 man-to-man attack, 48–49
  adjustments, 48
  best ball handler, 48
  compact 1-2-2 offensive setup, 48
  left-post man, 48
  left-wing man, 48
  low-post men, 48
  numbering players and positions, 49
  point man, 48
  right-post man, 48
  right-wing man, 48
  "turning offense over," 49
  used 80% of time, 48
  wing men, 48
 zone press defenses, 198–213
  (see also Zone press defenses)
Five Cutter Offense, 49–65
 (see also Man-to-man)
Five Cutter Offense with Ball Movement, 168–172
Five Cutter Offense with Player Movement, 159–168
Floor balance, 29, 41–42
Fluctuating defenses, 188–190
Forced shot, 21
Formations, two all-purpose percentage offensive, 46–47
Front-court pressure, tight man-to-man, 113–114
Full-court:
 Identical Inside Option, 140–146
 operating stack, 146–148

Index

G

Give-and-go maneuver, 74
Give-and-go option, 19
Going over top, 98–99, 101–102

H

Half-and-half duty, 79
Half-court facing, 151–152
Hand signals, 38
Hogging ball, 33

I

Identical Inside Option, 84–93, 96–99, 116, 134–136, 140–146, 184–188
Identifying the press drill, 232
"Inside," term, 64–65
Interchanging, Outside Options and Identical Inside Option, 96–99

J

Jump shot, 21

L

Layups, 23

M

Man-to-man attack:
  adjustment techniques, 98–113
    against sagging, switching and anticipating defenses, 99–113
    circling defense, 98, 106–108
    double screening defense, 98, 102–103
    going over top, 98–99, 101–102
    screen rolling defense, 98, 103–106
    team special offensive, 108–113
  Auxiliary Offense to Five Cutter Attack, 121–126
  backtrap screen, 52
  continuity for 1 play, 69–73
  denial pressure overplay, 50
  diagrams, 49–67, 70–83, 85–92, 94–96, 100–111, 113, 115–126
  dribble release move, 114–116
  easy layup, 53
  Five Cutter Formation, 48–49
  Five Cutter Offense, 49–65
    development brought about, 59–60
    getting into, 60–65
  handling tight front-court pressure, 113–114

Man-to-man attack (cont'd)
  Identical Inside Option, 84–93
  Interchanging Outside Options and Identical Inside Option, 96–99
  1 play, 66–69
  Outside Options, 66–84
    (see also Outside Options)
  positions players assume in original formation, 49
  rotating, 93–96
    Identical Inside Option, 95–96
    Outside Option, 93–95
  setting up attack, 48–126
  signals, 55–59
  stack to Identical Inside Option, 116
  stationary screen, 51
  strong-side safety valve, 117–121
  "topping the defense," 102
  2 play, 73–74
  verbal release call, 114
  weak-side–strong-side formation, 50, 52, 56
Man-to-man offense, maneuverability to zone offense, 43–44
Man-to-man pressure defenses:
  active presses, 128–129
  aims, 128
  Auxiliary Offense to Five Cutter Attack, 136–140
  Box Specials, 148–151
  diagrams, 130–141, 143–151
  dribbling into Identical Inside Option, 134–136
  dribbling into the Outside Options, 129–134
  facing half-court, 151–152
  meeting, 127
  operating the stack full-court, 146–148
  passive presses, 129
  using Identical Inside Option full-court, 140–146
  X play, 149–151
Merits, 18–19
  (see also Advantages)
Movement:
  ball, 38, 168–172, 180–184
  players, 37–38, 157–158, 159–168, 172–180
Moving layup, 19

N

Numbering, players and positions, 49

O

Odd-front half-court zone presses, attacking, 225, 227, 229
Offensive rebound power shots, 24
One-hand set shooter, 24
One-hand set shot, 21
1 play, 66–69, 69–73
1-2-2 formation, 46–47
1-2-2 press, forcing into 1-3-1 press formation, 214
Options:
    cross-court pass, 223, 225
    disciplined, 36–37
    give-and-go, 19
    Identical Inside, 84–93, 96–99, 116, 134–136, 140–146, 184–188
    Outside
    (*see also,* Outside Option)
    play, simplified signals, 38–39
    sideline-to-middle, 221, 223
    signals for each, 29
Outside Options:
    alternating 1 play and 2 play, 82–84
    continuity for 1 play, 69–73
    dribbling into, 129–134
    interchanged with Identical Inside Option, 96–99
    1 play, 66–69
    rules for defensive responsibility, 69
    2 play, 73–82
"Outside," term, 64–65

P

Passing skills, 28
Passive presses, 129
Patterns, 28, 29
Percentage-controlled attack:
    advantages, 29–31
    attack, 29
    coach, 27–28
    disadvantages, 31–32
    essential attributes, 27–29
    players, 28
Percentage shots:
    areas, 24–25
    ball-control theory, 26–27
    criteria for selecting, 21–24
    game charts illustrated, 25, 26
    getting against any defense, 25–26
    moving layup, 19
    penetrating patterns designed to get, 39–40

Percentage shots (*cont'd*)
    6-foot area in front of basket, 24
    6- to 15-foot zone, 24
    6 to 15 footers, 21
    16-foot to 21-foot distance, 24
    stationary power, 20–21
    three types, 19–21
    21- to 25-foot distance, 25
"Play," 39
"Play run," 84
Player movement offenses, 157–158
Players:
    attributes, 28
    disciplined, 23
    movement, 37–38, 157–158, 159–168, 172–180
    positioning, 35–36
    reaction to playing on percentage-controlled team, 32–34
    shooting ability, 23
Point man:
    best ball handler, 48
    rotating, 93
Positioning:
    offensive rebounders for second and third shots, 40–41
    players, 35–36
Power shot, 68, 77, 78
Presses:
    active, 128–129
    passive, 129

Q

"Quarterback," 98

R

Rear screen, 76, 84
Records, success, 28
Responsibility, 28
"Rotate," 93
Rotating:
    Identical Inside Option, 95–96
    Outside Option, 93–95
        point man, 93
        wing man, 94–95
Rule One, 195
Rule Two, 195, 198
Run-and-shoot offense, 26

S

Safety outlet pass, 219, 221
Sag, 39, 102
Sagging defenses, 39

Index

Screen rolling defense, 98, 103–106
Screens:
    backtrap, 51, 75, 101, 108–109
    backtrap rear, 76
    double, 98, 102–103
    rear, 76, 84
    side, 76, 80
    stationary, 51
Self-control, 28
Shooting:
    ability, 23
    policies, 23
Shots:
    moving layup, 19
    percentage
        (*see* Percentage shots)
    6 to 15 footers, 21
    stationary power, 20–21
Shuffle continuity, 49
Shuffle offense, 36
Side screen, 76, 80
Sideline-to-middle option, 221, 223
Signals:
    easy, identifiable, 29
    Five Cutter Offense, 55–59
    hand, 38
    Identical Inside Option, 99
    Outside Options, 99
    verbal, 38
6- and 7-man zone presses, 232, 234
6 to 15 footers, 21
Stack to Identical Inside Option, 116
Stationary power, 20–21
Stationary screen, 51
Stopwatch, 44–45
Strong-side safety valve, 117–121
Success records, 28
Switch, 39
Switching defenses, 99

T

Tap-ins, 24
Team, essentials, 27–29
Tempo, 17
10-point lead, 32
3-on-1 and 3-on-2 drills, 232
Throw-in:
    combating pressure, 204, 209, 225
    screening zone press, 209
Time clock, 44–45
Timing the press offense, 232
Topping defense, 98–99, 101–102
"Turning the offense over," 49

Two-handed overhead pass, 66
2 play, 73–74
Two Rule Play, 195–198
2-3 low setup, 47

U

Unmolested layup, 23
Up-and-down, 26

V

Verbal release call, 114
Verbal signals, 38

W

Weak-side–strong-side formation, 50, 52, 56
Wing man, rotating, 94–95

X

X play, 149–151

Z

Zone defenses:
    All-Purpose Percentage Attack, 188–190
    attacking combination defenses with Identical Inside Option, 184–188
    Auxiliary Five Cutter Offense with Player Movement, 172–180
    Auxiliary Formation, 156–157
    Auxiliary Formation with Ball Movement, 180–184
    ball movement offenses, 158–159
    diagrams, 154, 156–158, 160–165, 167–183, 185–189
    Five Cutter Formation, 155–156
    Five Cutter Offense with Ball Movement, 168–172
    Five Cutter Offense with Player Movement, 159–168
    fluctuating, 188–190
    mixing the movement attacks, 158–159
    player movement offenses, 157–158
Zone offense, maneuverability from man-to-man offense, 43–44
Zone press defenses:
    Auxiliary Formation against odd-front full-court and half-court zone presses, 213–229
    attacking odd-front half-court zone presses, 225, 227, 229

Zone press defenses (*cont'd*)
  Auxiliary Formation (*cont'd*)
    combating pressure on throw-in, 225
    cross-court pass option, 223, 225
    forcing the 1-2-2 press into 1-3-1 press formation, 214
    4 man's cutting angle keyed on the middle defender, 216, 219
    objective of odd-front zone press offense from Auxiliary Formation, 214
    positioning ball to middle lane, 214–215
    safety outlet pass, 219, 221
    sideline-to-middle option, 221, 223
    3 man's decision, 215–216
  back-and-forth drill, 231
  breaking, 192–195
  coaching offenses, 229–234
  cover areas on floor, 192
  diagrams, 193–194, 196–199, 201–203, 205–208, 210–213, 215, 217–220, 222–224, 226–228, 230–231, 233
  disciplined full-court zone press offense, 192

Zone press defenses (*cont'd*)
  double-team traps, 192
  dribble-or-pass drill, 231–232
  Five Cutter Formation against even-front full-court and half-court, 198–213
    attacking the even-front half-court zone presses, 209, 211, 213
    combating pressure on the throw-in, 204, 209
    getting ball to middle, 200, 202, 204
  identifying the press drill, 232
  method of our attack, 192
  Middle Lane Blitz, 192
  objectives, 191–192
  simulating game conditions, 234
  6- and 7-man zone presses, 232, **234**
  summing up offenses, 234
  3-on-1 and 3-on-2 drills, 232
  timing the press offense, 232
  Two Rule Play, 195–198
    Rule One, 195
    Rule Two, 195, 198
Zone press offenses:
  drills, 231–234
  summing up, 234